# MODERNISM

## Second edition

The modernist movement radically transformed the late nineteenth- and early twentieth-century literary establishment, and its effects are still felt today. *Modernism* introduces and analyses what amounted to nothing less than a literary and cultural revolution.

In this fully updated and revised second edition, charting the movement in its global and local contexts, Peter Childs:

- details the origins of the modernist movement and the influence of thinkers such as Darwin, Marx, Freud, Nietzsche, Saussure and Einstein;
- explores the radical changes that occurred in the literature, drama, art and film of the period;
- traces 'modernism at work' in anglophone literatures, especially in writings by a range of key figures including James Joyce, Virginia Woolf, Samuel Beckett, Nella Larsen, Gertrude Stein, Katherine Mansfield, T. S. Eliot, and many others;
- reflects upon the shift from modernism to postmodernism.

At once accessible and critically informed, *Modernism* guides readers from their first steps in the field to an advanced understanding of one of the most important cultural movements of the twentieth century.

**Peter Childs** is Professor in Modern English at the University of Gloucestershire. He is the author of many books on literature post-1900, including *The Twentieth Century in Poetry* (1998).

# THE NEW CRITICAL IDIOM

SERIES EDITOR JOHN DRAKAKIS, UNIVERSITY OF STIRLING

*The New Critical Idiom* is an invaluable series of introductory guides to today's critical terminology. Each book:

- provides a handy, explanatory guide to the use (and abuse) of the term
- offers an original and distinctive overview by a leading literary and cultural critic
- relates the term to the larger field of cultural representation

With a strong emphasis on clarity, lively debate and the widest possible breadth of examples, *The New Critical Idiom* is an indispensable approach to key topics in literary studies.

Also available in this series:

# MODERNISM

Second edition

Peter Childs

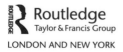
Routledge
Taylor & Francis Group

LONDON AND NEW YORK

First edition published 2000
Reprinted 2001, 2002, 2003, 2004, 2005 (twice)
Second edition published 2008
by Routledge
2 Park Square, Milton Park, Abingdon, Oxon OX14 4RN

Simultaneously published in the USA and Canada
by Routledge
270 Madison Ave, New York, NY 10016

*Routledge is an imprint of the Taylor & Francis Group, an informa business*

© 2000, 2008 Peter Childs

Typeset in Garamond and Scala Sans by
Taylor & Francis Books
Printed and bound in Great Britain by
TJ International Ltd, Padstow, Cornwall

*British Library Cataloguing in Publication Data*
A catalogue record for this book is available from the British Library

*Library of Congress Cataloging in Publication Data*
Childs, Peter, 1962-
    Modernism / Peter Childs. – 2nd ed.
        p. cm. – (The new critical idiom)
    Includes bibliographical references and index.
    1. Modernism (Art) 2. Arts, Modern–19th century. 3. Arts,
    Modern–20th century. I. Title.
    NX454.5.M63C48 2007
700'.4112–dc22                    2007018342

ISBN13 978-0-415-41544-6 (hbk)
ISBN13 978-0-415-41546-0 (pbk)
ISBN13 978-0-203-93378-7 (ebk)

# Contents

# SERIES EDITOR'S PREFACE

*The New Critical Idiom* is a series of introductory books which seeks to extend the lexicon of literary terms in order to address the radical changes which took place in the study of literature during the last decades of the twentieth century. The aim is to provide clear, well-illustrated accounts of the full range of terminology currently in use and to evolve histories of its changing usage.

The current state of the discipline of literary studies is one where there is considerable debate concerning basic questions of terminology. This involves, among other things, the boundaries that distinguish the literary from the non-literary; the position of literature within the larger sphere of culture; the relationship between literatures of different cultures; and questions concerning the relation of literary to other cultural forms within the context of interdisciplinary studies.

It is clear that the field of literary criticism and theory is a dynamic and heterogeneous one. The present need is for individual volumes on terms which combine clarity of exposition with an adventurousness of perspective and a breadth of application. Each volume will contain, as part of its apparatus, some indication of the direction in which the definition of particular terms is likely to move, as well as expanding the disciplinary boundaries within which some of these terms have been traditionally contained. This will involve some resituation of terms within the larger field of cultural representation and will introduce examples from the area of film and the modern media in addition to examples from a variety of literary texts.

# Acknowledgements

For generous advice given to me during the writing and rewriting of this book, I would like to thank Liz Brown, Polly Dodson, John Drakakis and the many readers, reviewers and report-writers who provided helpful comments on the first edition.

# INTRODUCTION

## ANSWERING THE QUESTION: WHAT IS MODERNISM?

### Romance

> In medieval literature, a verse narrative [recounts] the marvelous
> adventures of a chivalric hero. ... In modern literature, i.e., from the
> latter part of the 18th through the 19th centuries, a romance is a
> work of prose fiction in which the scenes and incidents are more or
> less removed from common life and are surrounded by a halo of
> mystery, an atmosphere of strangeness and adventure.
>
> (William Rose Benét, *The Reader's Encyclopedia*)

### Realism

> A mode of writing that gives the impression of recording or 'reflect-
> ing' faithfully an actual way of life. The term refers, sometimes con-
> fusingly, both to a literary method based on detailed accuracy of
> description (i.e. verisimilitude) and to a more general attitude that
> rejects idealization, escapism, and other extravagant qualities of
> romance in favour of recognizing soberly the actual problems of life.
>
> (Chris Baldick, *Oxford Dictionary of Literary Terms*)

## Modernism

> Modernist art is, in most critical usage, reckoned to be the art of what Harold Rosenburg calls 'the tradition of the new.' It is experimental, formally complex, elliptical, contains elements of decreation as well as creation, and tends to associate notions of the artist's freedom from realism, materialism, traditional genre and form, with notions of cultural apocalypse and disaster ... We can dispute about when it starts (French symbolism; decadence; the break-up of naturalism) and whether it has ended (Kermode distinguishes 'paleo-modernism' and 'neo-modernism' and hence a degree of continuity through to post-war art). We can regard it as a timebound concept (say 1890 to 1930) or a timeless one (including Sterne, Donne, Villon, Ronsard). The best focus remains a body of major writers (James, Conrad, Proust, Mann, Gide, Kafka, Svevo, Joyce, Musil, Faulkner in fiction; Strindberg, Pirandello, Wedekind, Brecht in drama; Mallarmé, Yeats, Eliot, Pound, Rilke, Apollinaire, Stevens in poetry) whose works are aesthetically radical, contain striking technical innovation, emphasize spatial or 'fugal' as opposed to chronological form, tend towards ironic modes, and involve a certain 'dehumanization of art.'
>
> (Malcolm Bradbury, in Childs and Fowler 2005)

## Postmodernism

> The new avant-garde literature (neomodernist or postmodernist) partly carried modernism further, partly reacted against it – for example against its ideology and its historical orientation. What it consistently pretended to be (and sometimes actually was) was *new*. Determinedly self-destructive, it attempted to cut off its branch of the past, by proposing entirely new methods, a fresh 'syllabus' or canon of authors (Nietzsche, Freud, Saussure, Proust) and a new register of allusions.
>
> (*A History of English Literature*, Alastair Fowler)

If the idea that identity exists through difference is taken as a starting point, then modernism can begin to be understood in terms of possible distinctions from other literary forms. Modernism is, for example, frequently distinguished from realism, the dominant mode of the novel from its inception in Britain in the eighteenth century with the rise of bourgeois capitalism to the present day. According to many critics, realism is characterised by its attempt to offer up a mirror to the world, thus disavowing its own culturally conditioned processes and ideological stylistic assumptions. Modelled on prose forms such as historiography and journalism, realist writing thus often presents itself as transparently representative of the author's society and so features characters, language, and a spatial-temporal setting familiar to its contemporary readers. Most importantly for a debate of literary history, it is apparent that the hegemony of realism as the dominant form of the novel was challenged by writers throughout the twentieth century as alternative ways of representing reality and the world were presented by modernists and then postmodernists. Realism itself was once a new, innovative form of writing, with authors such as Daniel Defoe (1660–1731) and Samuel Richardson (1690–1761) providing a different template for fiction from the previously dominant mode of prose writing, the Romance, which was parodied in one of the very first novels, Cervantes's *Don Quixote* (1605–15), and survives in Gothic and fantasy fiction. To the present day, realism remains the primary favoured style for most novelists, but many avant-garde, innovative, and radical writers have sought to undermine its dominance. Very broadly speaking, the vast majority of attempts to offer alternative modes of representation from the middle of the nineteenth century to the middle of the twentieth century have at one time or another been termed modernist, and this applies to literature, music, painting, film and architecture (and to some works before and after this period). In poetry, modernism is associated with moves to break from the iambic pentameter as the basic unit of verse, to introduce *vers libre*, symbolism, and other new forms of writing. In prose, it is associated with attempts to render human subjectivity in ways more real than realism: to represent consciousness, perception, emotion, meaning and the individual's relation to society through interior monologue, stream of consciousness, tunnelling, defamiliarisation, rhythm, irresolution and other terms that will be encountered later in the book. Modernist writers therefore struggled, in Ezra Pound's brief phrase, to 'make it new', to modify if not overturn existing modes and subjects of representation, partly by pushing them towards the abstract or the introspective, and to express the new sensibilities of their time: in a compressed, condensed, complex literature of the city, of industry and technology, war, machinery and speed, mass markets and communication, of internationalism, the New Woman, the aesthete, the nihilist and the *flâneur*.

The dominant post-war conception of modernism has accentuated these aspects to its key texts; however, emphases in recent studies have moved towards alternative conceptualisations. Instead of the progressive model whereby literary modes eclipse or supersede older ones in a teleological line of development, like Virginia Woolf's gig-lamps symmetrically arranged, there is acknowledgement of, first, styles existing alongside one another in the text, and second, of modernism's involvement in the broader social structures of the period and with the mass movements and popular cultures of modernity. Here, the literary complexion starts to change once the dominant view of a break from previous, or indeed contemporary, forms and cultural practices is questioned, and marginalised voices from the *fin de siècle* and the Empire, as well as voices of those excluded for reasons of gender or sexuality, are placed closer to the centre of modernism's narrative. Also, a critic such as Lawrence Rainey explores the role played by various individuals, such as patrons and collectors, and institutions, such as the academy and the law courts, in initially promoting the avant-garde to a wider reading public, beyond which point literary modernism, whose engagement with popular culture is evident in the works of James Joyce and T. S. Eliot for example, would require the influence of the mass media as well as both 'critical approbation and some degree of commercial viability to ratify its status as a significant idiom' (Rainey 1998: 170). Starting with the little discussed pre-war visits to England of the Italian futurist Filippo Tommaso Marinetti, Rainey's sociologically oriented *Institutions of Modernism: Literary Elites and Public Culture* reconstructs formative moments in the making of modernism, focusing on the decade after 1912 up to the publication of Joyce's *Ulysses* and Eliot's *The Waste Land* in 1922, and then Ezra Pound's *Draft of XVI Cantos* in 1925. Rainey pitches modernism between the age of journalism and the coming of the universities, seeing it as situated between a passing elite bourgeois culture and the coming middle-brow world of media aesthetics. Most importantly, it was ambiguously caught between its inclinations away from and towards contemporaneous common cultural practices in the wider civil society. In his conception of modernism, Rainey sees a greater importance for all kinds of cultural institutions than has previously been acknowledged: the idea of the deluxe edition and *Ulysses*, the rise of the little review and *The Waste Land* (both forms of publication indebted to massive patronage), politics for Pound and 'a coterie politics' for H.D. Thus, the significance of popular and even demotic culture to 'high modernism' can be reacknowledged, from such seeming extremes as Joyce's interest in pornography to Eliot's 1923 essay on the extremely successful comedian and singer Marie Lloyd. But, the wider influence of jazz, art, music, romance, machinery and the sheer frenzy of economic, cultural and social change, from market forces to machines, is increasingly felt in the myriad depictions of modernism.

## PLUNGING IN

With regard to literature, modernism is most readily understood through the work of the avant-garde authors who wrote in the decades before and after the turn of the twentieth century. It is a contentious term and should not be discussed without a sense of the literary, historical and political debates that have accompanied its usage. The problems of definition are such that many critics avoid providing one, even though they freely use the term. David Ayers avoids the issue of definition by stating a starkly contrasting problem with regard to *Ulysses*: Joyce's novel is such a touchstone for uses of the term in literature that it has become almost impossible to read it in any terms other than 'modernist', which means reference will be made to its symbolism, its variety of textual forms, and range of methods (see Ayers 2004: 66), and no matter how much contemporary critics try to analyse the novel's content, in terms of gender, nationalism, colonialism and so on, rather than its form, content and form remain inseparable, and so do, it seems, *Ulysses* and modernism.

One of the first aspects of much modernist writing to strike contemporary readers was the way in which such novels, stories, plays and poems immerse them in an unfamiliar world with little of the orienting preambles and descriptions provided by most nineteenth-century realist writers, such as Jane Austen, Charles Dickens and George Eliot. In other words, modernist writing 'plunges' the reader into a confusing and difficult mental landscape which cannot be immediately understood but which must be moved through and mapped in order to understand its limits and meanings (see Mahaffey 2007). In this Introduction, I will briefly sketch features of this landscape so that some of the contours of modernism can be visible, but I recommend that the reader returns to the Introduction having read the entire book, at which time its broad brushstrokes will be better appreciated with the knowledge accrued from the later chapters.

But before plunging into the terms and the definitions employed by critics, I would like to plunge into a fictional narrative and discuss what is going on at the start of a modernist text which is in some ways exemplary but which would actually be sidelined by some definitions of modernism and by some overviews of modernist writers. Samuel Beckett's *Murphy* was published in 1938, supposedly eight years after modernism started to wane and be replaced by the neo-realism of writers such as Graham Greene, George Orwell, Ernest Hemingway, Rosamond Lehmann and Evelyn Waugh. It is also by a writer who is often cited as the first *post*modernist. However, the elements of religious scepticism, deep introspection, technical and formal experimentation, cerebral game-playing, linguistic innovation, self-referentiality, misanthropic despair overlaid with humour, philosophical speculation, loss of faith and cultural exhaustion all exemplify the preoccupations of modernism. I shall quote the opening page of the novel, to give a strong flavour of the writing, and then offer a commentary on it.

> The sun shone, having no alternative, on the nothing new. Murphy sat out of it, as though he were free, in a mew in West Brompton.

Here for what might have been six months he had eaten, drunk, slept, and put his clothes on and off, in a medium-sized cage of
5   north-western aspect commanding an unbroken view of medium-sized cages of south-eastern aspect. Soon he would have to make other arrangements, for the mew had been condemned. Soon he would have to buckle to and start eating, drinking, sleeping and putting his clothes on and off, in quite alien surroundings.

He sat naked in his rocking-chair of undressed teak, guaranteed not to crack, warp, shrink, corrode, or creak at night. It was his own, it never left him. The corner in which he sat was curtained off from the sun, the poor old sun in the Virgin again for the billionth time. Seven scarves held him in position. Two fastened his shins to the
15   rockers, one his thighs to the seat, two his breast and belly to the back, one his wrists to the strut behind. Only the most local movements were possible. Sweat poured off him, tightened the thongs. The breath was not perceptible. The eyes, cold and unwavering as a gull's, stared up at an iridescence splashed over the cornice moulding, shrinking and fading. Somewhere a cuckoo-clock, having struck between twenty and thirty, became the echo of a street-cry, which now entering the mew gave *Quid pro quo! Quid pro quo!* directly.

These were sights and sounds that he did not like. They detained him in the world to which they belonged, but not he, as he fondly
25   hoped. He wondered dimly what was breaking up his sunlight, what wares were being cried. Dimly, very dimly. He sat in his chair in this way because it gave him pleasure! First it gave his body pleasure, it appeased his body. Then it set him free in his mind. For it was not until his body was appeased that he could come alive in his mind, as description in section six. And life in his mind gave him pleasure, such pleasure that pleasure was not the word.

(Beckett 1973: lines 1–33)

When beginning to interpret or decode these lines, we should remember that modernist prose is enormously compressed, which means that it ought to be read with the attention normally reserved for poetry or philosophy. Brief lines allude to complex ideas; comic set pieces enact philosophical theories; and there is little attempt to relate the extreme situations and mental conditions in the novel to anything the reader might consider to be representing 'normality'. This opening contains many of the features associated with modernist stylistics and preoccupations: a solipsistic mental landscape, an unreliable narrator, psychological and linguistic repetition, an obsession with language, a quest(ioning) towards 'reality', uncertainty in a Godless universe, the constraints of convention against the drives of passion and black humour.

A Dubliner in London, Murphy is a quite typical Beckett (anti-)hero. This is at least in the sense that he follows Beckett's idea of the human condition and so has a supple mind shackled to an imperfect, cumbersome body: the one a sanctuary to which he wishes to retreat, the other a chaos which he wishes to control. This is one reason he is literally tied up at the opening of the novel, as he attempts to negate the body and escape into his mind by achieving some kind of nirvana through meditative contemplation. For our purposes, this immediately signals a greater interest, typical of modernism, in the workings of the mind than of the body. As discussed below, it is also a starting point for consideration of how the mind works and, in particular, how a mind in extremity works.

As would be common in a modernist narrative, the novel has been read as a search to climb inside the mind, away from the body's needs and wants: to be free from desire. On the superficial level, Murphy is a young man with a gull's eyes and a yellow complexion who suffers from violent heart attacks. His girlfriend Celia is a prostitute who is described via a perfunctory list of measurements and passport details at the start of Chapter 2 and yet is the most sympathetically portrayed of all the characters – Beckett calls them puppets – in his novels. It is Murphy's predicament that he is to be sought by each of the other characters in the novel while he only wishes to escape from himself. Murphy wants to flee the physical world and seek refuge in the indivisible, unextended, pain-free mental world, which is one reason why he later takes a job in a mental asylum. Beckett's interest is in the Cartesian problem of dualism: how do the mind and the body interact? They coexist together like the yolk and albumen sealed within an egg, but no one knows how they are connected. In an attempt to represent this dilemma, Beckett toys with several theories such as Descartes's belief that there is a connection through the pineal gland and also the theological explanation, related to the issue of free will, that whenever the individual wills their body to move, God causes the action to be performed. Such concerns, though flavoured by Beckett's peculiar preoccupations, exemplify modernism's fascination with the way the mind processes or projects a reality which surrounds the individual but which is often alienating and oppressing.

The novel is also deeply concerned with religious explanations of the universe and with questions of what it means to be human with or without God. The opening line of this, Beckett's first novel, reminds us that there is nothing new under the sun (cf. Ecclesiastes 1:9) and also hints at the belief that there is no free will in the universe. The sun has no alternative but to shine, and in the second sentence we find Murphy sitting out of the sun 'as though he were free', suggesting that he, like the sun, is actually determined by his nature, driven by biological and psychological impulses of which he knows very little. This comment on restriction has a more literal embodied relevance in the next paragraph when we learn that Murphy is tied to a chair, a predicament that is quite possibly a parody of the philosopher Wittgenstein who famously used to sit on a deckchair beneath a fan in his otherwise bare room at Cambridge. The third sentence tells us as much about Beckett's narrator as it does about Murphy. This is because the narrator, who at most later times will appear omniscient, is undecided about the length of time Murphy has been at West Brompton: 'what might have been six months' (l. 3). It is one of the first hints that the narrator, who we have already realised is playful, is not going to follow the usual conventions of story-telling, but will mock them instead. So he has little time for the normal realist descriptions of homes and is content to describe Murphy's condemned mews as 'a medium-sized cage of north-western aspect.' The final sentence of the paragraph introduces another of Beckett's favourite techniques: repetition. Lines 8 and 9 repeat the round of eating, drinking, sleeping and dressing mentioned in lines 3 and 4. In this case, the echoing underlines the point that, though Murphy will soon have to move, there will indeed be nothing new for the sun to shine on. This is a modernist preoccupation with repetitive, cyclical rather than chronological, teleological time which will be discussed later.

The second paragraph immediately matches Murphy's undressed body with the undressed teak of his rocking chair, the perfect vehicle in which to be constantly moving and yet going nowhere. The difference between the two is that Murphy's body is not guaranteed not to 'crack, warp, shrink, corrode, or creak at night' (l. 11). The reader is then once more reminded of nature's unremitting cycles at the level of the cosmos and of animal sexuality, with 'the poor old sun [son] in the virgin again for the billionth time' (l. 13). The extra significance of this is that Beckett substitutes astrology for God as a system of faith for Murphy. The following sentences concerning Murphy's bondage are a typical Beckett set piece in that they contain the detailed but flawed over-explanation of a situation containing permutations. Murphy is tied up with seven scarves: two on his shins, one round his thighs, two at his torso, and one round his wrists. The inadequate or delinquent rather than unreliable narrator leaves the reader with two questions: where is the seventh scarf, and how did Murphy on his own achieve this Houdini-like position, in which his hands are tied and he is restricted to 'the most local movements' (ll. 16–17)? Beckett's points here are that, first, mathematics, the purest science, does not adequately represent the world; for example, try to work out, to as many decimal places as your mind can tolerate, the exact number of weeks in a year by dividing the number of days in a year [365] by the number of days in a week [7]); and, second, that Murphy's mind is always ensnared in and unable to escape from his body, and hence is always 'tied up'. Bringing these two points together provides a clue to why Murphy later calls another character 'Thou surd' (Beckett 1973: 47). A surd is an irrational number, such as the square root of minus one. The mathematical way of recording these imagined figures which exist in theory but not in practice is with the symbol $i$, which, curiously, is also when capitalised the pronoun used to represent the individual, who is always an irrational and *ab*surd figure in Beckett's imagined fiction, where the perverse, neurotic, thought-tormented characters of modernism find their fullest expression.

Murphy sits, sweats and watches the sunlight's play on the ceiling. A cuckoo clock strikes the improbable time of between twenty and thirty and echoes the barterer's shout *Quid pro quo!* (one thing in exchange for another). This business cry, signalling the difference between the commercial preoccupations of the capitalist world against which the modernists pitted artistic freedom, is a precursor of one of the novel's major speculative philosophical themes: that the amount of suffering in the world is always constant, though it may change in form. The argument is that life is a closed system, that 'For every symptom that is eased, another is made worse ... Humanity is a well with two buckets ... one going down to be filled, the other coming up to be emptied' (Beckett 1973: 36–7). The supposed comfort of this theory is that though things cannot overall get better they cannot get worse either. Things 'will always be the same as they always were' (Beckett 1973: 36); or, to return us to the start of the book, there is 'nothing new' under the sun, there is only redistribution: quid pro quo. Beckett suggests that this also operates on the divine level by reference to the fact that in one of the gospels it is stated that one of the thieves on the cross beside Jesus was saved and the other one damned, the moral being that the individual should neither despair nor presume. This suggests a balanced if inexplicable and unfair universe, to which Beckett often wants to draw our attention in a phrase which occurs in several of his works, as in *Murphy*: 'Remember also one thief was saved' (1973: 121; from St Augustine).

The third paragraph tells us that Murphy does not like such distractions breaking into his consciousness because they detract from his pleasure, which is to 'set him free in his mind', which again raises the question of free will. Murphy believes that the freedom of the mind depends upon the appeasement of the body, a fact that the narrator, again breaking the frame of the narrative, tells us we will have to wait until section six to have described. Such metafictional comments are anticipatory of many post-modernist techniques. The last sentence tells us that 'pleasure was not the word' for the pleasure in Murphy's mind and this is a repeated trope in the book (cf. 'hardly the word' (Beckett 1973: 21), 'not quite the right word' (1973: 39), and 'pleasant was not the word' (1973: 66)). This is partly a questioning of language's ability to represent the world adequately and is also a questioning of boundaries: can pleasure be pushed so far that it becomes something else, such as pain, which leaves aside the other question as to whether pleasure is felt by the body rather than the mind?

The chapter ends by returning to its beginning: the narrator contemplates 'most things under the moon' while Murphy rests back in his rocking chair: 'Soon his body would be quiet, soon he would be free.' Murphy is eventually freed from his desires, when, while he is seated in his rocking chair, a gas leak is ignited and Murphy at last achieves the oblivion he has sought in a final 'big bang'. It is an ending that is inevitable in a world in which, reminding us of the novel's fatalistic opening sentence, 'all things hobble/limp together for the only possible' (Beckett 1973: 127 and 131). *Murphy* is a very funny but deeply pessimistic novel, and it is entirely appropriate that Murphy's will asks for his burnt remains to be flushed down the toilet in the Abbey Theatre, Dublin, 'where their happiest hours have been spent'. It is appropriate to Beckett's sense of life's irony and futility that they will actually be scattered across the floor of a London pub in a brawl.

Having plunged into an in-some-ways-representative modernist piece of writing, and thus offered a microcosmic bottom-up perspective of a segment of modernism through one literary example, I want now to move to the other end of the spectrum of approaches and offer a top-down macrocosmic overview of the terms and critical stances associated with modernism. It is only through the negotiation of these two understandings of modernism, as specific textual examples and as a number of gross cultural movements, that the word itself can become meaningful.

## WORDS, WORDS, WORDS: MODERN, MODERNISM, MODERNITY

Modernism is variously argued to be a period, style, genre or combination of the above; but it is first of all a word, one that exists alongside cognate words. Its stem, 'modern-', is a term that, from the latin *modo*, means 'current', and so has a far wider currency and range of meanings than 'modernism'. In the late fifth century, for example, the Latin *modernus* referred to the Christian present in opposition to the Roman past; modern English is distinguished from Middle English; and the modern period in literature is considered to be from the sixteenth century on, although it is sometimes used to describe twentieth-century writing. More generally, 'modern' has been frequently used to refer to the avant-garde, though since the Second World War this sense has been embraced by the term 'contemporary' while 'modern' has shifted from meaning 'now' to 'just now' (Williams 1989). It is this sense of the avant-garde, radical, progressive or even revolutionary side to the modern that was the catalyst for the coinage 'modernism', and it is to this meaning that Rimbaud appealed when insisting 'Il faut être absolument moderne' (One must be modern absolutely).

It is now, however, perhaps both impossible and undesirable to speak of a single 'modernism,' and the practice of referring to 'modernisms' dates back to the 1960s. Some critics argue that the term is simply an imposition, applied after the fact to a small group of unrelated authors and a series of genuine movements such as imagism and vorticism. Undoubtedly, there has developed in literary studies a recognisable but not immutable canon of modernist authors and texts, just as there has more recently arisen an ever-growing body of critics since the 1980s foregrounding alternative and other writers: female authors in particular, but also, for example, the writers of the Harlem Renaissance and, more recently, novelists and poets from outside Euro-America, whose work contests the ground that has been staked by the assertions, claims and practices of the familiar names and their critics. It is consequently invidious to have to say what modernism was, precisely because any history or definition insinuates many implicit exclusions. Modernism has predominantly been represented in white, male, heterosexist, Euro-American middle-class terms, and any of the recent challenges to each of these aspects either reorients the term itself and dilutes the elitism of a pantheon of modernist writers, or introduces another one of a plurality of modernisms. This reveals that there is sufficient currency and investment in the term itself that writers and critics seek to contest its parameters and scope, its application(s) and meaning(s). Even the assertion that modernism was internationalist (in the sense of European and transatlantic) raises a question mark over the extent to which critics can speak of a 'British' literary modernism, just as in fine art the assumed precedence of continental painters has been questioned in the light of re-examinations of neglected and previously unfashionable British artists from the turn of the century. While the works of Picasso and Matisse have had more impact, there is an alternative history of modern(ist) art to be deduced from paintings such as those of the Camden Town Group and the London Group.

Despite those critics who argue that it is a specious label, the term 'modernism' appears to be here to stay; though most of the points that would have been asserted of it in the 1970s are challengeable. For example, that it is fundamentally Euro-American is open to immediate querying, when it can as persuasively be argued that modernism marked the regeneration of a tired Western artistic tradition by other cultures: African, African-American, Asian, Chinese, and, more generally, diasporic. Similarly, the view that modernist writers simply rejected or broke away from Victorian literature, for example, has been more and more challenged as critics point out connections with rather than departures from the writings of such figures as Robert Browning, Walter Pater, A. C. Swinburne and even Rudyard Kipling.

'Modernist' is a comparatively old word which in the late sixteenth century named a modern person and came by the eighteenth century to denote a follower of modern ways and also a supporter of modern over ancient literature. By contrast, 'modernism' was first used in the early eighteenth century simply to denote trends characteristic of modern times, while in the nineteenth century its meaning encompassed a sympathy with modern opinions, styles or expressions. In the later part of the nineteenth century, 'modernism' referred to progressive trends in the Catholic Church. In literature, it surfaced in Thomas Hardy's *Tess of the D'Urbervilles* (1891), to denote what he called a general and unwelcomed creeping industrial 'ache of Modernism'. The term also gained wider and earlier use in relation to other arts, but in literary criticism, the context with which this book is concerned, the expression emerged most notably – but failed to gain currency – with Robert Graves's and Laura Riding's 1927 study *A Survey of Modernist Poetry*. However, it is also true that a conviction that there was a 'modern movement' came into broad circulation before the Second World War, and the spirit of Ezra Pound's 'make it new' was consciously embraced by many and disparate writers such that, while it is commonplace to maintain that 'modernism' is a partial version of literary history constructed and mythologised long after the fact, it is nonetheless true that many writers and especially their harshest critics recognised in the early decades of the twentieth century multiple trends toward radical, innovative, challenging and experimental writing that would remain even if the retrospective label itself were removed.

It was only in the 1960s that the term 'modernist' became widely used as a description of a generation of writers and of a literary phase that was both identifiable and in some sense over. Its literary roots have been said to be in the work of the French poet and essayist Charles Baudelaire and the novelist Gustave Flaubert, in the Romantics, or in the 1890s *fin-de-siècle* writers, while its culmination or apogee arguably occurred before the First World War, by which point radical experimentation had impacted on all the arts, or in 1922, the *annus mirabilis* of James Joyce's *Ulysses*, T. S. Eliot's *The Waste Land*, Katherine Mansfield's *The Garden Party*, May Sinclair's *The Life and Death of Harriett Frean*, and Virginia Woolf's *Jacob's Room* (see North 1999). Postwar dates for modernism's high-point make sense in terms of British and also US literature but, perhaps, not in terms of any other in Europe. Its end is variously defined, in terms of time, as 1930, 1940, 1950, or even yet to happen, and, in terms of literary reaction, as neo-realism or postmodernism. As an international art term, it covers the many avant-garde styles and movements that proliferated under the names of expressionism, imagism, surrealism, futurism, Dadaism, vorticism, formalism and, in writing if not painting, impressionism. Modernist writing is most particularly noted for its experimentation, its complexity, its formalism and for its attempt to create a 'tradition of the new'. Its historical and social background includes the emergence of the New Woman, the peak and downturn of the British Empire, unprecedented technological change, the rise of the Labour Party, the appearance of factory-line mass production, war in Africa, Europe and elsewhere. Modernism has, therefore, almost universally been considered a literature of not just change but crisis.

'Modernity' is a word first used by Baudelaire in the mid-nineteenth century. In his essay 'The Painter of Modern Life', Baudelaire describes modernity as the fashionable, fleeting and contingent in art, in opposition to the eternal and immutable. In relation to modernism, modernity is considered to describe a way of living and of experiencing life which has arisen with the changes wrought by industrialisation, urbanisation and secular-isation; its characteristics are disintegration and reformation, fragmentation and rapid change, ephemerality and insecurity. It involves certain new understandings of time and space: speed, mobility, communication, travel, dynamism, chaos and cultural revolution. This societal shift was differently theorised at the turn of the century by, for example, Émile Durkheim, Max Weber and Ferdinand Tönnies. Durkheim focused on the increased division of labour inherent in modern production, Weber on the disen-chantment of a rationalised world, and Tönnies on the gradual move from the interrelations of the close-knit rural community, the *Gemeinschaft*, to the heterodoxy and anonymity of urban society, which he termed the *Gesellschaft* (see the Introduction to Bradbury and McFarlane 1976). The foundations of sociology lie in these attempts to come to terms with changes that were also being processed by the modernists.

The most notable writers on modernity in the first half of the twentieth century were the Frankfurt School of Critical Theor-ists, such as Theodor Adorno, Max Horkheimer and Walter Benjamin. Benjamin's ninth thesis in his 'Theses on the Philo-sophy of History' provides a famous image of 'the nightmare of history' as the modernists saw it. He describes an 'Angel of History':

> His face is turned toward the past. Where we perceive a chain of
> events, he sees one single catastrophe which keeps piling wreckage

upon wreckage and hurls it in front of his feet. The angel would like to stay, awaken the dead, and make whole what has been smashed. But a storm is blowing from Paradise; it has got caught in his wings with such violence that the angel can no longer close them. The storm irresistibly propels him into the future to which his back is turned, while the pile of debris before him grows skyward. This storm is what we call progress.

(Benjamin 1973: 259–60)

This image complements the emerging view of history, as detritus and shored ruins, in the world of Charles Baudelaire and then Franz Kafka, of Eliot and Joyce. Modernity is both the culmination of the past and the harbinger of the future, pinpointing a moment of potential breakdown in socio-cultural relations and aesthetic representation. It is not surprising that artistic reactions and responses bifurcated into the largely celebratory (Marinetti, Le Corbusier, Mayakovsky) and, particularly in the British Isles, the primarily condemnatory or apocalyptic and despairing (T. S. Eliot, W. B. Yeats, Ezra Pound, T. E. Hulme, D. H. Lawrence).

More generally, 'modernity' is an imprecise and contested term. It has been said to encompass Western history from the Renaissance, or the epoch that began with the seventeenth-century scientific revolutions of Galileo, Hobbes, Newton, Leibniz and Descartes; it has also been argued to have been inaugurated by the eighteenth-century Age of Enlightenment and its drive to a mastery of nature and society through reason, since which rationality has been considered the key to justice, morality, control, organisation, understanding and happiness. One influential critic, Marshall Berman (1983), divides modernity into three phases, 1500–1800 (when people struggled to find a vocabulary to describe modern life), the 1800s (from the American and French Revolutions through the great upheavals across Europe in the nineteenth century), and the 1900s (in which almost the whole world became involved in the process of modernisation). Alternatively, modernity has been said to be an attitude rather than an epoch (Foucault 1986). Above all, it is characterised by the attempt to place humanity and, in particular, human reason at the centre of everything from religion and nature to finance and science. Modernity describes the rise of capitalism, of social study and state regulation, of belief in progress and productivity leading to mass systems of industry, institutionalisation, administration and surveillance. Defended by its supporters as a universal endeavour that leads to the gradual emancipation of all human beings, its adversarial critics contend that reason and knowledge are merely used to enslave and control people in alternative ways to premodern society, which employed coercion, religion and 'natural' authority to achieve social domination. One of modernity's staunchest defenders, the critic Jürgen Habermas, argues that 'The project of modernity, formulated in the eighteenth century by the philosophers of the Enlightenment, consisted in their efforts to develop objective science, universal morality and law, and autonomous art according to their inner logic . . . for the rational organization of everyday life' (Habermas 1981: 9). For Habermas, modernity is an incomplete project because it continues to attempt its own self-redefinition through many instances and utterances of identification and projection. But, the counter-argument runs, while the dominance of reason and science has led to material benefit, modernity has not fostered individual autonomy or profitable self-knowledge. It has not provided meaning to the world or to spiritual life, religious or otherwise, perhaps reducing humans merely to rational(ising) animals who are increasingly perceived as more complex and consequently more emotionally, psychologically and technologically dependent. Humanity arguably appears without purpose and is instead merely striving for change and transformation, which produce only momentary satisfaction or meaning. Modernity is also associated with the period of European global expansion, such that its universalising thrust has been concomitant with and dependent upon near-global systems of subjugation and navigation despite its Eurocentric focus. Suggestions of countermodernities based on colonial or post-colonial models have been made by critics such as Homi Bhabha (1991) and Paul Gilroy (1993) among others.

Modernism has, therefore, frequently been seen as an aesthetic and cultural reaction to late modernity and modernisation. On the one hand, modernist artists kicked against the homogenisation required by mass systems. On the other, they celebrated the new conditions of production, circulation and consumption engendered by technological change (Harvey 1989: 23). There were paradoxical if not opposed trends towards revolutionary and reactionary positions, fear of the new and delight at the disappearance of the old, nihilism and fanatical enthusiasm, creativity and despair.

## PERIODS, GENRES, MODELS

Modernism is regularly viewed as either a time-bound or a genre-bound art form. When time-bound, it is often primarily located in the years 1890–1930, with a wider acknowledgement that it develops from the mid-nineteenth century and begins to lose its influence in the mid-twentieth century. This is certainly the period in which most modernist literature was written, but, conversely, most literature written in the period was not modernist. When genre-bound, modernism is associated with innovation and novelty and has been stretched to include such British and Irish figures as John Donne, William Blake, Samuel Taylor Coleridge and Laurence Sterne: typical aspects to this kind of 'modernist' writing are radical aesthetics, technical experimentation, spatial or rhythmic rather than chronological form, self-conscious reflexiveness, scepticism towards the idea of a centred human subject and a sustained inquiry into the uncertainty of reality. Any adequate discussion, however, has to take note of both views and of their meeting point in the intense international and interdisciplinary artistic revolutions around the start of the twentieth century.

Another approach is to attempt to construct a description of the representative features of modernist writing or style (for example, see Whitworth 2007). One critic, Norman Cantor, has offered what he calls a Model of Modernism (Cantor 1988: 35), with the following characteristics. Modernism favoured anti-historicism because truth is not evolutionary and progressive but something requiring analysis. It focused on the micro- rather than the macrocosm, and, hence, the individual more than the social. It was concerned with self-referentiality, producing art that was about itself and texts that were self-contained rather than representational. It leant towards the disjointed, disintegrating and discordant in opposition to Victorian harmony. Modernism also advocated that an object exists in terms of its function; a house is, therefore, seen as a machine for living in (Le Corbusier) and a poem 'a machine made for words' (William Carlos Williams). It was frequently and unashamedly elitist, in that, for example, modernist art stressed complexity and difficulty and also emphasised that culture had changed in response to the machine age. In terms of sexuality and the family, modernism introduced a new openness with candid descriptions often sympathetic to feminism, homosexuality, androgyny and bisexuality beside a questioning of the constraints of the nuclear family which seemed to hamper the individual's search for personal values. Modernists did not view ethics as superior to art, seeing the latter instead as the highest form of human achievement. If Victorian literature was concerned with morality, modernist writing was concerned with aesthetics. Lastly, Cantor notes a tendency towards feelings of apocalypse and despair following decades of creeping Victorian doubt. In this spirit, modernist texts often focus on social, spiritual or personal collapse and subsume history under mythology and symbolism.

Other oft-noted characteristics are a focus on the city and a championing as well as a fear of technology; technical experimentation allied with radical stylistic innovation; a suspicion of language as a medium for comprehending or explaining the world; and an attack on nineteenth-century stalwarts such as empiricism and rationalism. Above all, however, from the mid-nineteenth century onwards, what has come to be called modernism appears retrospectively to have been a wide-ranging and far-reaching series of vigorous and persistent attempts to multiply and disturb modes of representation. Its artistic expansion seemed to follow on from other kinds of growth: scientific, imperial and social. These lucrative material changes were accompanied by individual and collective crises, especially spiritual, which issued in a new literature that was rebellious, questioning, doubtful and introspective but confident and even aggressive in its aesthetic conviction. In 1857, the cultural commentator and poet Matthew Arnold gave a lecture entitled 'On the Modern Element in Literature'. He described this modern style in terms of repose, confidence, tolerance, free activity of the mind, reason and universals (Arnold 1857). Fifty years later the avant-garde of literature expressed the opposite: alienation, plight, chaos, unreason, depression and a disenchantment with European culture.

Modernism can be taken as a response by artists and writers to several things, including industrialisation, urban society, war, technological change and new philosophical ideas. Because the nineteenth century experienced a spreading disillusionment with existing models of the individual and the social, the Western world was transformed and reinterpreted by Marx, Freud and Darwin, who respectively changed established notions of the social, the individual and the natural, as will be discussed in Chapter 1 prior to an overview of their effects on literary and cultural genres in Chapter 2. Imperialism had exposed European sensibilities to alternative cultures, ethics and social structures. The First World War, and the years immediately before and after it, brought about the demise of many institutions and beliefs: the class system was rocked by the rise of trade unions and the Labour Party; beliefs in King and Country, patriotism and duty were betrayed by the carnage of the war; the strength of patriarchy was challenged as women went to work outside the home and the suffrage movement gained hold. In terms of the trauma of the war itself, the effect on modern consciousness cannot be overstated. It resulted in the invention of new weapons, such as submarines, aeroplanes, poison gas and cannons with ranges over 75 miles, and produced more than 33 million military casualties, and an additional 5 million civilian deaths, not counting the millions of war-related influenza deaths. With devastation on such a scale, it became absurd to celebrate noble ideas like human dignity in art, or blithely to assert a belief in human progress. The war produced a deep distrust of optimistic secular or teleological understandings of history and seemed a climactic, severing event that showed conclusively the failures of nineteenth-century rationalism. As will be discussed in Chapter 3, the war was a defining moment in terms of both society and the individual, such that the fracturing of minds that came to be known as shell shock seemed to represent in miniature what was happening to societies and nations, as much of the world went to war, Europe was torn apart, and Russia was thrown into revolution.

Technological changes meant that modernism was an art of a rapidly transforming world of industrial development, mechanisation, urbanisation, secularisation and mass forms of social interaction. By 1900, there were on the planet eleven cities with populations of over 1 million. London and New York stood at over 5 million people, while Paris had 3 million inhabitants and Berlin 2 million. At the end of the nineteenth century, there were several key areas of technological advancement whose importance has also to be appreciated: motor power (internal combustion engine, diesel engine, steam turbine); fuel (electricity, oil and petroleum as new power sources); transport (automobile, motor bus appeared in London in 1905, aeroplane, tractor); communication (telephone, typewriter, tape machine – all leading to modern office organisation); synthetic materials (chemical industry was revolutionised, man-made fibres, plastics). Also, in 1895, modern physics began with the use of X-rays, the discovery of the radioactive properties of uranium and the initial work with radium; in 1897 electrons were detected for the first time, and the quantum theory of energy was proposed in 1900. Albert Einstein's Special Theory of Relativity appeared in 1905, and when his theories of a fourth dimension appeared a decade later, the accepted picture of the physical universe, which had been fixed by the 1884 Prime Meridian Conference which enshrined the universal day with Greenwich as its zero point, was fundamentally altered. Such changes created modern living, which was now about distance, speed, consumption, communication and mechanisation. Most famously, Marinetti openly celebrated change in 'The Founding and Manifesto of Futurism':

> We say that the world's magnificence has been enriched by a new beauty: the beauty of speed. A racing car whose hood is adorned with great pipes, like serpents of explosive breath – a roaring car that seems to ride on grapeshot – is more beautiful than the *Victory of Samothrace* . . . Time and Space died yesterday. We already live in the absolute because we have created eternal, omnipresent speed.
>
> (Cahoone 1996: 187)

There was also a new perception of reality and the function of art. The previous dominant modes had been a poetics of mimesis, verisimilitude and realism. By contrast, modernism marked a movement towards increased sophistication, studied mannerism, profound introversion, technical display, self-scepticism and anti-representationalism. In music, modernists responded to the lush symphonies of the nineteenth century with atonalism; in art, they progressively undermined realism in movements like post-impressionism, expressionism, cubism, symbolism, imagism, vorticism, Dadaism, futurism and surrealism (see Chapter 2). Each presented a different way of viewing reality. In fiction, new writers spearheaded a rejection of several of the fundamentals of classic realism, such as a dependable narrator; the depiction of a fixed stable self; history as a progressive linear process; bourgeois politics, which advocated reform not radical change; and the tying up of all narrative strands, or 'closure'.

Modernism can also be discussed in terms of its exclusions and its critical reformulations. I have mentioned its Eurocentric bias, but, in its reactionary aspects, it has also been characterised as a response to mass culture and to feminisation, and thus as resting upon a masculinist elitism. This construction chimes with many of the pronouncements, in fiction and in essays, by male writers of the time, and it also describes the character of much criticism on modernism until recently. Around the turn of the century, literature was increasingly perceived as a 'profession' and as, therefore, supposedly outside of women's domestic sphere, and it was beginning to be seen as a serious academic discipline, one that had to be assessed and regularised. Previously, literary study had been considered suitable for women and not for men, but in the early 1900s it was more and more thought that instead of being an escapist amusement, literature could teach codes of behaviour and define national identity. Consequently, the literary 'world' became colonised by various benign commercial and didactic interests: the *Times Literary Supplement*, the Oxford University Press' series of World's Classics and the Everyman imprint, the Nobel Prize for Literature (founded in 1901), and the creation of the English Association (1907) to establish the essential role English literature should play in British culture.

This growing emphasis on a masculine national culture culminated in the setting up in 1910 of the Academic Committee: a coterie of male writers gathered together with the aim of establishing all that was best and most important in English letters. It included Thomas Hardy, W. B. Yeats and Joseph Conrad and, at times, constituted a dining and debating club which was to a degree set upon establishing a virile, manly English literature. One of the Committee's conclusions was that Victorian literature had been too feminine and moralistic, and that writers such as George Eliot, whose reputation has never been lower, had held back the English novel in comparison with its European equivalents. Much of this can be easily read as a reaction to the rise of the suffragette movement and its equivalent in writing, the New Woman, against whom Kipling composed 'The Female of the Species', Henry James created Henry Ransom in *The Bostonians* and Edmund Gosse railed in 'The Decay of Literary Taste' (Ledger 1997: 177–98). Since the 1980s, modernist writing has been questioned and broadened, in terms of both its authors and its poetics. For example, writers such as Katherine Mansfield, Mina Loy, Dorothy Richardson, Sylvia Warner and Charlotte Mew have been added to Virginia Woolf's token inclusion in the modernist canon, which was previously summarised as *The Men of 1914: T.S. Eliot and Early Modernism* or *The Pound Era*, in the titles of well-known books (replied to in Scott's *Refiguring Modernism: The Women of 1928*). Critics such as Alice Jardine (1985) and Rachel Blau DuPlessis (1985) have also registered the commonality between modernist writing and *écriture féminine*, irregular, fluid and experimental 'feminine' writing theorised by French feminist critics such as Julia Kristeva and Hélène Cixous (see Moi 1985).

However, claims by such critics as Andreas Huyssen that there is a 'powerful masculinist mystique' explicit in modernism seem too passive in their acceptance of the self-definition embarked upon by certain male writers and critics. Huyssen suggests that even more than an exclusion of women (for example, Jean Rhys, Elizabeth Bowen, Mary Butts) in established modernist criticism, there is a celebration of maleness, a phallic triumphalism which informs the 'movement', and this has often characterised the canon celebrated by critics of US literature in particular. Others, however, have sought to reconstruct the idea of the literary experimentation and newness of the period by avoiding the hegemonic claims of a literary elite as the avant-garde in favour of a more inclusive apprehension of challenges to accepted aesthetic and formal or social and political norms coming from various underprivileged or embattled quarters. There has also been greater emphasis on the texts of Caribbean and African-American literary modernism since studies like Houston A. Baker's key 1989 tract *Modernism and the Harlem Renaissance*. These critiques contrast the traditional picture of modernism as an urban movement, centred on Paris, London, New York, etc., with newer emphases on, *inter alia*, the black Atlantic (see Paul Gilroy), modernism in anticolonial resistance movements (see Boehmer), new mythologies of the Caribbean in writers such as Wilson Harris and Kamau Brathwaite (see Pollard).

From these divergent viewpoints, the three highly structured chapters, on influences, genres and texts, that form the rest of this book sketch a syncretic picture while introducing the precursors, writers and theorists of modernism as well as summarising the key formal, thematic and aesthetic preoccupations of a range of influential fiction and poetry written by avant-garde authors. Chapter 1 explains the impetus that Darwin, Marx, Freud, Nietzsche, Saussure and Einstein gave to experimental writers at the end of the nineteenth and the start of the twentieth centuries. Chapter 2 illuminates the pan-European origins of the radical literary changes that occurred in the novel, poetry and drama, as well as the many revolutions in art and film. Chapter 3 then analyses modernist elements in the texts of familiar writers such as Joyce, Woolf, Mansfield, Lawrence, Yeats, Eliot and Conrad, as well as in the work of less commonly studied authors such as Charlotte Mew and Rebecca West.

To develop a reasonable grasp of the subject, there is, of course, no substitute for reading modernist texts themselves, but, from a critical standpoint, the best follow-up to the introduction offered here is to read one of the many edited books of manifestos, extracts and documents that have been published on modernism, of which I would particularly recommend the valuable anthology of important background material by Kolocotroni, Goldman and Taxidou (1998), and, for a more recent but very different assembly, Rainey (2005).

## INTERNATIONAL ANGLOPHONE MODERNISMS

The broader phenomenon of transatlantic modernism pivots on what Malcolm Bradbury has called 'dangerous pilgrimages': the heavy traffic between the old and new worlds, whose dangers and attractions would be repeatedly analysed by myriad writers (such as Henry James, Edith Wharton and Ford Madox Ford). Most important here is the fact that American writers came to Europe to help revivify language and literature. Before Pound and Eliot came to Britain, Gertrude Stein came to Paris in 1903, and, for thirty years, turned her quiet courtyard apartment on the rue de Fleurus, adjacent to the cafés of Montparnasse, into 'the great hub of cosmopolitan aesthetic activity' (Bradbury 1995: 253). Paris itself burnt into life in the pre-war years as, *inter alia*, Diaghilev and Stravinsky, Proust and Gide, Picasso and Apollinaire took centre stage. Stein herself came into her own at this time but entered the prime of her influence in the 1920s when every visiting American writer had to stop and sojourn at her studio. As C. Barry Chabot notes, American literature would have been both very different and much poorer if Gertrude Stein had not taken up residence in Paris and 'made her home a shrine to everything that was culturally up-to-date' (Chabot 1997: 10).

It is also true, however, that prior to the vogue for Paris, London had drawn more than its fair share of writers, and it continued as a cultural centre to attract artists through the decades up to the Second World War. After Henry James and George Bernard Shaw came to London in 1876, the list of exiles and émigrés includes Conrad, Pound, Eliot, Mansfield, H.D., Wilde, Olive Schreiner and many others. London also served as a magnet for those within Britain who were fighting feminist and socialist causes, making the influx to the capital from around the country and the world one of the most important stimuli to a revolution in culture that would probably have been matched by a revolution in politics had not the Great War intervened. As far as the effects on British life are concerned, as Lyn Innes has argued, the coming together of some of the most gifted and articulate representatives of countries and cultures throughout the empire produced 'the readiness to question the assumptions, traditions, [and] doctrines of the English ruling class' (2002: 178). Edward Said goes further. He argues that modernist form was *necessary* to 'deal with' a new sense of Europe's vulnerability occasioned by texts and artefacts from the Empire. The familiar symbol of this is the shock not of the new but of the African mask with all that it signified to Europe of primitivism and transgression, marking a primal moment of modernism in Picasso's painting *Les Demoiselles D'Avignon* (1907).

An example of transatlantic connections is Mina Loy (1882–1966), a radical poet whose involvement with Gertrude Stein and Ezra Pound, modern art and futurism, free verse and free love, produced poems from 1910 onwards that gained a contemporary notoriety, about 'Joyce's Ulysses', 'Brancusi's Golden Bird', 'The Ineffectual Marriage' or 'Parturition' – a poem whose form mimics a woman's contractions in labour. Her characteristic cynical wit and violent imagery in poems such as 'Love Songs' led one of her editors to declare: 'To reduce eroticism to the sty was an outrage, and to do so without verbs, sentence structure, punctuation, even more offensive' (Scott 1990: 233). Loy's influence on modernism has often been underestimated, as has the role of the feminist movement on changing aesthetics more generally. For instance, it is fundamental to the course of imagism's development that on 15 June 1913, Dora Marsden and Harriet Shaw Weaver produced the first edition of their paper, the *New Freewoman*. They entrusted Ezra Pound with soliciting literary contributions, and he duly accepted work from Wyndham Lewis, Robert Frost, William Carlos Williams, Amy Lowell, H.D., Richard Aldington and other imagists. From the start of 1914, the *New Freewoman* was transformed into *The Egoist*, the journal which was to last for a year longer than the war and, after serialising James Joyce's *A Portrait of the Artist as a Young Man* in its first two years, was to introduce as its assistant editor, in 1917, an American expatriate called T. S. Eliot (Ross 1967: 60–70).

Considering Anglo-American intersections, a further dimension to modernism's experimentation particularly crucial to the US context is noted by Michael North:

> Writers as far from Harlem as T. S. Eliot and Gertrude Stein reimagined themselves as black, spoke in a black voice, and used that voice to transform the literature of their time. In fact, three of the accepted landmarks of literary Modernism in English depend on racial ventriloquism of this kind: Conrad's *Nigger of the 'Narcissus'*, Stein's 'Melanctha', and Eliot's *The Waste Land*. If the racial status of these works is taken at all seriously, it seems that linguistic mimicry and racial masquerade were not just shallow fads but strategies without which modernism could not have arisen.
>
> (North 1994: Preface)

In his first sentence, North is alluding to the Harlem Renaissance, a term that has come to be used to refer to a range of artists, musicians and writers of the 1920s, including Claude McKay (1890–1948), Nella Larsen (1891–1964), Langston Hughes (1902–67), Countee Cullen (1903–64), and Jean Toomer (1894–1967), who were some of the first African-American cultural and social commentators to engage the idea of the modern. Influential early book-length publications were the British Jamaican poet Claude McKay's new black urban poetry in *Harlem Shadows* (1922), which Michael North says in *The Dialect of Modernism* inaugurates the movement (North 1994: 8), and Jean Toomer's fragmented, impressionistic, mixed-genre prose in *Cane* (1923). The heyday was the 1920s, but important works relevant to the movement were published up to 1940, and one of the most important writers of the 1930s was Zora Neale Hurston (1901–60), whose anthropological analysis of her ethnicity influenced the writers of the Harlem Renaissance as well as many other black authors.

Alain Locke's anthology *The New Negro: An Interpretation* (1925) was a key publication that included nearly all those who would later be seen as a part of the Renaissance. However, in his influential book *Modernism and the Harlem Renaissance*, Houston A. Baker Jr locates the beginning of African-American modernism in a speech by Booker T. Washington on 18 September 1895, which was given as the opening address at an Atlanta Exposition where he 'offered guiding premises and discursive strategies' that would be expanded in his autobiography *Up from Slavery* (1901). The extensive use of rhetoric and distinctive forms of expression are then what come to define African-American modernism for Baker, but the Renaissance was also highly notable for its engagement with issues such as black poverty, racism and African-American identity. More recently, it has been noted how, in terms of the relationship between modernisms, it can be argued that, when Jean Toomer's novel *Cane* (1923) alludes to Eliot's *The Waste Land* (1922) and Claude McKay's 'Home to Harlem' has allusions to Hemingway's *The Sun Also Rises* (1926), African-American texts may be shown to 'signify' upon white texts repeatedly. Baker in fact says that

> Modernist 'anxiety' in Afro-American culture does not stem from a fear of replicating outmoded forms or of giving way to bourgeois formalisms. Instead, the anxiety of Modernist influence is produced, in the first instance, by the black spokesperson's necessary task of employing audible extant forms in ways that move clearly *up*, masterfully and re-soundingly away from slavery.
>
> (Baker 1987: 101)

Another key influence on African-American writing and the Renaissance was W. E. B. DuBois (1868–1963), and especially his tract *The Souls of Black Folk* (1903), with its idea of black 'double-consciousness' in white society and the famous opening line of its second chapter: 'The problem of the twentieth century is the problem of the color-line' (DuBois 1994: 9). In 1909, DuBois founded the National Association for the Advancement of Colored People, and he wished African-American art to be directed towards political ends, but most of the authors declined to channel their efforts that way or see their works in terms of propaganda. The broader interest of the period in the primitive inspired many Harlem writers, while the intellectual community DuBois represented wanted a greater emphasis on economic improvement and social conscience.

Considering Locke's *The New Negro* the key manifesto of black modernism, Simon Gikandi concludes: 'one can see how advocates of cultural blackness existed both inside and outside the dominant notions of the Modernist aesthetic. For one, the continuous insistence on the newness of the Negro echoed Baudelaire's definition of Modernism as the art of the fleeting and the new.' (Gikandi 1997: 161) Locke himself declared that Harlem 'has the same role to play for the New Negro as Dublin has had for the New Ireland or Prague for the New Czechoslovakia' (Locke 1968: 17). Locke saw a new psychology and a new spirit at work in the texts of many African-American writers, and it is this that aligns the interior focus of black modernism with that of traditional Anglo-American modernism.

Explaining his desire to put the Harlem Renaissance into the mainstream of discussion about modernism, Baker says that for an 'Afro-American student of literature like me', it is difficult 'to find intimacy either in the moderns' hostility to *civilization* that, in its prototypical form, is exclusively Western, preeminently bourgeois, and optically white' (Baker 1987: 6). However, in partial disagreement with Baker, Gikandi argues that high modernism's ideological emphases, from the critique of civilisation to the privileging of the bourgeois subject, might be said to stand against the drive in the Harlem Renaissance for

> the transformative power of civilization and progress and its evocation of the collective character of the masses. But this radical difference conceals, I believe, an identity of means. In other words, 'black modernism' set out to deploy the aesthetic ideology of modernism to affirm and sustain what we may call the incomplete project of 'black modernity'.
>
> (Gikandi 1997: 161)

This identity of means in some ways has helped to reorient discussion of Anglo- and especially American modernism away from its conventionally heavy accent on largely apolitical concerns. In common with several of the authors above, C. Barry Chabot in his 1997 book *Writers for the Nation* argues that American modernists (including Willa Cather, Allen Tate (1899–1979), Jessie

Fauset (1882–1961), Langston Hughes and Wallace Stevens) were deeply concerned with social values, community and the political life of the country. Chabot and others have thus helped to deflect analyses of modernism away from the more traditional emphases on experimentation and artistic innovation towards an engagement with history. Such reconceptualisations of Anglo-American modernism have also occurred alongside non-Eurocentric studies that have looked at the work of writers inventing new literatures outside of the West.

While many critics see the aesthetic revolutions of modernism shaped by disillusion at the failure of imperialism, Elleke Boehmer argues for an 'expanded picture of a globalized and constellated modernism' enveloping the modernist-inflected writings of nationalist movements in the empire's outer regions:

> the eclecticism of the 1900s Bengal art movement pioneered by E. B. Havell [1861–1934], Abanindranath Tagore [1871–1951], and Sister Nivedita [Margaret Elizabeth Noble, 1867–1911]; the Jamaican Claude McKay's 1910s articulations both in Caribbean patois and standard English; the atmospheric 1920s poetry of the Australian Ken Slessor [1901–71] or the Fauvist paintings of his compatriot Margaret Preston [1875–1963]; and the Eliot-influenced progressive Hindi poetry of Ajneya [1911–87] and Gajanan Madhav Muktibodh [1917–64] in the 1940s and 1950s.
>
> (Boehmer 2002: 175)

For Boehmer, experimental writing can be seen in a post-colonial context as 'a nexus of uneven developments' in which it is emphasised that modernism was shaped by global influences and modernist self-scrutiny is understood to have taken place in a period of imperial expansion and colonial contact.

Though Boehmer argues for a broader understanding of experimental literature of the period in her book *Empire, the National and the Postcolonial, 1890–1920: Resistance in Interaction*, literary modernism outside of the Harlem Renaissance remains a largely white phenomenon in critical studies – but only if one retains a restricted, and especially a time-bound, notion of modernism. The works of writers such as Wilson Harris, from Guyana, and

Gabriel Okara, from Nigeria, have a great deal in common with modernist forms and styles though these authors use them to different ends in non-European contexts, while Latin American and Hispanic Caribbean writing has been said to use the poetics of modernism for anti-colonial struggle (see Iris Zavala's *Colonialism and Culture*, 1992). Indeed, in *The Black Jacobins* (1938), the influential critic C. L. R. James made this claim long ago for Aimé Césaire, who uses Eliot's vision of a unified human time in 'The Dry Salvages' to found Negritude (James 1980: 402). Charles Pollard thus goes on to talk about the 'New World Modernisms' of the Caribbean in writers such as Wilson Harris and Kamau Brathwaite.

Caribbean writers such as Harris and Césaire have openly adopted modernist linguistic strategies and formal approaches, and such realignment of modernist aesthetics has altered modernism's relationship to history, colonialism and political systems. Simon Gikandi maintains 'that a consideration of modernity and modernism from the margins of the modern world system inevitably forces us to question previous definitions of the term itself and to recognise its variegated genealogies and contradictory categories' (Gikandi 1992: 254). Noting that the key foundational works of Caribbean modernism were written outside the West Indies (Aimé Césaire's *Cahier d'un Retour au Pays Natal*, Frantz Fanon's *Black Skin, White Masks*, C. L. R. James's *The Black Jacobins*, George Lamming's *In the Castle of My Skin*, V. S. Naipaul's *A House for Mr Biswas*), Gikandi also argues that exile for Caribbean modernists was used 'as an instrument for transcending the prison-house of colonialism. In both a psychological and an ideological sense, exile would be adopted as an imaginary zone distanced from the values and structures of colonialism; it would hence be posited as the point of departure for ... anticolonial discourse' (Gikandi 1992: 34)

Considering a generation of diverse writers from George Lamming (1927–) and Sam Selvon (1923–94) to Wilson Harris (1921–) and Paule Marshall (1929–), Gikandi argues that

> Caribbean modernism has evolved out of an anxiety toward the colonizing structure in general and its history, language and ideology in particular; ... this modernism, which is closely related to creolization,

develops as a narrative strategy and counter-discourse away from outmoded and conventional modes of representation associated with colonial domination and colonizing cultural structures.

(Gikandi 1992: 5)

While Anglo-American modernism often wanted to escape history through aesthetics, writers of Caribbean origin and influence sought to exorcise enslavement and the ahistorical positioning of colonial subjectivity. Thus, alongside the arrival at a Caribbean concept of history, a parallel decolonisation of the mind required working through the terminology of Western political history and its totalising ideological concepts to understand and depart from those gestures of control. Caribbean modernism thus came to challenge colonial history through the creation of a form of representation that emphasises or acknowledges displacement, otherness, contradiction and reversal.

However, the convergence of modernism and late colonialism remains a particular matter of anxiety for Caribbean writers who have borrowed from the European literary avant-garde, naturalising European language to West Indian culture. However, this syncretic approach has been symptomatic of the broader thrust and 'creolization has come to represent a unique kind of Caribbean Modernism, one that resists the colonizing structures through the diversion of the colonial language and still manages to reconcile the values of European literacy with the long-repressed traditions of African orality' (Gikandi 1992: 16).

It is also significant that for both Caribbean and Anglo-American modernists, a key issue was how to remake subjectivity, narrative and language for the purposes of liberation. The figure of the Maroon, or escaped slave, provided a model for this in the Caribbean, indicating a strategy for literary reworking by using knowledge of a dominant culture to oppose it. The tropes of doubling, displacement and linguistic invention are as common in Caribbean as in Anglo-American modernist writers. Gikandi writes: 'exile and the displacement it engenders constitutes the ground zero of West Indian literature, its radical point of departure; exile generates nationalism and with it the desire for decolonized Caribbean spaces' (Gikandi 1992: 33).

Finally, it remains true that a partial critique of empire lies at the heart of canonical modernism in central works such as *Ulysses*, *The Waste Land* and *Mrs Dalloway*. In the first novel by Woolf to feature the Dalloway family, *The Voyage Out* (1915), the restrictions of patriarchy are already linked explicitly to Empire. In this, her debut novel, Woolf casts Richard Dalloway as the supporter of imperialism who says, 'I can conceive no more exalted aim – to be the citizen of the Empire' (Woolf 1978: 63). This is the culmination of his discussion of Empire with Miss Vinrace, who has asked him what is his ideal. For Richard Dalloway, 'unity' and 'dominion' emerge as expressions of the ideals of progress, and for him the 'voyage out' concerns the spread of ideas from the imperial centre.

The sentiments associated with Dalloway in Woolf's *A Voyage Out* stands as the opposite to those in Edward Said's concept of the 'voyage in' which brings colonial values back to the metropolis: 'the conscious effort to enter into the discourse of Europe and the West, to mix with it, transform it, to make it acknowledge marginalized or suppressed or forgotten histories ... I call this effort *the voyage in*' (Said 1993: 260–1). As a result of the voyage in, Said thinks the high-point of modernism marks the beginning of the end for the Grand Narratives that reinforced patriarchy and Empire, signalled by the disquieting appearance in Europe of various people from the Empire who by their very presence challenged and resisted familiar metropolitan understandings, aesthetic beliefs and histories in the works of writers like Eliot, Conrad, Mann, Proust, Woolf, Pound, Lawrence, Joyce and Forster.

As Henry Louis Gates has pointed out, it can thus be argued modernism was a 'mulatto movement' in which newness came to art and culture through syncretism and fusion, typified by the art of the Harlem Renaissance and Paul Gilroy's theory of the black Atlantic, which brings an explicitly intercultural perspective on modernity that focuses on a complex cultural system: the transmigration of people, goods and capital between Europe, Africa and the Americas (the term 'black Atlantic' denotes a webbed intercontinental network of the local and the global, as opposed to nationalist cultural histories which fail to explain transcultural and transnational mixtures of ideas, categories and identities in the involved genealogy of black Atlantic culture that alone can explain such topics as the development of hip-hop, soul and jazz).

It is almost certainly incontrovertible that the apogee of modernism marks a time at which Western art forms were shaped by international culture. In addition to the influence of Japanese and Chinese art on key figures such as Pound, there is the impact of African art on European artists like Derain and Picasso and the popularity of jazz rhythms with classical musicians and poets. There are the allusions to Indian subjects and imagery in the poetry of Yeats and T. S. Eliot, Eliot's use of African-American references and Conrad's questioning of the prevailing assumptions of racial superiority justifying European imperialism, matched by Leonard Woolf (1880–69) in his fiction and letters about Sri Lanka.

Which is to say that, increasingly, modernist art and writing appear to critics as in some ways a consequence of the growing awareness of different cultures in the oscillation of the voyage out and the voyage in. Additionally, this double voyage was not simply a geographical one but a temporal one also, as both mythology and anthropology brought the traditions of other cultures into contemporary Western thinking. Thus, when asked in 1919 what he thought comprised *modern* culture, T. S. Eliot first listed 'Byzantine, Polynesian, African, Hebridean, [and] Chinese . . .' art (1988: 317). There is also the regard held by Pound and Yeats for Chinese and Japanese drama and poetry, as well as the allusions to Indian subjects and Eastern imagery in the poetry of Yeats and Eliot.

Modernism was a metropolitan phenomenon that drew on the outposts of empires, yet a critic such as Fredric Jameson has argued that only Joyce is uniquely placed to treat imperial issues within modernist form. In this, he reveals a common blindness with regard to modernism outside of Euro-America. As Edward Said notes,

> Most histories of European aesthetic modernism leave out the massive infusions of non-European cultures into the metropolitan heartland during the early years of this century, despite the patently

important influence they had on modernist artists like Picasso, Stravinsky, and Matisse, and on the very fabric of a society that largely believed itself to be homogenously white and Western. In the interwar period students from India, Senegal, Vietnam, and the Caribbean flocked to London and Paris; journals, reviews, and political associations formed – one thinks of the pan-African congresses in England, magazines like *Cri des nègres*, parties like the *Union des Travailleurs Nègres* established by expatriates, dissidents, exiles, and refugees, who paradoxically work better in the heart of the empire than in its far-flung domains, or of the invigoration provided African movements by the Harlem Renaissance. A common anti-imperialist experience was felt, with new associations between Europeans, Americans, and non-Europeans, and they transformed disciplines and gave voice to new ideas that unalterably changed that structure of attitude and reference which had endured for generations within European culture. The cross-fertilization between African nationalism as represented by George Padmore, Nkrumah, C.L.R. James on the one hand, and, on the other the emergence of a new literary style in the works of Césaire, Senghor, poets of the Harlem Renaissance like Claude McKay and Langston Hughes, is a central part of the global history of modernism.

(Said 1993: 292–3)

# 1

## INTERPRETING AND CHANGING

In 1845, Karl Marx stated that 'The philosophers have only *interpreted* the world in various ways; the point, however, is to *change* it' (Marx and Engels: 286). This stands as a warning for the second half of the nineteenth century and a battle cry for the Modernist period. Certain writers in different fields did change the world in the sense at least of massively altering people's most fundamental interpretations of the world. Not least in any such list would be the six figures given prominence in this chapter: Freud, Darwin, Saussure, Nietzsche, Einstein, and Marx himself. They are not all from the same generation but were all born in the nineteenth century and for a short time their lives overlapped around 1880, at the threshold of the artistic revolutions that would be collected under the heading of Modernism. In this chapter, these names will be used as shorthand for the fundamental breaks with previous understandings that occurred in Victorian Britain and across the Western world at this time; in terms of politics and history, religion and evolution, psychology, philosophy, language and science.

Modernism is a literature of the twentieth century but its clarion call is sounded throughout the nineteenth century in voices as diverse as those of Kierkegaard and Carlyle, Strindberg and Melville, Ibsen and Baudelaire. Their Janus-faced perspectives allow a bleak condemnation of the rejected past and an optimistic vision of a refashioned future, an outlook which peaks in the Italian Futurists' recommendation to eschew history, burn its books and recreate the human in the image of the machine. Here, the belief in a possibility of wholeness, whether of society or the individual, is still evident. The Modernists who followed after the First World War were more noticeable for their pessimism and their sense of a failed, fragmented society, in which the uncomprehending individual was swallowed up by huge forces outside of personal control, leaving many writers with the sense that they should withdraw into their art and an intense, aesthetic world where sense, shape and order could be achieved. Such reactions are, for example, arguably evident in the immersion in memory of Marcel Proust, the paranoid visions of Franz Kafka, and the solipsism of Samuel Beckett.

## MARX (1818–83)

Karl Marx was a social, political and economic theorist grounded in French political history, German philosophy and English economics. Educated at Bonn and Berlin, he was born into a Jewish family in Germany who had to hide their religion to escape anti-Semitism. He emigrated to Paris in 1843, where he met Friedrich Engels, and there developed his idea of the alienation of humans in capitalist society and the necessity for a proletarian revolution in order to effect social change. He moved to Brussels in 1845 and wrote with Engels the *Communist Manifesto* (1848) and *The German Ideology* (posthumously published). After the failure of newspapers of which he was editor, and under political pressure, Marx and his family moved to London in 1849, and in the British Library, he worked on his masterpieces *Grundrisse der Kritik der politischen Ökonomie* (1857–8) and the three volumes of *Das Kapital* (1867, 1884 and 1894). In these, he expounds the theory of surplus value, inherent class conflict, the inevitable historical evolution from capitalism to socialism and the attenuating of the state with the successful rise of the classless society achieved by communism.

Marshall Berman has argued that

> In the first part of the *Manifesto*, Marx lays out the polarities that will shape and animate the culture of Modernism in the century to come: the theme of insatiable desires and drives, permanent revolution, infinite development, perpetual creation and renewal in every sphere of life; and its radical antithesis, the theme of nihilism, insatiable destruction, the shattering and swallowing up of life, the heart of darkness, the horror.
>
> (Berman 1983: 102)

It is not surprising, therefore, that the large cluster of individuals and theories that cohere around the name of Marx and Marxism have been extremely important in their influence upon and conceptualisation of modernism. Modernism has not only been theorised as an alienation from capitalism, by commentators from Georg Lukács through to Fredric Jameson, it has also had its most radical aspect in Marxist criticism and theory, as evidenced in the writings of Walter Benjamin, Bertolt Brecht and Theodor Adorno. An understanding of the nineteenth-century shifts from country to city, land to factory, individual to mass production, can best be arrived at in terms of the influence of Marx's analysis of history, politics and society. Modernism has repeatedly been characterised as a literature of crisis, and it is Marx who places crisis at the centre of capitalist development. On the one hand, Marx sees that crises 'by their periodic return put the existence of the whole bourgeois society in question, each time more threateningly' (*Communist Manifesto*) and texts such as E. M. Forster's *Howards End*, T. S. Eliot's *The Waste Land*, D. H. Lawrence's *Women in Love*, and W. B. Yeats's 'The Second Coming' are driven by a similar fear of crisis and longing for rejuvenation. Also in the *Communist Manifesto*, Marx realises how such a society, through its competitive drive, flourishes through its crises: 'on the one hand, by enforced destruction of a mass of productive forces; on the other, by conquest of new markets and more thorough exploitation of the old ones' (Berman 1983: 103). Much modernist writing also understands this cyclical movement but ascribes it to natural not economic forces: the importance of circles and cycles, whether deduced from Darwin, James Frazer's *The Golden Bough*, or Nietzsche's Zarathustra, is clear in the work of D. H. Lawrence, Malcolm Lowry and many others. Lawrence, for example, insisted that 'we have to drop our manner of on-and-on-and-on, from a start to a finish, and allow the mind to move in cycles, or to flit here and there over a cluster of images. Our idea of time as a continuity in an eternal, straight line has crippled our consciousness cruelly' (1932: 97–8).

From a Marxist viewpoint, modernist art grows out of a European loss of communal identity, out of alienating capitalism and constant industrial acceleration. The work of avant-garde artists was fuelled by the rise of urban living, the invention of the proletariat and the bringing together of the human with the machine, epitomised by Jacob Epstein's *Rock Drill* sculpture. According to Fredric Jameson (1984: 78) Modernism is the middle part in a triad of cultural periods that begins with realism and ends with postmodernism and that parallels social and economic upheavals precipitated by technological innovations, such as the shift from steam to electric motors to electronic machines, and the development of a mass commodity culture. Modernity, in classical Marxism, is a double-edged phenomenon in which capitalism and the rise of the bourgeoisie eliminated feudalism and brought enormously significant forms of communication, transport and production but also created a serially exploited proletariat which would eventually overthrow it.

Over the second half of the nineteenth century, the vision of an organic society is gradually eroded, and conflict is increasingly seen as the basis of life in the industrialised West, as Marx and Engels had pictured all history at the start of the *Communist Manifesto*. Indeed, the *Manifesto* may be viewed as in some senses the first of the many modernist proclamations of (the need for) a radical break from the past. Modernist writers were most clearly affected by this in that they attempted to represent alienated urban living. The elements of defamiliarisation and difficulty in modernist writing arguably stemmed from this disaffection; the *Communist Manifesto* can be said to be the first modernist manifesto in that its dialectical contrariness appears to presage the contradictions, ambivalences and double consciousness of modernism.

Marx argues that capitalism thrives on disturbance, uncertainty and the progress that is needed to stave off stasis, and so describes the symptoms from which the modernist writers would consider themselves to suffer. The flattening of status introduced by the authority of exchange-value also strips away many of the distinctions fundamental to previous societies. The elitism ascribed to modernist writers can again be read in terms of the loss of authority suffered by professional, spiritual and artistic elites, who all become paid labour alongside every other wage-earner. The market economy recognises no privileges or externalities but considers all commodities and competitors equally. In fact, questions of value and vulgarity are at the heart of the bourgeois mentality but seep into the economy only in terms of the vagaries of supply and demand: Van Gogh's paintings are valueless in the 1890s and priceless in the 1990s. Many modernist artists reacted against this by creating a new importance for art, by elevating aesthetics above everything, including morality and money, and by condemning the everyday and the humdrum, often including ordinary life. We may take as an example T. S. Eliot's disapproval of his contemporary figures in *The Waste Land*, which is more usual than Joyce's celebration of his characters in *Ulysses*. The shift to abstraction in avant-garde art has also been seen as a symptom of this alienation from social reality. Even before the turn of the century, from Charles Baudelaire through to Oscar Wilde, there is a systematic elevation of art above truth, completing the shift from 'art imitates life', through 'art imitates art', to 'life imitates art'.

The separation between art and economics within society is a theme of E. M. Forster's novel *Howards End* (1910) and indicates one way in which, though the book is in many ways realist, Forster's social analysis reaches towards a modernist sensibility; for example, Cyril Connolly wrote in his 1938 survey of modern literature that *Howards End* showed 'a great departure from the writing of the nineteenth century. Extreme simplicity, the absence of relative and conjunctive clauses, an everyday choice of words ... constitute a more revolutionary break from the Mandarin style than any we have yet quoted' (1938: 38). The novel's organisation and outlook rest upon a division between the male, practical, solidly middle-class English Wilcoxes and the female, artistic, upper-middle-class German Schlegels, in which the former have power and money while the latter have culture and pedigree. Forster, like most liberal or left-wing modernists, was also anti-colonial, and so it is additionally important to note that the Wilcoxes' money largely comes from their Anglo-Imperial Rubber Company.

For Marx, modernity is a constant impulse to renewal engendered by the dynamics and crises of capitalism. He divides history not into two stages of the premodern and modern but into modes of production. Marx's vocabulary is also, in many ways, that of the modernists, with its apocalyptic images of earthquakes, abysses, eruptions, tidal movements, powers and forces. Marshall Berman recognises that Marx provides the definitive vision of the modern environment in his characterisation of the bourgeois era in the *Communist Manifesto*:

> Constant revolutionizing of production, uninterrupted disturbance of social relations, everlasting uncertainty and agitation, distinguish the bourgeois epoch from all earlier ones. ... All that is solid melts into air, all that is holy is profaned, and men at last are forced to face ... the real conditions of their lives and their relations with their fellow men.
>
> (Marx 1983: 21)

Marx sees capitalism as driven to creation and recreative destruction, renewal, innovation and constant change; which are also the dynamics of modernism.

In contrast to the social-realist novelists of the nineteenth century, modernist writers focused on psychology, introspection and individual consciousness. Also, while realists depicted history using a similar set of tools to historiographers, the modernists felt that authorial omniscience and third-person narration were misleadingly 'objective' techniques which did not allow for the position of the storyteller. Similarly, the present always surely stood in the way of any clear and direct explanation of the past. In James Joyce's *Ulysses*, Stephen Dedalus declares pessimistically and introvertedly that 'History. ... is a nightmare from which I am trying to awake' (1969: 40). Writers such as Joyce turned against forms of historical understanding, seeing greater meaning in the individual than in society. The ideology expressed by this stance has been hotly disputed by Marxist writers, and their debate is frequently contextualised in terms of the opposed stances of the Hungarian critic Georg Lukács and the German dramatist Bertolt Brecht, a dispute which was continued by Lukács and the German social philosopher Theodor Adorno after the Second World War. Lukács's position is best outlined in his late essay 'The Ideology of Modernism' (1957), in which he argues that modernism involves a 'negation of history' by self-consciously pitting itself against the past and by rejecting modes of historical understanding (Lukács 1957). Modernism, he argues, was there- fore profoundly anti-Marxist. By this, he means that modernist writers were interested in the personal, spiritual or mystical transcendence of their surroundings, and so the social environ- ment in their texts is little more than a backdrop. Lukács argues that this concern for the human rather than the social condition manifests itself in two ways: first, the protagonist is delimited by personal experience, unmarked by historical specificity, and, second, the individual is isolated, neither forming nor formed by the world. Such a subjective representation of reality seemed to Lukács profoundly reactionary, suggesting that culture could be separated from history, human beings from their actual material conditions. Lukács championed what he saw as historical rea- lism's dynamic presentation of dialectical change in preference to Joyce's historical stasis, which Lukács thought reflected the individualism of bourgeois society.

Against this viewpoint, the dramatist Bertolt Brecht countered that the purpose of art for Marx and Marxists was not to reflect social conditions but to attempt to change them, and this could only be done through the shock tactics of avant-garde modernist aesthetics. Real social conditions such as poverty and inequality should not be shown as either fixed or acceptable, as suggested by their naturalised depiction in most realist writing, but as abhorrent, outrageous and unjust. Brecht's approach in his own plays, which intentionally alienated the audience from the char- acters and conditions they saw on stage, was in many ways the (formal but not ideological) incarnation of the American poet Ezra Pound's dictum that modernist artists should always 'make it new' (1934). As social conditions changed, as capitalist forces adjusted to and assimilated revolutionary forms of art, those means of artistic representation had themselves constantly to change in order to force people to reappraise their lives. Brecht argued against Lukács in 1938 that

> Realism is not a pure question of form. Copying the methods of these realists [Honoré de Balzac and Leo Tolstoy], we should cease to be realists ourselves. For time moves on ... new problems flare up and demand new techniques. Reality alters; to represent it the means of representation must alter too. Nothing arises from nothing; the new springs from the old, but that is just what makes it new.
>
> (Brecht 1975: 424–5)

However, there are different views which take us beyond these polarised opinions and interpret modernist writing in other ways which are illuminating. Theodor Adorno, a major figure in the Frankfurt School of critical theorists, maintained that art and literature, and particularly modernist art, could function as a kind of negative or contradictory criticism of society, in thought-provoking experimental texts. Adorno argued that difficult texts provoked new, unfamiliar, estranged conceptions of life – which is to say that the dissonances and fractures of modernist art expressed the individual's loss of control, centredness and harmony in the contemporary world. For Walter Benjamin, a champion of Brecht's attempt to prise art from the confines of traditional bourgeois forms, such fragmented existence was reflected in the work of Baudelaire, whose graphic portrayal of urban life was to influence Eliot's London scenes in *The Waste Land*. Another important critical text is Benjamin's 'The Work of Art in the Age of Mechanical Reproduction', written in 1936, which analyses aesthetic works in terms of alienation and commodities (Benjamin 1973). Benjamin argues that in a world of printing, duplication and photography, artistic works have lost the 'aura' that their uniqueness once gave them. The rising technologies of artistic reproduction dispensed with the idea of a work's authenticity; for example, the idea of an authentic photographic or film print makes no sense. Benjamin thought this moved art's function from the realm of ritual, where it is magical and revered, into that of politics, where it is mass-produced for purposes of marketing and propaganda, with dire consequences for a politically polarised Europe after the Great War. The relation between politics and art, he felt, was radically different under fascism, which renders politics aesthetic, as in the choreography and stage-management of Hitler's Nuremberg Rallies, and Communism, which politicises art, as in the work of Brecht. These dialogues and debates amongst Marxist critics can be profitably studied in the collected volume *Aesthetics and Politics: Debates between Bloch, Lukács, Brecht, Benjamin, Adorno* (Bloch et al. 1977).

The last critic I want to discuss in this connection is Fredric Jameson. In his 1982 book *The Political Unconscious*, Jameson again takes up the issue of modernism's relation to history. In particular, he is interested in the division between realism's transparent representation of history, based on a principle of verisimilitude, and modernism's insistence on the difference of each individual's experience and interpretation of life. Jameson argues that all interpretations are, in fact, ideological, but that many deny this and repress historical forces through 'strategies of containment', such as symbolism. The purpose of interpretation is therefore to penetrate to the text's 'political unconscious', to the historical contradictions and the social conflicts it has repressed. In fact, it is only through this analysis of the ideological subtext that history can be approached. History is, therefore, the absent cause of the text which must be read back into the text. In this light, the formal experiments of the modernists appear as textual attempts to resolve the problems of contemporary society. Modernism's strategies of relativity and stream-of-consciousness narrative are compensations for the dynamics of late capitalism. Jameson, therefore, argues that while modernist writers appear to sideline history, they are, in fact, dealing with it constantly, through their efforts to transcend or contain it. In expressing new worlds, they are not only implicitly criticising but perhaps slowly changing the old.

## DARWIN (1809–82)

Charles Darwin, grandson of physicist Erasmus Darwin, was an English naturalist born in Shropshire and educated at Edinburgh and Cambridge, where his interest in geology and zoology was encouraged. From here, he took a post as naturalist on the HMS *Beagle*'s scientific survey of South American seas (1831–6), visiting, among other places, Tenerife, Brazil, Buenos Aires, Chile, the Galapagos Islands, Tahiti and New Zealand. Having private means, he devoted himself afterwards to studying the findings of that expedition, which were developed into a sketch of conclusions in 1844, at which point he had begun to formulate his principle of evolution by natural selection, the cornerstone of his theory. However, wary of controversy, Darwin delayed publication, and it was only when Alfred Russel Wallace put forward a fundamentally similar idea that he moved to publish *The Origin of Species by Means of Natural Selection*, in 1859. Subsequent work was effectively a series of supplements to this book and included *The Descent of Man and Selection in Relation to Sex* (1871), which related the progenitors of humanity to apes. Darwin was not the first to expound a belief in evolution, but his principle of natural selection turned it from a speculation into a verifiable theory.

Natural selection's emphasis on the propagation and survival of the fittest can be seen from a Marxist viewpoint as one of the main underpinnings of a capitalist morality legitimised by selfish genes, the struggle for self-preservation and -promotion. Marxism, in turn, can be viewed from an evolutionary perspective as societies mutate and develop from feudal to capitalist to communist systems.

Alongside the Marxist critique of capitalism, the impact of evolutionary theory was also felt in modernist writing, though neither was often explicitly discussed: both evolution and capitalism were great levellers, supposedly liberating individuals from archaic rule by the clergy and the aristocracy but dividing humanity between the strong and the weak, either physically or financially. Darwin's argument that sex and natural selection were at the root of human development suggested a different kind of species from the previous belief in one unchanging humanity modelled on God's image. Humans were closer to animals than to a God, and nature was evolving not static. This suggested different narratives of human history, not one of a single progression towards a final judgement day; but a cyclical movement within nature, in which reproduction and survival of the fittest increasingly became recognised as the forces behind human endeavour, not rational thought or spiritual belief.

For several sciences, such as zoology, geology and botany, Darwin's *The Origin of Species* (1859) represented a sea change in the thinking of their practitioners. Throughout the nineteenth century, the rationalism of science and philosophy attacked the validity of religious faith, but Darwin's is the name most often associated with the overthrow of the old order. To many people, Darwinian evolution and, subsequently, social Darwinism embodied the assault on traditional beliefs concerning God, the universe and humanity's position in relation to each. Even in England, Darwin was not alone in this attack, but was a figurehead, alongside the philosopher Herbert Spencer (1820–1903) and the theologian Bishop Colenso (1814–83), for the advance guard of scientists questioning religion's ideological dominance over science; and even their theories were in some ways carrying on from the implications of Charles Lyell's *Principles of Geology* of the early 1830s. All these thinkers, while offering liberating ideas of human change and progress, also proposed theories which overwhelmed individual agency or will within new systems of vast collective social and biological forces.

On the negative side, late nineteenth-century theories of 'degeneracy' also fit in to this general area of new ideas about human development and social manipulation. The translation of Max Nordau's influential book *Degeneration* in 1895 was perhaps the most important of many works published in Britain on the theme from the 1880s onwards. Degeneration was the term used to describe a sense of a social status quo under threat from the freer values of a younger generation sceptical about the worth of their society's strictures on morality, customs and proprieties, especially sexual, raising fears over chastity, homosexuality or same-sex love, perversity, masturbation, morbidity and syphilis. According to Nordau, the end of civilisation could be foretold from contemporary trends in the arts, such as naturalism or mysticism and decadents such as Oscar Wilde. The rise of the New Woman and the suffrage movement were also co-opted into this apocalyptic vision. The joint preoccupation with sin and disease led to the former being considered a species of the latter, and any deviation from conventional morality was deemed a sign of madness as much as depravity. After Darwin's outline of the progress of the species, it was inevitable that theorists would speculate on human adaptations that were not for the better and on the possibility that evolution could be regressive. Edwin Ray Lankester, a close follower of Darwin, published *Degeneration: A Chapter in Darwinism* in 1880, in which he speculated on the decline of not the species but the white races, who might become socially parasitical. A discourse which originated in medical circles soon began to dominate social theories.

A fascinating text in this respect is H. G. Wells's pioneering science-fiction romance *The Time Machine* (1895). *The Daily Chronicle*, reviewing the novel on its first publication, praised the last pages of the story and called it 'that last fin de siècle, when earth is moribund and man has ceased to be'. *The Time Machine* caught the mood of the decade, because, written at the end of the century when society was full of discussion of end-points, it envisioned both the end of humanity and the end of the world. In fact, the popular literature of the 1880s and 1890s in general produced a number of fantasy genres reflecting current issues of human development, degeneration and depravity. The horror fiction of monstrous selves and others is present in Bram Stoker's *Dracula*, Oscar Wilde's *The Picture of Dorian Gray* and Robert Louis Stevenson's *Dr Jekyll and Mr Hyde*, all of which have been read partly as cautions against a rise in *fin-de-siècle* promiscuity and its concomitant evils of prostitution, syphilis and adultery. However, these texts are also related to themes of Empire and colonialism, facets of European expansion which were suffused with images of fearful tribal varieties and threatening animalistic human natures. *Dracula* certainly warns of the threat to Christianity posed by Eastern paganism. *Dr Jekyll and Mr Hyde* and *The Picture of Dorian Gray* each caution against the 'savage' side of humanity which is only kept in check by culture and civilisation.

Again, at the very end of the century, Joseph Conrad's *Heart of Darkness* warns against this explicitly. Its social argument is that the civilised veneer of European nations actually functions through constraints and is primarily composed of a series of occupations like those of butchers and the police who shield people from violence and so create the illusion of an evolving non-aggressive community that is becoming progressively more 'civilised'. Social Darwinism argued that human societies can improve and evolve in the same way that species do, but societies too, therefore, have their origins and their antecedents. Just as apes are considered to be related but under-evolved humans, so then, in the 1890s, are non-European societies perceived as related but underdeveloped or degenerate civilisations. Many of these theories, such as those of the Scottish anatomist Robert Knox (1791–1862) and the French Orientalist Comte de Gobineau (1816–83), have been grouped together with social Darwinism as kinds of scientific racism. Indeed, Gobineau has also been considered the intellectual ancestor of Nietzsche and the true originator of Nietzsche's 'over-man' philosophy (see Comas 1961).

The theory of degeneration threatened Europe with the possibility of a reversion to a less complex and more barbaric form of society. Notions of 'evolution', 'progress' and 'reform' led to an urgent fascination for their apparent opposites: 'regression', 'atavism' and 'decline'. For the Victorians, evolution was meant to turn the primitive into the civilised, to lead from African society to European; but, at a later stage, Darwin and his followers, unconcerned with the racism inherent in their argument, began to think that perhaps evolution was not synonymous with 'progress'. Degeneracy then became a byword for modern Western civilisation, and it was supposedly witnessed in all the new tendencies in the arts. Dandyism, naturalism and mysticism were all manifestations of degeneracy. That other 'races' had supposedly evolved less far – such as in Africa – or had developed into decadence – such as in the East – hinted that signs of European weakness might be genetically determined rather than socially controlled. This threat to European society was felt to also be a threat to imperial dominance. The moral justification for colonialism was based precisely on a rhetoric of social and racial superiority. If a country had not independently achieved an advanced stage of industrialisation, it signified a social and cultural backwardness, an inferiority on behalf of the country's people. According to this logic, it then became the duty of the developed nations to educate, civilise and improve what they called primitive peoples. In this way, exploitation, encouraged by fear as well as greed, appeared as education (see Trotter 1993).

This was also the era of eugenics, championed by Darwin's cousin Francis Galton, of the study of selective breeding and the delineation of racial qualities. Interbreeding or miscegenation was frowned upon, and it was argued that a nation that fails to ensure that 'its better elements have a dominant fertility' has destroyed itself more effectively than its foes ever could. In *The Time Machine*, the positive effects of eugenics are alluded to in the distant future's elimination of disease and the cultivation of new beautiful flowers. However, one of the book's twists is that the reason why animals have died out is not because humans have become vegetarian but because they have started eating each other instead (see Rich 1986).

*The Time Machine* is an example of a novel about degeneracy because it is a story about the loss of mental and physical strength: as Wells's Traveller says at one point, 'This has ever been the fate of energy in security; it takes to art and eroticism, and then come langour and decay'. It is also significant that Wells's Traveller finds only what he considers to be inferior people in his travels. This sense of a superiority to anything or anyone who might be encountered on an English adventurer's travels is typical of Victorian imperial *hubris*. Both of the tribes the Time Traveller encounters in the future, the Eloi and the Morlocks, are characterised by mental and physical degeneracy. The Eloi are described thus:

> one of them suddenly asked me a question that showed him to be on the intellectual level of one of our five-year-old children — asked me, in fact, if I had come from the sun in a thunderstorm! It let loose the judgment I had suspended upon their clothes, their frail light limbs, and fragile features.
>
> (Wells 1972a: 25)

So, the Eloi, Wells's fey, Grecian aesthetes, are children both mentally and physically. Wells uses the idea of degeneracy literally and argues that the human race might return to a 'child-like' state: to the innocence and ignorance symbolised by Adam and Eve in Eden. As the Traveller says at one point: 'The too-perfect security of the Upper-worlders had led them to a slow movement of degeneration, to a general dwindling in size, strength, and intelligence' (Wells 1972a: 50).

By contrast, the underground Morlocks, who are representative of the basement dwellers, miners, underground travellers and down-stairs servants of Wells's own period, are described in this way:

> I turned with my heart in my mouth and saw a queer little ape-like figure, its head held down in a peculiar manner ... it was a dull white, and had strange large greyish-red eyes; also there was flaxen hair on its head and down its back. ... I cannot even say whether it ran on all-fours, or only with its forearms held very low ... a small, white, moving creature with large bright eyes which regarded me steadfastly as it retreated. It made me shudder. It was so like a human spider! ... But, gradually, the truth dawned on me: that Man had not remained one species, but had differentiated into two distinct animals: that my graceful children of the Upper-world were not the sole descendants of our generation, but that this bleached, obscene, nocturnal Thing, which had flashed before me, was also heir to all ages.
>
> (Wells 1972a: 46–7)

The Eloi are again children, but the Morlocks have regressed differently, into animals walking on all fours, devoid of facial characteristics. Once more, Wells employs the theory of degeneracy literally, but instead of positing a return to childlike or Judeo-Christian innocence, he takes the model of evolution and draws the Morlocks along the lines of prehistoric cave-dwellers and animals, likening them to apes, rats, spiders and ants. The world represented here, with effete Eloi above ground and squalid Morlocks below, would seem to be one in which the Victorian middle class have been lost, have been expunged by history. The book thus appears, from one perspective, as a novel that promotes the image of the scientific, educated middle classes gathered at the beginning in the Time Traveller's dining room as the foundation of society, keeping in check the excesses of a decadent aristocracy and a barbaric proletariat.

However, these two attitudes – towards others as children or primitive humans – also meet in another contemporary discourse of Wells's own time. If we view the novel as neither a prediction nor a comment on class but as a statement of the current English view of the world, these two visions of other people blend into one. Wells is writing at the time of the 'Scramble for Africa', when European nations were competing with each other for trade routes and territory. The European attitude to Africans was pre-cisely that of Wells's Traveller towards the Eloi and the Morlocks: on the one hand, they were children in an arcadian wilderness, incapable of self-rule and in need of European administration and government. On the other hand, Africans were considered aggres-sive savages and cannibals, creatures of darkness in need of the constraints of an enlightened civilisation.

*The Time Machine* is, in this reading, akin to a modernist vision of social apocalypse built on contemporary observations of racial inequalities. It is a journey into time in the same way that a novel such as Defoe's *Robinson Crusoe* is a journey across space, into the terrifying possibilities that other cultures represented for European civilisation. The egocentricity of the dominant Victor-ian worldview is also echoed by the Traveller's interpretation of the future civilisation he finds. Though there is a period of 800,000 years between his society and that of the Eloi and the Morlocks, the Traveller sees a direct correlation between his society and theirs. He is unable to consider the insertion of any significant social structure between the two. He believes *his* civilisation to be the origin of a society aeons into the future. This is the usual stuff of allegory: the projection of a different society in terms that correspond directly but imaginatively with the writer's own social background. But it is also an articulation of Victorian imperial confidence and racial fear. Moreover, in the light of Germany's rebuilding and industrialisation after the First World War, Wells's vision is replicated in a key modernist text, Fritz Lang's futuristic nightmare *Metropolis* (1926), a film which also consigns its workers underground while the children of the capitalist owners play in Elysian fields above the city. Indeed, the powerful motifs of Wells's fiction inform numerous kinds of social division that are found in twentieth-century fiction and many postmodernist post-apocalyptic films, from Ridley Scott's *Blade Runner* (1982) to John Carpenter's *Escape from New York* (1981).

Wells's book is not considered a modernist novel but in English fiction it comes right at the start of the period of modernist experimentation carried out by writers such as Henry James, with whom Wells debated the role of the novel as art or entertainment in their correspondence with each other. James felt that while Wells dealt with the circumstances of subjects of crucial contemporary interest, such as evolution, he did not consider the value of the knowledge, facts and details he was presenting. James thought that novels by such writers as Wells and Arnold Bennett were not unified artworks but monuments of 'the quarried and gathered material' they happened to contain – their interest lay in their accumulation and display of learning, not the analysis and value of that knowledge or its expression through consistent, life-like, rounded characterisation. In effect, James was asking for a shift from the models of Victorian 'baggy monsters', to concentrated, crafted fiction-writing which would fully express the complexity of human character. Wells brought in ideas of Darwinian evolution and of Marxist social organisation but did little to consider the value of these models of human development. At the end of the nineteenth century, novels of such a kind were not to be found in England, but in France and Russia.

An earlier novel than *The Time Machine*, one written in Russian, does have all the hallmarks of a very different sensibility from Wells's, one that is much closer to James's: Fyodor Dostoevsky's *Notes from Underground* (1864). In this book, an alienated narrator angrily dissects several of the issues also evident in *The Time Machine*, but Dostoevsky has them sarcastically articulated in a psychologically complex way which would be called modernist or proto-modernist. The unnamed narrator rails against Darwinism's attempt to explain the present by the past, as though the fact that humans are descended from apes adequately accounts for them individually. In this precursor to much twentieth-century fiction, Dostoevsky also scathingly attacks contemporary idealism in Russia. One of the novel's key targets is a book published in the previous year by an imprisoned political radical, Nikolai Chernyshevsky's *What Is to Be Done?*, a book that championed the idea of 'rational egoism', the belief that in a properly organised social system all people will act in their own best interests, benefiting from shared goals and mutual aid. Dostoevsky's narrator likens this vision, of all gaining from doing what is best for each, to an anthill, where every member is catered for and knows their place but where there is no individuality. The Underground Man compares Chernyshevsky's utopian dream of a supreme Crystal Palace (the new building unveiled in London in 1851 at the Great Exhibition) to vaudeville, in which suffering is also absent but life is vacuous and false. Against Chernyshevsky's faith in evolving human rationalism and positivism, Dostoevsky pits the world of 'underground' and asserts that people's wills and their deeper unconscious desires are far more important in shaping actions, accounting for wars and such human behaviour as lying and cheating.

What Chernyshevsky and Dostoevsky share is a radical passion for life, and their separate visions express the optimistic and the pessimistic poles of thinking that would characterise the modernists' attitude to urban, secular, planned industrialised society. Dostoevsky's narrator also fulminates against trends towards logic, as well as philosophical and social systems, because he believes humans' lives are more characterised by choice, perversity and doubt. He illustrates how people are more mentally complex than rationalists allow by attacking the mathematical tyranny that $2 \times 2 = 4$. Though impossible for logic, it is possible for human beings that $2 \times 2 = 5$. Reason abhors the equation, but the human imagination may find it beautiful or preferable. A further offensive is launched against the vogue for determinist philosophies, which are seen as 'blank walls' whose logical conclusion is that individuals are not responsible for what they do, nor can they be blamed for their actions or choices. The Underground Man maintains that determinism is only a logical exercise, and human beings are in fact driven by their volition, their free will. He admits that, against the idea of a perfect society, the possibility of individuality, of choices and preferences will also necessitate hardship and pain; however, he asserts many values at the same time, such as spontaneity, faith, beauty, will power and freedom, even though the book is most famous for its excoriating bitterness.

Henry James aimed for 'psychological realism' and Dostoevsky for a 'Higher Realism'. For both, reality lay in human consciousness and the fathomless workings of the mind. Unsurprisingly, Dostoevsky's assertion of the individual becomes a common one among later avant-garde writers, to the extent that Katherine Mansfield's husband, the critic John Middleton Murry, stated in his influential essay 'The Break-Up of the Novel' that for the modernist writers across Europe and America 'inner consciousness [is] reality'. Similarly, in *Fantasia of the Unconscious* (1923) D. H. Lawrence remarks that there is 'only one clue to the universe. And that is the individual soul within the individual being' (1971: 150). Realism had proposed a shared world perceived in largely the same way by all members of society; by contrast, the modernists argued that reality was as varied as the individuals who perceived it. While in many ways empowering, for many people, such an emphasis on the individual also brought with it feelings of alienation and existential angst after centuries of shared religious certainties.

At the turn of the century, Western humanity's belief in a purposeful universe was crumbling, alongside the spreading suspicion that God, if not dead, was absent from human affairs, a view that percolated down from intellectuals to the masses such that, in the years 1886 to 1903, church attendance in London declined by a quarter. Running parallel with this was a burgeoning growth in the 1870s and 1880s in alternative institutions, such as the theosophy societies, the Christian Scientists and the Salvation Army, as well as a rising interest in rival, often Eastern, religions, psychical investigations and, more obviously, secularist movements. The word 'agnostic' was itself only coined in 1870 to express the new-found conviction that to the empirical mind, belief and unbelief were equally impossible. However, the important seeds of doubt were sown soon after the mid-century;

for example, Tennyson's *In Memoriam* (1850) has often been signposted as a key literary turning point. This was not just precipitated by Darwinian evolution but by other theories, such as the German philosopher Arthur Schopenhauer's pessimism, the German naturalist Ernst Haeckel's determinism and Herbert Spencer's Darwinian 'synthetic philosophy'. In the forty years before the First World War, humanity increasingly found itself in a world which seemed hostile towards its species and a universe which, because, rather than in spite of, the advances of science, was steadily decreasing in its comprehensibility (see Lester 1968). People had lost many of their beliefs in external authorities and found themselves increasingly unsure not only of the universe but also of themselves; they were now seen as Godless primates sharing ancestors with other 'savage' animals. Not least for this reason, the world was ripe for Freud and for therapy, a situation anticipated by Darwin at the close of *The Origin of Species* when he states that because of the preservation of favoured races in the struggle for life, 'In the distant future ... psychology will be based on a new foundation' (1968: 458).

## FREUD (1856–1939)

Sigmund Freud was born of Jewish parentage in Austria and studied medicine at Vienna, where he worked as a neurologist at the general hospital from 1882. His first significant work was with Josef Breuer (1842–1925) in the treatment of hysteria via reminiscences under hypnosis. He moved to Paris in 1885 where he shifted his interest to psychopathology. On returning to Vienna, he established conversational 'free association' as an alternative to hypnosis for recovering repressed memories. Freud broke with Breuer in 1897 and went on to further develop his own views on psychoanalysis and the importance of infantile sexuality. In 1900, he published *Die Traumdeutung* (*The Interpretation of Dreams*), which argued that dreams were the product of repressed desires, akin to neuroses. His work, including *The Psychopathology of Everyday Life* (1901) and *Three Essays on the Theory of Sexuality* (1905), met with great controversy and widespread incomprehension. In 1910, he founded the International

Psychoanalytical Association with Carl Gustav Jung, its first president. Not many years later, Freud broke with Jung, as he had with Breuer before. After the First World War, he went on to produce his theories of the divided mind in *Beyond the Pleasure Principle* (1919–20) and *Ego and Id* (1923), identifying a primitive 'id' and a socialised 'superego' exerting sway over an embattled 'ego'. For Freud, a well-balanced ego is fundamental to healthy mental life, and a dominance of the ego by the id leads to psychosis and by the superego results in neurosis. The London Psychoanalytic Society was founded in 1913 by Ernest Jones, but none of Freud's works was translated into English until 1915. By the 1920s, most British intellectuals were familiar, if only at second hand, with Freudian concepts and terminology.

By the end of the nineteenth century, religion was in decline for a number of reasons. Science had in many ways dismantled the certainties of previous ages. Darwinism had shaken people's faith in the Book of Genesis or in a divine creator, and the churches were ceasing to perform a therapeutic role in helping individuals to cope with life's crises. According to one critic:

> The starting point of Modernism is the crisis of belief that pervades twentieth century western culture: loss of faith, experience of fragmentation and disintegration, and the shattering of cultural symbols and norms. At the centre of this crisis were the new technologies of science, the epistemology of logical positivism, and the relativism of functionalist thought – in short, major aspects of the philosophical perspectives that Freud embodied.
>
> (Friedman 1981: 97)

Freud is the one figure who all reviews of modernism privilege, and yet his work's impact has to be understood within the general increased level of inquiry at the turn of the century into the workings of the mind and its relation to society, by, among others, Carl Gustav Jung (1875–1961), Henri Bergson (1859–1941), William James (1842–1910), C. S. Pierce (1839–1914), J. W. Dunne (1875–1949), and Ernst Haeckel (1834–1919). The start of the new century is marked by a hunger for interpretation and an urge to decode societies, minds and personalities.

Besides Freud, an important figure in discussions of modernism's borrowing from psychology and philosophy is the French philosopher Henri Bergson. In *Time and Free Will* (1889), Bergson maintained that facts and matter, which are the objects of discursive reason, are only the outer surface that has to be penetrated by *intuition* in order to achieve a *vision in depth of reality*. Bergson thought that 'reality' was characterised by the different experience of time in the mind from the linear, regular beats of clock time which measure all experience by the same gradations. Bergson argued that psychological time was measured by *duration*, defined as the varying speed at which the mind apprehends the length of experiences according to their different intensities, contents and meanings for each individual. His work changed the way many modernists represented time in fiction. For example, in Virginia Woolf's *Mrs Dalloway* (1925), whose working title had been 'The Hours', a few pages are frequently given to the discussion of thoughts dwelt upon by a character while only a few seconds of common clock time elapse (see appendix to Easthope 1991).

Also relevant to any discussion of Woolf's mature fiction is the fact that when Bergson distinguished between chronological time and what he called 'duration', he did so by arguing that chronological time is the time of history (hours, minutes and seconds), while duration encompasses those times in a life which are significant to an individual and which are necessarily different for each individual. If you are asked to talk about your own life, the time that matters to you is to do with events in your growing up or subsequent achievements and crises – in short, experiences which have turned you into the person you are. You may have several significant moments in your life which matter to you, and the backdrop of clock time is irrelevant. As Proust famously noted, 'Reality takes shape in the memory alone'. Therefore, because individuals order reality differently from external time, fiction for the modernists had to represent the individual's actual experience, as with John Dowell's not chronologically but subjectively ordered meandering narrative in *The Good Soldier* by Ford Madox Ford (1873–1939). As T. S. Eliot put it in *The Waste Land*, mental life is composed of 'memory' and 'desire': the past and the future organised in the individual mind in the present. Chronology is a continuum our bodies unavoidably move through, but our minds are not held in a linear, one-dimensional universe except in as much as they are embodied. Bergson's *Time and Free Will* was enormously influential, impinging on the work of writers such as Woolf and Joyce and underpinning Wyndham Lewis's massive *Time and Western Man* (1927). Lewis, who was also influenced by Nietzsche, opposed the idea of any kind of continuity to time, seeing it instead as fragmented and people as inhabiting time only in memory and projection.

For many modernists, it is the clock, which regulates and parcels out time, that is to blame for the tyranny of space over the psychological flow of time in the mind. It is, of course, only in the mind that the past is preserved, and Bergson, like many others, argued that nothing was forgotten: all was stored in the mind even if it was not brought to the surface. Understandably, this new conception of the world led to the use of different techniques in art, such as the abrupt beginning and open-ended conclusion to many modernist novels. Bergson's conviction that experience is understood by intuition rather than rational reflection, combined with Freud's belief that past events shape the psyche, resulted in the view that reality only exists in subjective apprehensions becoming widespread in artistic circles.

What Bergson did for ideas about the mind's understanding or ignorance of time, Freud did for ideas of the mind's awareness of its own functioning. Freud's theories influenced the modern artist as much as any other's; he began publishing on psychoanalysis in 1895 and wrote his first influential paper on human sexuality in 1898, which was followed by *The Interpretation of Dreams* in 1900. With the publication of Freud's work, it became clear to many writers that there wasn't a unitary normative self to which each of us might conform, and many modernists were sufficiently influenced by advances in psychology to change the way they represented human character. For Lawrence, Woolf, Joyce and others, the self was not fixed and stable but evolving, fluid, discontinuous and fragmented. Where Marx had seen religion as a numbing drug, psychoanalysis as an explanation and diagnosis of the individual and also of the 'modern condition' came to substitute for religion, particularly for many artists.

In literature after Freud, many writers felt it was no longer sufficient to present the outsides of personalities and the surfaces of minds, as predominated in realist fiction; instead, the writer needed to explore hidden drives and desires, to deal in what Henry James called 'psychological realism'. For example, according to the editors of Freud's works in English, his 'most fundamental' theory was the Principle of Constancy, that the mind attempts to keep constant the quantity of emotion (or affect) within it, which is to say that the individual feels a need to discharge emotions, or, in other words, to express their feelings. In line with this, in many modernist novels, the inability to purge the mind of particular strong feelings results in madness, murder and pathological behaviour. From another angle, the Principle of Constancy is evident in the extract from Beckett studied in the Introduction. I mentioned that one of Beckett's major concerns was with the idea that the amount of suffering and of desire in the world is always the same. He described this as the constancy of 'the quantum of wantum', a philosophical notion that finds a psychological counterpart in Freud's belief that the quantity of, not energy or suffering, but feelings is constant as the individual strives to keep it to a minimum. Freud's interest in language, not least in *Jokes and their Relation to the Unconscious* (1905), is particularly well complemented by the use of puns and wordplay in the Irish modernists such as Beckett, Joyce and Flann O'Brien.

Freud's mapping of the unconscious also seemed to vindicate art's concern with symbolism and contingency; psychoanalysis (a term coined in 1896), both an art and a science, now seemed to suggest that life is full of hidden meanings and, for the conscious mind, haphazard events. This had a great effect, for example, on W. B. Yeats, who developed a range of mythopoeic symbols, which he worked up into a system described in *A Vision* (1925). Similarly, there are obvious connections between Freud's 'free association' and the modernist novelists' associative technique of 'stream of consciousness', most linked with Joyce but coined by the philosopher brother of Henry, William James; in 'Principles of Psychology' (1890), James writes that consciousness 'is nothing jointed; it flows. A "river" or a "stream" are the metaphors by which it is most naturally described. . . . Let us call it the stream of thought, of consciousness'.

Freud's use of therapy in which the patient's mind is allowed freely to associate ideas in order to uncover insights is reflected in many writers' interest in the novel as (a representation of) 'talking cure', as in Dostoevsky's confessional first-person novels, like *Notes from Underground*, or Ford's *The Good Soldier*, in which Dowell says his mind is 'circling in a weary baffled space of pain' and so he has embarked upon a painful but cathartic talking cure. Dowell says that the purpose of telling the story is 'to get it out of his head', as though he could transfer his distress onto the page. He imagines that he is talking to a silent listener in a domestic environment, and, as such, he seems to take on the role of a patient unburdening to a therapist. Hence his constant plea to the reader to 'sort it out' for him. Also, at one point, Dowell says: 'I don't know that analysis of my own psychology matters at all to this story' (Ford 1972: 99), and yet the reader soon divines that this matters more than anything else. Dowell goes on to say that while his psychology doesn't matter, he thinks he has at least given enough of it to anyone who believes that it does, placing the reader firmly in the position of psychological as well as textual decoder. The role of the reader as interpreter of the manifest matter of the novel beneath which lies latent content has often been compared to Freudian dream analysis. In fact, the language of psychotherapy and literary criticism shares, broadly speaking, many approaches and terms in common, not least 'analysis', and literature and psychoanalysis are almost unique and probably equally vigorous in their quest for insights into mental life.

This is not to say that many modernists were directly influenced by Freud's writing but that commonalities are easy to plot because so many writers and thinkers were keen to explore their own and their characters' psychological recesses. Freudian theory can easily be applied to Joyce's *Ulysses*, Lawrence's *Sons and Lovers*, or Woolf's *Mrs Dalloway*; not because these authors were translating Freud's theories into art. Joyce was damning of Freud, and, for his part, Lawrence, despite the obvious Oedipal entanglement of *Sons and Lovers* and his fascination with sexuality, avoided following Freud and was openly hostile to many of Freud's theories, looking instead to the work of Haeckel. Consequently, Lawrence's *Psychoanalysis and the Unconscious* (1921) can be more profitably read for its illumination of Lawrence's work than Freud's. The connections between Freud and these writers are instead because all were part of the widespread contemporary interest in psychical states and psychological motivations.

Freud was able to convince himself that his observations revealed universal conditions when he was able to observe neurotic symptoms in all people. His belief that every individual developed an unconscious which would affect their behaviour, to the extent suggested by his 1901 book *The Psychopathology of Everyday Life*, was echoed in the intense interest the modernists took in the drives, obsessions and compulsions motivating ordinary people. After his theory of the conscious, pre-conscious and unconscious, Freud's second tripartite map of the mind from 1923 postulated three agencies: a wilful, primal id; a socialised, prohibitive superego; and a part-conscious, part-unconscious rationalising ego in the middle, and this also finds numerous parallels in the tense confrontations between passion and convention in modernist novels. With the advent of psychoanalysis, among other new ideas, the theological search for God had been replaced by the epistemological quest for self-knowledge; enlightenment was not to be found in Christianity or in society but in the self, in individual subjective consciousness.

## NIETZSCHE (1844–1900)

Friedrich Wilhelm Nietzsche was an unconventional philologist and anti-idealist philosopher born in Saxony and educated at the universities of Bonn and Leipzig. His father, who died when Nietzsche was a child, was a Lutheran pastor whose religious beliefs were not shared by a son who was scathing of Christianity and of liberalism. A brilliant student, greatly influenced by Schopenhauer early on, at twenty-four Nietzsche became Professor of Classical Philology at the University of Basel. His first books were *The Birth of Tragedy* (1872), which divided experience between the two categories 'Dionysian' (aesthetic pleasure) and 'Apollonian' (rational discourse), and *Untimely Meditations* (1873–6), after which he had to retire from the university for reasons of ill health in 1878. He suffered a complete mental breakdown in 1889 after finishing his autobiography *Ecce Homo: How One Becomes What One Is* (published in 1908). A prolific, idiosyncratic and epigrammatic writer, his mature and best-known works (for which he accepted the term 'aristocratic radicalism') are *Beyond Good and Evil: Prelude to a Philosophy of the Future* (1886), *On the Genealogy of Morals* (1887), and *Thus Spoke Zarathustra: A Book for Everyone and No One* (1883–92), in which he expounds his theories of the *Übermensch* (super- or over-man) who is above societal morality, of the 'will to power', eternal recurrence and the death of God.

In the 1886 edition of his first book, *The Birth of Tragedy*, Nietzsche added a prefatory piece entitled 'Essay in Self-Criticism', in which he foreshadows the modernists' self-scrutinising and their concern with aesthetics as the primary responsibility of the artist if not of all individuals, overthrowing a Victorian fetishisation of morality:

> Art – and *not* morality – is represented as the actual *metaphysical* activity of mankind ... it is only as an aesthetic phenomenon that the existence of the world is *justified*. The whole book, indeed, recognises only an artistic meaning and hidden meaning behind all events ... One may call this whole artist's metaphysics arbitrary, idle, fantastical – the essential thing about it is that it already betrays a spirit who will one day and regardless of the risk take up arms against the *moral* interpretation and significance of existence.

In line with this, modernism was the first secular literature, in which natural selection replaced God's ordering of creation and a human will to power eclipsed the divine will. The First World War shattered any remaining belief in natural or supernatural benevolence, in terms of aristocratic *noblesse oblige* or providence. However, almost every article of faith challenged by the modernists had previously been attacked by Nietzsche, whose pronouncement in *Thus Spoke Zarathustra* that 'God is Dead' makes him an important figure to follow Marx, Darwin and Freud, but his influence is much wider. Nietzsche was a prophet, an iconoclast and a brilliant original scholar. Increasingly, he seems to be the figure who most overshadows twentieth-century critical theory; however, his position was not unique, and his ideas had parallels and precursors (Søren Kierkegaard is the most often cited), as well as followers in the existentialists of the twentieth century, such as Albert Camus and Jean-Paul Sartre.

Arthur Schopenhauer (1788–1860), the greatest influence on Nietzsche's early work, developed a philosophy of the will founded on a deeply pessimistic view of the universe (see *The World as Will and Idea*). An atheist, he believed, along with Plato and Immanuel Kant, that the world is only a physical manifestation of an underlying cosmic reality, which for Schopenhauer was 'the will' – whether the human thought of movement behind action or the timeless force of desire that Schopenhauer believed animated the universe, and led meaninglessly to all suffering because the will was never sated. While for Schopenhauer the 'will' denoted something metaphysical, which led him to recommend the denial of life, for Nietzsche it described a physiological complex of drives and impulses, and he moved increasingly to advocate its joyful celebration. Unfortunately, in a diagnosis that would appeal greatly to Yeats, Nietzsche felt that far from attending to the positive forces of its will, a repressed and enervated modern society was sick, led by frivolity and morbidity: a wilderness in need of a prophet.

If this view were true, as Nietzsche thought, it might explain why his idea of the driven will was co-opted by aggressive temperaments and oppressive political factions. Nietzsche's holistic view of universal will, most strongly expressed in *The Will to Power* (1885–8, published 1901), identified not 'power' but relations of power between forces, the driving energy behind human life. Life was to him, therefore, an endeavour to maximise one's own feelings of power over other people or things; an idea which, if not checked by other convictions, could result in such extremes as dictatorship, asceticism, self-punishment or sadism. Such beliefs, as well as being influential on modern theorists such as Foucault, Lyotard and Derrida, also led to political, especially fascistic, interpretations of Nietzsche's designations of different moralities for 'masters' and 'slaves'. This was compounded by his famous theory of the 'over-man', the *Übermensch*. Nietzsche believed that the highest goal humanity could achieve was an 'over-man', a new creative being who could transcend religion, morality and ordinary society, could further culture not reason, and whose life-affirming slogan would be 'Become what you are'.

Better than anyone, in texts like *Beyond Good and Evil* (1886, translated into English in 1907), Nietzsche expresses the contradictions and contrariness of a new aesthetic: 'We moderns, we half-barbarians. We are in the midst of our bliss only when we are most in danger'. He yearns for a new individual to create for the future new values – 'the revaluation of all values' – and to reject the present as already fading into the past. Nietzsche is also the theorist of nihilism, a term coined by Ivan Turgenev for *Fathers and Sons* (1861) but more fully explored in the misanthropic protagonist of Dostoevsky's *Notes from Underground* (1864), discussed above. In *The Will to Power*, a posthumously published book compiled from Nietzsche's 1880s notebooks by his sister, later a Nazi supporter, Nietzsche describes 'European Nihilism', in the title of Book 1, in terms of the centralising and secularising processes of modern politics. In Sections 22–3, he says of nihilism: 'It is ambiguous: A. Nihilism as a sign of increased power of the spirit: as *active* nihilism. B. Nihilism as decline and recession of the power of the spirit: as *passive* nihilism'. The first is actively, violently destructive; the second is marked by futility, resignation and cynicism. Both kinds would be evident in the attitudes of different movements banded together under the heading of modernism, in which a climate of revolution was as evident in the calls to destroy as in those to create.

In his first book, where he delineated the now dominant ordered, rational Apollonian mentality and the suppressed creative, aesthetic Dionysian spirit, Nietzsche had argued that one of the problems of the modern age was that people had lost touch with tragic myth, with the sensuality, intuition and truth found in Greek tragedy, and especially the Dionysian principle of dream and chaos expressed in Greek music. Both Darwin and Freud also contributed to an increased interest in myth. For many modernists, mythology, such as the story of Oedipus's murder of his father and marriage to his mother in Sophocles's *Oedipus Tyrannus*, was thought to obey a logic much closer to the subjective and associative promptings of the unconscious mind than to the formal progression of scientific inquiry. To writers like Yeats, Eliot and Joyce, the importance of myth applied to contemporary literature was in its ordering power, which the disharmony of modern society and culture had lost and only art could recapture. One critic has concluded that

> In writers, the search for order and pattern began in its own nega-
> tion, in the overwhelming sense of disorder and fragmentation
> caused by the modern materialist world. The artist as seer would
> attempt to create what the culture could no longer produce: symbol
> and meaning in the dimension of art, brought into being through the
> agency of language.
>
> (Friedman 1981: 98)

Sir James Frazer's *The Golden Bough* (12 vols, 1890–1915), which was greatly influential on Eliot's *The Waste Land*, is a key text which charts the connections between pagan rites and Christian religion. In literature, a progressive shift can be detected from the dismantling of religious narrative elements to the construction of new mythological models. For example, Hardy expressed a new set of values in his later novels which are nonetheless haunted by biblical allusions, archetypes and punishments, but the modernist writers who followed turned instead to classical models, most famously in *Ulysses* and *The Waste Land*. They also set about creating their own myths and bibles in all-encompassing works such as Joyce's *Finnegans Wake* (1939) or Proust's *À La Recherche du temps perdu* (1913–27).

In Britain, Nietzsche's ideas were propagated by the literary and cultural journal *The New Age*, which also, for example, first published most of Katherine Mansfield's early short stories, and his opinions became widely known after the publication in English of *Beyond Good and Evil* in 1907. He had admirers in

Wyndham Lewis and D. H. Lawrence. Lawrence's most admired novels, *The Rainbow* (1915) and *Women in Love* (1920, but completed 1916), are suffused with Nietzschean language. Consider, for example, this speech by Birkin to Ursula in *Women in Love*:

> 'But your passion is a lie,' he went on violently. 'It isn't passion at all, it is your *will*. It's your bullying will. You want to clutch things and have them in your power. ... You have only your will and your conceit of consciousness, and your lust for power, to *know*.'
>
> (Lawrence 1986: 92)

The earlier novel, whose second half is concerned with Ursula's emergence as a mature, sexual individual, also takes the assertion of 'will' as the principal motivation behind battling egos, such as that of Ursula's father: 'He was abstract, purely a fixed will' (Lawrence 1986: 117). Ursula's own key problem is the Nietzschean one of how to 'become what you are': 'How to become oneself, how to know the question and the answer of oneself, when one was merely an unfixed something-nothing, blowing about like the winds of heaven, undefined, unstated' (Lawrence 1986: 268).

For writers in Britain and across Europe, Nietzsche's assault on religion was particularly influential, as was his emphasis on the individual mind, which he opposed to the mass of the mindless 'herd'. In writers such as James, Conrad and Forster, there is also a clear artistic approach to fashioning chaos into an order of some kind, expressing the mind's unique subjective view in an essentially purposeless universe without authority or structure. Nietzsche's attack on science as not explanation but description also appealed to the artists who wanted to express better worlds, to seize the future for aesthetic principles. Another key belief expressed by Nietzsche was 'eternal recurrence', a theory misrepresented as simply the view that all experience is eternally repeated but best comprehended as an axiom for affirmative life: the individual *should* live each moment as though it were to be eternally repeated. An emphasis on not linear but cyclical time, brought to many Europeans by African culture, became a frequent modernist stylistic device, and many critics have commented on the circularity of works like Joyce's *Ulysses*, which at the most basic level, for example, starts and ends with the same letter, or *Finnegans Wake*, in which the opening and closing sentences to the novel run into and complete each other. But Nietzsche was recommending far more than an acknowledgement of life's cyclical patterning; eternal recurrence insisted upon the need to experience life to the full, to make the most of every moment, and to accept responsibility for present actions – whatever the individual chooses to do should be for all time, and so every person ought to strive to fulfil their potential or simply to 'become' what they are, and so should live as if they wanted each moment to come back again.

Lastly, Nietzsche's hatred for systematisers is visible in the modernists' earnest desire to speak for and as individuals, to express the internal not describe the external world, which was, in almost every respect, the product of a constricting social and aesthetic hegemony which needed questioning. Such systems included the philosophical, social, political and moral guidelines people turned to for convictions which were not their own; for example, Nietzsche railed against the debilitating influence of concepts such as guilt, pity, equality and democracy. After the straitlaced public morality professed by the Victorians, it was liberating for writers such as Lawrence and Joyce that Nietzsche deemed ethical beliefs the instinct of the herd, because he thought convictions of this kind are always held by groups, made up of weak individuals who are only strong collectively. Morality, thus, with the death of God, had been exposed as a function of self-interest and power. New criteria of judgement, based on aesthetics, were needed for art, and in many ways for life too.

Nietzsche's questioning of all certainties, in his assertions that truths are undisclosed errors or that facts are temporary, and his emphasis on relativity, interpretation and uncertainty, anticipates not only the art but also the science of the twentieth century. Nietzsche's original understandings of morality, aesthetics, truth and language are reminders of literature's many roots in philosophical ideas, and, in this respect, his contributions to Western thought were crucially added to by such thinkers as Martin Heidegger (1889–1976), who first stated the idea that individuals do not speak through language so much as language speaks through them, and Ludwig Wittgenstein (1889–1951), who conceived the idea that all human reasoning is a kind of 'language game' rather than an objective engagement with reality or truth. Nietzsche was the first philosopher to consider extensively human responsibility and freedom in a universe without God, but perhaps his primary legacy is to persuade philosophers and writers that truth is an 'army of metaphors' and that human reality is composed, first and foremost, of language, a subject of study revolutionised, if posthumously, by the Swiss linguist Ferdinand de Saussure.

## SAUSSURE (1857–1913)

Saussure was born in Geneva and became a professor of, first, Indo-European and then general linguistics at the University of Geneva. He was arguably the first person to question the accepted theoretical foundations of linguistics and then to reformulate if not change its object of analysis. His *Course in General Linguistics* (1916) was edited and completed from lecture notes by his students after his death. Saussure shifted the study of linguistics from a genealogy of changes in word and grammar usage over time to an investigation into language as a social phenomenon. His desire to detect systems resulted in the distinction between synchronic (descriptive and analytical) and diachronic (historical) perspectives, the separation of *langue* (language as structured system) from *parole* (language as particular utterance or speech act), and the formulation that 'language is a system with no positive signs', which, as a principle, was crucial in the theoretical development of structuralism and post-structuralism. '[W]hat was it that Saussure in particular reminded us of? That "Language (which consists only of differences) is not a function of the speaking subject". This implies that the subject ... is inscribed in the language, that he is a function of language' (Jacques Derrida).

The importance of language to the modernist sensibility is as great as to the postmodernist, but the emphasis is quite different. For realist writers, language had provided a tool to describe the world, almost to the extent of figuring as a window onto reality. For postmodernist writers, language constitutes reality; it does not describe the world but constructs it. As we saw in relation to Heidegger earlier, individuals have no access to 'reality' except through language, just as their minds have no knowledge of the world that is not provided by the senses. For the modernists, temporally and theoretically between these two positions, language was still a medium for conveying the world, but they found it increasingly difficult to deliver a common reality through words, which seemed not to be in agreement with the things they were meant to describe but in Eliot's phrase began to 'slip' and 'slide' ('Little Gidding'). Where postmodernists argue that 'reality' can only be engaged in and through language, modernists believed that there was such a shared world but that language was breaking down as it struggled and bent to encompass it. Language was in crisis because its simple relationship to the world, of naming and describing, no longer appeared to apply transparently, as ambiguity, irony, misunderstanding and the ineffable seemed commonplace. As Homi K. Bhabha has argued, Kurtz in Conrad's *Heart of Darkness* can express his vision only as 'The horror!', while the message of the Marabar Caves in Forster's *A Passage to India* amounts only to 'Ou-boum!'. Without a God to underwrite the Word, and without the old Victorian authority and confidence gained from God, the Empire and progress, words, as Alice found in Wonderland, could mean so many things that they were difficult to control; they had become unstuck from their respective referents such that individuals struggled both to express clear meanings and to tender authoritative accounts or descriptions.

A revolution in thinking about language occurred. Poetry could move to free verse, imagism, expressions of unconscious thoughts in surrealism, and to the cut-and-paste approach of the Dadaists. Narrative in fiction ceased to be either confident or consistent. After Dostoevsky's Underground Man could both say, 'I was a bad civil servant' and, half a page later, 'I was lying when I said just now I was a bad civil servant', Eliot's Prufrock could complain 'That is not what I meant, at all', Conrad's Marlow in *Heart of Darkness* could ask, 'Do you see the story? Do you see

anything? It seems to me I am trying to tell you a dream –
making a vain attempt', and Beckett's Unnamable could aver, 'I
can't go on. I'll go on'. And then stop. Most explicitly, Katherine
Mansfield ends her best-known story with Laura in 'The Garden
Party' searching for words: '"Isn't life," she stammered, "isn't
life—" But what life was she couldn't explain' (1951: 87). A
crisis in language also led to a crisis in communication, as when
Conrad's narrators ask repeatedly if we 'see' what they mean,
Ford's narrators ask if what they are saying makes sense, Beckett's
characters give up on the possibility of understanding, and, to
take an example we will look at in the next chapter, the Father
in Pirandello's *Six Characters in Search of an Author* concludes:
'We think we understand each other, but we never really do
understand'.

The figure whose thinking best marks this shift is Saussure, a
theorist who expressed and went beyond the modernists' crises of
language and inaugurated a linguistic turn which has given birth
to the theoretical perspectives offered by structuralism, semiotics
and post-structuralism. If, with world-changing consequences,
Freud decentred the individual and Marx decentred history, it
was Saussure's decentring of language that made possible so
much subsequent theoretical work across the arts, social sciences
and humanities in the second half of the twentieth century. His
importance to modernism lies in his parallel attempt to explore
the relationship between language and meaning. In revealing
language as a system of differences with no positive terms,
Saussure implicitly put in question the 'metaphysics of presence'
which had dominated Western philosophy. Signs owe their
capacity for signification not to the world but to their difference
from each other in the network of signs that is the signifying
system (see Belsey 1980: 136). Which is to say, there is an
absolute difference between (concepts of) objects in the real
world and the lexical sounds or marks used to denote them, such
that their yoking together is always arbitrary, just as using the
colour red to indicate 'stop' at traffic lights is arbitrary, as is its
use to mean 'in deficit' on a bank balance and 'danger' or 'anger'
in other sign systems. The importance of this is, first, that language is socially constructed, not divinely or naturally given,

and, second, that each term in the system only has a meaning in relation to the other terms in the system.

Saussure was, thus, not concerned, like other philologists, with the development of a language over time, but, like the modernists, with the way language was made to function by people, and the way that it made people function. He was, thus, most interested in establishing rules or structures of language which governed speech, in particular, and writing. For this purpose, he distinguished between *parole*, the utterance of an individual, and *langue*, the commonality or generality of language. His interest was the latter, deeming each speech act within the system merely a variant within the rules of discourse. This view came to lie behind the generalities and systems of structuralism.

Saussure has been accused of trying to replace God with structure, just as the modernists were accused of trying to compensate via art for the chaos created by God's absence from the universe. Perhaps most importantly, in his seminal essay 'Structure, Sign and Play in the Discourse of the Human Sciences', Jacques Derrida, thinking of Freud, Nietzsche, Heidegger and, especially, Saussure, argues that in the modernist period language became the key issue in discussions of truth and knowledge that it has since remained and 'everything became discourse'. In such discussions, another key term is undoubtedly 'relativity', the cultural belief already evident in much modernist writing, such as Conrad's, and boosted by the theories of Einstein, that because of differences in society, language, gender, sexuality, ethnicity and perspective, each person regards the world, and its meaning, differently.

## EINSTEIN (1879–1955)

Educated at Munich, Aarau and Zürich, Albert Einstein was born in Bavaria (to Jewish parents) but, by his death, had had German, Swiss and American citizenship. He was a mathematical physicist but was working as an examiner in the Swiss Patent Office when he began to publish his revolutionary papers on theoretical science. His Special (1905) and General (1916) Theories of Relativity overturned Newtonian physics and showed that in the case of objects travelling near the speed of light, strange occurrences such as diminished size and decreased mass can be expected. Einstein's belief in a space-time continuum, his equation for matter transformed into energy, $E = MC^2$, and, above all, his Theory of Relativity effected an irreversible paradigm shift in understandings of the physical universe.

> 'We should ask for no absolutes, or absolute. Once and for all and for ever, let us have done with the ugly imperialism of any absolute. There is no absolute good, there is nothing absolutely right. All things flow and change, and even change is not absolute'.
>
> (Lawrence 1971a: 186)

For Baudelaire, the modern individual had to embrace the transformations brought about by changes in physics, optics, chemistry and engineering, and the modern artist had to re-enact the new technological processes and energies: to bring them to life. This was an idea perhaps not fully realised until the early twentieth-century revolutions in cinema, painting and literature, represented through collage, montage, free verse and stream of consciousness (see Berman 1983: 145). At the same time as these early twentieth-century upheavals in art, a scientific revolution complemented the radical forms and perspectives offered by writers and painters and, indeed, appeared to serve as a perfect analogy for many avant-garde opinions about social relations.

While the natural sciences had been revolutionised by Darwin, physics and astronomy were turned around by Max Planck's work on quantum theory (1900–19) and Einstein's relativity theory (1905–15), to which could be added Werner Heisenberg's Uncertainty Principle of 1923, which undermined the claim to know anything absolutely about the material universe. This compounded Einstein's assertion that no physical law is entirely reliable but that the observer's position will always affect the result, will make the result relative and contingent. By the time of Heisenberg's principle, relativity was widely and excitedly debated in artistic circles as writers fondly embraced what they took to be the scientific backing for their ideas of individual perspective. The tendency towards narrative relativity, before and after Einstein, is perhaps the most striking aspect to modernist fiction, from Conrad and James to Proust and Woolf, in its use of perspective, unreliability, anti-absolutism, instability, individuality and subjective perceptions. The Uncertainty Principle seemed to describe the stance taken by several authors, Forster's on religion in *A Passage to India*, for example, or Ford's Dowell on people: 'After forty-five years of mixing with one's kind, one ought to have acquired the habit of being able to know something about one's fellow beings. But one doesn't' (Ford 1972: 39). Also, from a philosophical and aesthetic perspective, the idea of relativity cannot be underestimated in its impact on the way the world was viewed from multiple, overlapping, intercut or synthesised perspectives by art. In the realm of theory too, Mikhail Bakhtin (1895–1975) used Einstein's ideas of space-time to coin the term 'chronotope' to refer to his theory of the distinctive use of chronology and topology in particular genres of fiction.

A Newtonian universe found its reflection in the realist novel, where authors strove for principles and commonality in the strata of social life. Reliable, objective narrators encompassed the single perspective of a world governed by consistent, dependable scientific laws. Time was linear, and narrative moved along chronological lines. Observable physical rules governed spatial relationships, and empirical observation provided the key to predictable human behaviour. By contrast, modernism expressed time moving in arcs, flashbacks, jumps, repetitions and, above all, subjective leaps and swerves. Space was compressed, oppressive, threatening and subjectively perceived. Einstein's four-dimensional space-time continuum echoed the use of montage and collage in art. The intensity of space-time found parallels in the compression of the world into a single consciousness outlined by Joycean epiphanies and Woolfian moments of being, and detailed in Pound's 'Image', defined as an 'intellectual and emotional complex' in an instant of time. The physical universe under Einstein's theory had an ambiguity and flexibility that seemed to free experience from Newton's laws in a way that the modernist writers attempted to free their characters from social conventions and challenge the propriety, homogeneity and, as they saw it, absolutism of the social and aesthetic guidelines laid down for them by a previous generation. Einstein asserted that a frame of reference was needed to underwrite observations of position and velocity, and avant-garde writers employed unreliable, introspective, fallible, intensely subjective and even neurotic or insane narrators in their stories, which had to be taken as seen through the frame of reference of a Marlow (Conrad), Dowell (Ford), Septimus Smith (Woolf) or Maisie (James). In relativity and in modernism, the beginning of any analysis had to take into account point of view, perspective and parallax, the apparent change in the position of an object that is caused by an alteration in the observer's position. A new science seemed both to underwrite art's description of an uncertain world and to suggest alternative ways of understanding a universe that was in some ways as unpredictable and multifaceted as human behaviour. For example, in his collection *Pansies* of 1929, D. H. Lawrence published a short teasing poem entitled 'Relativity' which playfully reflects the artistic reception of new scientific theories by saying that, while not understanding them, Lawrence 'likes' the idea that atoms might change their minds, space might shift around, and matter might be 'impulsive'.

Finally, when turning to consider the influence in the early twentieth century of a scientist, whose job is either pure, as in Einstein's case, or applied, as in those of the scientists concerned with new technologies, it is worth at the same time dwelling on the spectacular influence of contemporary science on art more generally – in terms of ideas, certainly, but also in terms of direct material experience of a world whose bywords were progress and change. The growing mechanisation of the industrialised world produced the catastrophes of war on the one hand and the atomisation of human beings on the other. Science was changing not just the way humans viewed the world but also the notion of what it meant to be human. A brief overview of the period summarises the important shifts: the first air flight of the Wright brothers took place in 1903 and the first flight of the English Channel by Blériot in 1909. While the launch of the Model-T Ford in America inaugurated the era of the production line, technology was no longer affecting just industry, distribution and agriculture but also the home, private travel and entertainment, such that art would have to readjust to the perspectives offered by the camera and the motor car. In the last dozen years of the nineteenth century, machines that would revolutionise the twentieth century had been invented: the Kodak camera (1888), the electric motor (1888), the diesel engine (1892), the Ford motor car (1893), the gramophone (1894), Marconi's radio (1895), the Lumières' cinematograph (1895) and X-ray machines (1895). Powered flight, sound recordings and the discovery of radium were soon to follow. Domestic appliances such as electric kettles, telephones, electric irons and refrigerators were available, though too expensive for all but the richest households. In London, there were already 2 million electric lamps, on bicycles, at cinemas, in torches and so on. In cultural terms, this was the period in which it could be said, following the push for ever more trade markets, that the era of global knowledge had arrived. Peary reached the North Pole in 1909, while Amundsen made it to the South in 1911. The invention of the electric telegraph meant that communication across the planet could take place within hours. The fivefold expansion to 1 million kilometres of the world's railways between 1870 and 1914, and the doubling of merchant shipping brought increased trade and tourists into every major city (see Hobsbawm 1987: 62 and Childs 1999)

According to Robert Hughes, in his book *The Shock of the New*, the great symbol of modernism is the Eiffel Tower. Finished in 1889 as the focal point of the Centennial Exposition in Paris, it gathered the meanings of modernity together: metal and industry, abstract design and a metropolitan aspiration. It was then the tallest building in the world (1,056 feet). It did not represent a horizontal conquest of the land but a vertical expansion; it stood as the first architectural move to colonise the sky, and it could be seen from every point in Paris. Similarly, it meant that people could view a metropolitan landscape from a height of over 1,000 feet for the first time. Its construction in 1889, the centenary of the French Revolution, made it also emblematic of a cultural revolution: for Hughes it symbolises the dominance of both the city and the machine. In 1850, most Europeans had lived in the country; now, in the 1890s, most of them lived in cities. Like the poetry of Baudelaire, the Eiffel Tower celebrated urban life and artifice.

The emblems of this urban life were the train and then the car. The equivalent of the European cathedral of the past was the railway terminal, and for impressionists, such as Monet, train stations become a fitting subject for art. For example, in *Howards End*, Forster describes the way in which London's railway stations appear to encompass all of Britain, if not all of space:

> Like many others who have lived long in a great capital, [Margaret] had strong feelings about the various railway termini. They are our gates to the glorious and the unknown. Through them we pass out into adventure and sunshine, to them, alas! we return. In Paddington all Cornwall is latent and the remoter west; down the inclines of Liverpool Street lie fenlands and the illimitable Broads; Scotland is through the pylons of Euston; Wessex behind the poised chaos of Waterloo. ... To Margaret ... the station of King's Cross had always suggested infinity.
>
> (Forster 1975: 27)

The Railway gave a new experience and perspective to modern life: a sensation of speed and motion combined with views that were very different from those gained from the cart or the back of a horse. Time was compressed by the rapid career through the city and through the countryside, and the high-velocity trains created for passengers a world of glimpses and of parallax: a realisation, which would be key to cubism, that the landscape changed when it was viewed from a different position, that what was seen was always relative to where it was seen from. In a passage which also shows his indebtedness to impressionism, especially in relation to the effect of light on colour, Ford illustrated the pleasure of this new way of travelling from city to city through the country in *The Good Soldier*:

> I like the slow, smooth roll of the great big trains – and they are the best trains in the world! I like being drawn through the green country and looking at it through the clear glass of the great windows. Though, of course, the country isn't really green. The sun shines, the earth is blood red and purple and red and green and red. And the oxen in the ploughlands are bright varnished brown and black and

blackish purple; and the peasants are dressed in the black and white of magpies ... Still, the impression is that you are drawn through brilliant green meadows that run away on each side to the dark purple fir-woods.

(Ford 1972: 44)

The car, with its personal involvement of individuals, as though driving their own train, also changed perceptions of a world that now shot past like a film that changed colour, offered only snapshots, and altered and multiplied perspectives. What was to become the avant-garde in art had parallels with the avant-garde in engineering and architecture: interest in a faster movement through urban and rural landscapes, compressing space and creating a more intense experience of time: 'Cars, cars, fast, fast! One is seized, filled with enthusiasm, with joy ... the joy of power. The simple and naive pleasure of being in the midst of power, of strength' wrote the architect Le Corbusier in 1924. As Einstein, through theories that talked of vast distances covered at the speed of light, revolutionised humanity's understanding of the universe, modern engineering revolutionised its experience of time and space, which were now relative to the individual's own speed, direction and position. The universe was still the same, but new theories, most of which could be concretely applied to everyday life, had changed perceptions and experience of the world in irreversible ways that for many writers and painters made the traditional forms of art as outdated as the horse and cart in a world of trains and automobiles.

# 2

## GENRES, ART AND FILM

A work that aspires, however humbly, to the condition of art should carry its justification in every line. And art itself may be defined as a single-minded attempt to render the highest kind of justice to the visible universe, by bringing to light the truth, manifold and one, underlying its every aspect. It is an attempt to find in its forms, in its colours, in its light, in its shadows, in the aspects of matter, and in the facts of life what of each is fundamental, what is enduring and essential – their one illuminating and convincing quality – the very truth of their existence.

(Joseph Conrad, preface to *The Nigger of the Narcissus*, 1897)

Unlike the following one, this chapter is, in part, international in its summary of modernism's appearance in different genres and art forms. It is important to understand the significance of, for example, French poetry and Scandinavian drama, when considering early twentieth-century British writing. Like capitalism, art was becoming internationalist, and, in many ways, writers in Britain were late to acknowledge a modernist movement embraced far earlier on the Continent. In the arts, despite the efforts of Jacob Epstein, T. S. Eliot, Edith Sitwell, Ezra Pound, Wyndham

Lewis and D. H. Lawrence, the force of modernism would not be greatly felt in Britain until after the war. Yet, it had long been felt across Europe, and, as many critics have noted, a large number of the pioneering modernists writing in English were not from the British mainland: Pound, Conrad, Eliot, James, Yeats and Joyce. Therefore, I want in this chapter to give a background to the various changes, thematic and formal, that were wrought upon Western aesthetics, while noting that the sketches of aspects to modernism here are by no means exhaustive (movements and developments in architecture and music, for example, cannot be divorced from those in literature) and should serve as platforms for further reading.

## NOVEL

History provides many contexts for the emergence of modernism as a literary counterpart to the social and economic upheavals at the turn of the century: the fight for the vote by women up to 1918 is a crucial social and cultural aspect to the period; a second is the growing opposition between labour and capital (even in 1913, 1 per cent of the population owned two-thirds of the wealth), and strong unions were behind the miners' and dockers' strikes of 1912, after which Trades Union Congress (TUC) affiliation rose from 2.2 million in 1913 to 6.5 million in 1920; a third is the continued nationalist agitation for independence in Ireland and the campaigns in Ulster against Home Rule. Some critics have seen the pre-war period as one of mounting social disorder and political confrontation which, but for the war, would have led to revolution. There is certainly a literary history that can be charted in isolation from these political changes, as I shall outline below, but the social context should only be put in the background, not forgotten.

Modernist writing arises at a certain time in history and at a particular point in literary history. As I have mentioned before, in terms of the novel, it is most straightforwardly seen as a reaction to the hegemony of realist fiction. Realism has been an issue in philosophy and in aesthetic representation since Aristotle, but, as touched on in the Introduction, in discussions of the novel it is commonly used to denote a style of fiction which came to prominence in the eighteenth century and stylistically shared much with historical, journalistic or biographical writing. 'Classic realism', which flowered in the nineteenth century, has been delineated by the critics Roland Barthes, Colin MacCabe and Catherine Belsey. It is a term used to describe the work of such writers as the realists Honoré de Balzac, Charles Dickens, Elizabeth Gaskell and George Eliot: novels with reliable narrators who deal with representative characters immersed in contemporary social problems and delimited by a shared yet varied essential humanity:

> Classic realism presents individuals whose traits of character, understood as essential and predominantly given, constrain the choices they make and whose potential for development depends on what is given. Human nature is thus seen as a system of character-differences existing in the world, but one which nonetheless permits the reader to share the hopes and fears of a wide range of kinds of characters. This contradiction – that readers, like the central figures of fiction, are unique and that so many readers can identify with so many protagonists – is accommodated in ideology as a paradox. There is no character in *Middlemarch* with whom we cannot have some sense of shared humanity.
>
> (Belsey 1980: 74–5)

Alongside characters who are both recognisable and reflective of readers' self-images, the principal features of realism, opposed to the earlier Romance, are: narrative authority and reliability, a contemporary setting, representative locations, ordinary speech, linear plots and extensive use of free indirect discourse. Modernism challenged many of these conventions, particularly in terms of narrative technique, character portrayal, self-referentiality and linearity.

The transition from realism to a modernist style in fiction is accomplished not by one author, or even by writers in one country, but by a range of figures which would include Gustave Flaubert (1821–80), Fyodor Dostoevsky (1821–81), Émile Zola (1840–1902) and Henry James (1843–1916). Each of these can be associated with an attempt to improve upon the realist style and form. Flaubert wrote with scrupulous precision, as did Joyce, who in his first prose work *Dubliners* followed Flaubert's style, inflected by that of the English essayist Walter Pater, and developed the practice of channelling the narrative through the perceptions of one character. This was a technique perfected by Henry James in his quest for not social but 'psychological realism'. Dostoevsky strove for a 'higher realism' which would include spiritual as well as material truth. Zola, who was perhaps most closely matched by George Gissing in Britain, took the principle of verisimilitude in realism to a higher pitch in a style of authenticity which came to be called 'naturalism'.

What James developed from Flaubert was a linguistic intensity quite at odds with the Victorian idea of the novel as 'baggy monster'. In James's writing, syntax echoes content, on subjects as vast as the differences between America and Europe (from *The Europeans* [1879] through *The Ambassadors* [1903] to *The Golden Bowl* [1904]) or as close to home as the task, duty and responsibility of the artist. Most pertinently, James's novels concentrate on character in detail, drawing nice moral distinctions in social manners from minutely observed modes of behaviour. In his final phase (from 1902), he uses 'point of view' to mediate the story entirely through the filtering minds of particular characters, in a style that presages the stream-of-consciousness technique associated with James Joyce and Dorothy Richardson. Placing the consciousness of characters at the heart of the narrative world is one of James's chief determining influences on the modernist fiction that followed. In all of James's later work, there is, despite the wealth of detail, a necessary role for the reader in interpreting the narrative, in gradually comprehending more of the motives involved in the delicate situations described. This more demanding but empowering role for readers, requiring us 'to exercise our powers of inference', inviting us to set off 'in search of other kinds of relevance' than the literal is another name for modernism, according to David Trotter (1983: 74). For Roland Barthes, there is also here an important distinction to be made between realist and modernist fiction: that between the 'readerly' and the 'writerly' text. Readerly, usually realist, texts make up the vast majority of published novels; they rely upon shared conventions between writer and reader, such as closure or the tying up of strands of the narrative at its end, which encourage the reader to be passive, whereas writerly, commonly experimental, texts flout those conventions and require the reader to be more productive of the text's meanings, which are usually ambiguous (Barthes 1990). In the period we are primarily interested in, from 1890 to 1930, most novels published were undoubtedly traditional in form and 'readerly', while the experimental, 'writerly' modernist strain of fiction is not only out of the literary mainstream for the majority of the period, its novels sold far fewer copies than the authors who continued to write in the style of George Eliot and Anthony Trollope, such as Arnold Bennett (1867–1931) and John Galsworthy (1867–1933).

James's reliance on ambiguity, on careful revelation and on neither third-person omniscient narration nor first-person pseudo-autobiographical forms but on centres of consciousness, suggested alternative ways of writing fiction and implied that the novel was less a device for unravelling a story to a reader-as-consumer than a vehicle for conveying mental images to an active intelligence. To such methods was added the temporal reordering of the chronological story practised by Joseph Conrad (1857–1924). Time shifts, flashbacks and juxtapositions of events in Conrad's complex mosaic narratives intensified the psychological emphases found in James's novels. Conrad also introduced reappearing 'tellers' of his tales, most notably his partial alterego Marlow in *Lord Jim*, *Heart of Darkness* and other stories. But Conrad's moral tales are not those of social niceties and have more in common with the outlook of Hardy than James. Conrad is a sharp critic of economic, political and social pretensions, in narratives of greed and rapacity (*Nostromo* [1904] and *Heart of Darkness* [1899]), political folly (*The Secret Agent* [1907] and *Under Western Eyes* [1911]) and codes of honour ('The Secret Sharer' [1910] and *Lord Jim* [1900]). But, above all, his stories are about individuals at moments of crisis when they cross or falter at *The Shadow-Line* (1917), in the name of one short novel, between innocence and experience. Yet, what Conrad's stories are about is, generally speaking, less important than the way in which they are told; Cedric

Watts characterises Conrad's most complex novel, *Nostromo*, in terms of an enormous 'mobility of viewpoint', with regard to time, space, focalisation and other aspects. Watts argues that this mobility differentiates *Nostromo* from all previous novels; certainly, the handling of perspective and of time is an early and distinct example of modernist poetics: 'There are unexpected juxtapositions of events from different times; and Conrad is fond of delaying our decoding of large and small effects: experiences are thrust at us before we are in a position to comprehend their significance' (Watts 1982: 145). Less steeped in the English than the French novel tradition, Conrad started as an impressionist writer, as did his friend and collaborator Ford Madox Ford. I will consider below, in the section on Art, how writers adopted the techniques of painters to literary ends, but might briefly mention here what impressionist writing meant to Conrad and Ford: in brief, it can best be described as a method for accumulating impressions, a technique Ford called 'progression', in which the novel's incidents and even paragraphs follow a similar pattern whereby a series of connected elements reaches a culmination in terms of the development of the narrative. For example, a paragraph might contain a list of traits associated with the characters or a cumulative series of instances of their behaviour before ending with a statement that underlines their significance, like 'that's the way it was with us', in one example from *The Good Soldier*. Ford compared this method of finishing a paragraph of impressionistic details to shooting or slamming 'the bolt home'.

A last key figure to mention here because of her importance in changing the way writers rendered thought is Dorothy Richardson (1873–1957), a stylistic innovator of great significance even though her works, pre-eminent among which is the sequence entitled *Pilgrimage* (thirteen volumes beginning with *Painted Roofs*, 1915–38), are less studied than those of Joyce and Woolf. She was a major developer of the interior-monologue technique and attempted to write a 'feminine' prose to counter the dominance of 'masculine' realism. Her emphasis on psychology and female 'synthetic' consciousness led to a prose style which required a collaboration between author and reader to render fully the life of her characters, in a way Barthes would term 'writerly'. She pioneered the stream-of-consciousness technique and was one of the first writers to embrace fully a staunchly anti-realist mode.

Two confrontations, perhaps more than any others, illustrate the break from the realist mode in fiction represented by modernism. The first, between Henry James and H. G. Wells, I touched on in the last chapter but will expand on here. Wells criticised James in a semi-autobiographical novel, *Boon* (1915), in this way: 'To you literature, like painting, is an end, to us literature is a means, it has a use. ... I had rather be called a journalist than an artist'. James replied in two letters, saying that he considered the novel an admirable form of art because of

> its range and variety, its plasticity and liberality, its fairly living on the sincere and shifting experience of the individual practitioner. ... It is art that *makes* life, makes interest, makes importance, for our consideration and application of these things, and I know of no substitute whatever for the force and beauty of its processes.

For Wells, his fiction had a number of aims: education, social criticism and entertainment; whereas he thought James's work was about style and form only. Wells's novels were art for a purpose, like architecture, whereas James's were not, like painting. James replied that he thought the distinction 'null and void': all art was for a purpose, and all art was aesthetically determined. In a letter concerning Wells's *The New Machiavelli* (1911), James lamented the style of both that novel and *Boon*: 'That accurst autobiographic form which puts a premium on the loose, the improvised, the cheap and the easy'. James felt that the pseudo-autobiographical first-person form resulted in an overabundance of digressions and spurious personal opinions which added nothing to the novel's principal subject. Indeed, in Wells's most admired novel, *Tono-Bungay* (1909), the narrator, George, says that in choosing the autobiographical form he knows he may give 'an impression that I want to make simply a hotch-potch of anecdotes and experiences' (Wells 1972b: 5).

To warrant his friend's censure, Wells had formulated his own famous description of a Henry James novel:

> It is like a church lit but without a congregation to distract you, with
> every light and line focussed on the high altar. And on the altar, very
> reverently placed, intensely there, is a dead kitten, an egg-shell, a bit
> of string. . . . The chief fun, the only exercise, in reading Henry James
> is the clambering over vast metaphors.

These exchanges are collected under the title 'The Counter
Claims of Content and Form' in Richard Ellmann and Charles
Feidelson's *The Modern Tradition* (1965), and these respective
emphases, on story and on structure, have often been advanced as
the source of the chief ideological difference between James, as
one of the modernists, and Wells, as one of the realist writers, or,
as Virginia Woolf described them, 'materialists' and 'Bond-street
tailors' (Woolf 1924: 122–3).

  She uses these terms in the more well-known disagreement
between novelists which occurred when Woolf, in two essays,
attacked the fiction of the popular serious novelists of the time,
Arnold Bennett, Wells again and John Galsworthy. Galsworthy
also notably drew the opprobrium of D. H. Lawrence, who
thought he wrote 'documentary fictions' with characters 'lacking
a "real being"'. In particular, Woolf singled out Bennett, who
James also attacked for writing novels without principles of
organisation such that they resembled 'fluid pudding'. The dispute lasted from 1917 to Bennett's death in 1931. Woolf's first
essay is entitled 'Modern Fiction' (1919). It decries the 'materialists' for writing about 'unimportant things', spending immense
industry making the transitory appear enduring and important,
the same accusation levelled at James by Wells but for entirely
opposite reasons. Woolf admires the enormous number of details
assembled by Bennett and Wells, but, she says: 'Life escapes: and
perhaps without life nothing else is worthwhile'. In opposition to
the mass of facts accumulated by the realists, Woolf says that the
interest for modern(ist) authors 'lies very likely in the dark places
of psychology'. In the most well-known passage in the essay,
Woolf describes what she means by 'life': 'Examine for a moment
an ordinary mind on an ordinary day. The mind receives a myriad
impressions – trivial, fantastic, evanescent, or engraved with the
sharpness of steel. From all sides they come, an incessant shower

of innumerable atoms'. Instead of recording externalities like a person's appearance, home, family, town and job, exemplified in the opening to Bennett's most highly praised novel *The Old Wives' Tale* (1908), Woolf wanted novelists to explore character and thought, desire and memory:

> Life is not a series of gig-lamps symmetrically arranged but a luminous halo, a semi-transparent envelope surrounding us from the beginning of consciousness to the end. Is it not the task of the novelist to convey this varying, this unknown and uncircumscribed spirit, whatever aberration or complexity it may display, with as little mixture of the alien and external as possible?'

Woolf's second key essay is 'Mr Bennett and Mrs Brown' (1924), in which she argues that 'in or about December, 1910, human character changed'. It has been debated whether Woolf was referring to a change of government at the time, the accession of George V, or the post-impressionist exhibition organised by Roger Fry, another member of the Bloomsbury group. In any case, Woolf's belief was that the novel's purpose was to represent character. Yet, Bennett agreed with this, and, as the more prestigious novelist at the time, he had the greater opportunities in articles and reviews to put across his view of what character was, and why Woolf failed to capture it. He felt that the Georgians (Forster, Lawrence, Joyce) did not draw characters who were 'real, true and convincing', while the Edwardians (himself, Wells and Galsworthy) had invented societies, factories and even Utopias, together with recognisable people living in them. Here also, underlining that the disagreement between them was over *how* character should best be presented, Woolf agreed: 'Bennett convinces us so well that there is a house, in every detail, that we become convinced that there must be a person living there'. In many ways, the dispute boiled down to this principal issue of how to describe the representative figure of Mrs Brown, a woman sitting in a railway carriage invented by Woolf to illustrate the differences between the Georgians and Edwardians. Bennett, she decided, would describe every detail about Mrs Brown's dress, face and body, while delivering copious extra information about her life, but that the reader would never get inside Mrs Brown's mind and, consequently, would not know her in any meaningful sense, only about her. For Woolf therefore, it could be said that with the advent of the Georgian period, because literary approaches had changed, human character had changed. Woolf felt that character should and even could only be illuminated through a plethora of memories and thoughts, while the Edwardians were still representing characters through a mass of external details:

> You have overheard scraps of talk that filled you with amazement. You have gone to bed at night bewildered by the complexity of your feelings. In one day thousands of ideas have coursed through your brains; thousands of emotions have met, collided and disappeared in astonishing disorder. Nevertheless, you allow the writers to palm off upon you a version of all this, an image of Mrs Brown, which has no likeness to that surprising apparition whatsoever.

She concludes that with the coming of the new novelists there will be revolutionary changes: 'The literary convention of the time is so artificial ... that, naturally, the feeble are tempted to outrage, and the strong are led to destroy the very foundations and rules of literary society. Signs of this are everywhere apparent. Grammar is violated; syntax disintegrated'.

If we turn now to another of the foremost modernist writers, D. H. Lawrence's main contributions outside of his novels and stories to the revolution of fiction were essays written in the 1920s, though some were not published until his collected non-fictional prose was assembled under the title *Phoenix* in 1936. The most important are 'The Novel' (1925), 'Morality and the Novel' (1925), 'Why the Novel Matters' (mid-1920s, published 1936) and 'Surgery for the Novel – or a Bomb' (1923). In these essays, Lawrence, like Woolf, asserts his belief in 'life', though he defines it differently, as 'something that gleams, that has the fourth-dimensional quality' ('Morality and the Novel', 1971: 178). In 'Why the Novel Matters', he explains why the novelist is 'superior' to the philosopher or scientist, or even poet, who only deal with parts of 'life':

> Nothing is important but life. ... For this reason I am a novelist. ... The novel is the one bright book of life. Books are not life. They are

only tremulations on the ether. But the novel as a tremulation can make the whole man tremble. Which is more than poetry, philosophy, science, or any other book-tremulation can do.

(Lawrence 1971: 184–5)

In 'Morality and the Novel', in a sentence that partly explains the symbol in the title of one of his most important books, he adds: 'The novel is the perfect medium for revealing to us the changing rainbow of our living relationships' (Lawrence 1971: 180–1). It is the importance of relationships and relatedness to 'life' that Lawrence avers in this essay and which he puts forward as the reason why the novel, 'the highest example of subtle inter-relatedness that man has discovered' (Lawrence 1971: 177), is morally important. The essay begins: 'The business of art is to reveal the relation between man and his circumambient universe, at the living moment' (Lawrence 1971: 175), and goes on to say that 'life consists in this achievement of a pure relationship between ourselves and the living universe' (1971: 176). Arguably, his best, if still vague, example of what he means by this, and which reveals the expressionist component in Lawrence's philosophy, is that of a painter: 'When van Gogh paints sunflowers, he reveals, or achieves, the vivid relation between himself, as man, and the sunflower, as sunflower, at that quick moment of time. His painting does not represent the sunflower itself. We shall never know what the sunflower itself is' (Lawrence 1971: 175)' And, for Lawrence, morality is truth to life and to its inter-relatedness: 'The only morality is to have man true to his manhood, woman to her womanhood, and let the relationship form of itself, in all honour. For it is, to each, life itself' (Lawrence 1971: 179).

Lastly, if any figure influenced the novel's development in the way that Ezra Pound did poetry's, it was Ford Madox Ford. Friend to both the Edwardians and the Georgians, promoter of Joyce and James, discoverer of D. H. Lawrence, Wyndham Lewis and Jean Rhys, collaborator with Conrad and ally to the majority of innovative writers of the period, Ford was involved with almost every notable literary project in the modernist period. In 1908–9, he launched an influential magazine devoted to new experimental writing, *The English Review*, to defend the art of fiction against the commercial whims of publishers, and, in his own best fiction, he managed to reconcile the perspectives of James, Pound and Conrad with those of Bennett and Wells, while retaining the admiration of all of them. His sense of a clash between old and new worlds, expressed through personal crisis in *The Good Soldier* (1915) and historical breakdown in the war tetralogy *Parade's End* (1924–8), marked him as one of the most forceful modernisers to succeed in exploring the position of the individual in history. Indebted to the French novelists Flaubert and Maupassant and to the artistic ideas of impressionism, Ford encapsulated in personal tragedy the disintegration of traditional English society amid political and economic upheaval while affirming the ability of an innovatory modernism to develop with and not against the grain of realism. In this project, he also foreshadowed the aims of many novelists since the 1930s.

Backed by a jazz soundtrack, American modernism, far more than British, is characterised by the mix of experimental writing with popular culture. There is a breadth that reflects the multi-faceted development of a new, forward-looking twentieth-century nation; and the spectrum of writers sometimes discussed, albeit loosely, under the rubric of modernism spans from Willa Cather (1873–1947) to Ralph Ellison (1913–64), from F. Scott Fitzgerald (1896–1940) and Zora Neale Hurston (1891–1960) to Sherwood Anderson (1876–1941). For example, a range of fiction traverses urban landscapes, from *Sister Carrie* by Theodore Dreiser (1871–1945) in 1900 and *The Jungle* by Upton Sinclair (1878–1968) in 1906 through key works by John Dos Passos (1896–1970), Sinclair Lewis (1885–1951) and Waldo Frank (1889–1967) in the 1920s to *Call it Sleep* by Henry Roth (1906–95) in 1934, a coming-of-age novel set in the Jewish slums of New York. Yet, American modernism was far wider than an anatomy of the metropolis, as is apparent in the disparate work by authors that placed 'new writing' rather than experimentalism at the heart of American fiction of the period: Ernest Hemingway (1899–1961), F. Scott Fitzgerald, Willa Cather, William Faulkner (1897–1962), Richard Wright (1908–60) and Nathaniel West (1903–40).

## SHORT STORY

In the same way that much new-century fiction turned away from the nineteenth-century long novel, the American short-story cycle departed from the well-made tale of Nathaniel Hawthorne (1804–64), and its new guise was, perhaps, epitomised by Sherwood Anderson's *Winesburg* stories of individual small-town Ohio tragedies steeped in isolation and frustration: a transatlantic complement to James Joyce's story cycle *Dubliners*. Just as Henry James was a seminal figure in the development of much modernist theory and practice with regard to the novel, he was an important innovator in short-story writing. Where James's late novels, such as *The Golden Bowl* (1904), show an unprecedented degree of attention to aesthetic detail and intense reflection and his prefaces to his novels expound a theory of fiction whose claims elevated the form to a new height of artistic integrity, his almost plotless short stories seemed to apply an intricate stylistic delicacy and classical unity that epitomised many of the emerging precepts of modernism. James published 112 'tales', in the tradition but not the style of pioneering American short-story writers Hawthorne and Edgar Allan Poe (1809–49), which anticipated the enigmatic and elliptical stories of Katherine Mansfield, who was also indebted to Guy de Maupassant (French) and particularly Anton Chekhov (Russian), as well as to the economical but exquisite prosaical 'meanness' of Joyce's *Dubliners*, which also owed a great deal to George Meredith (English) and George Moore (Irish). Other modernists, such as Joseph Conrad, D. H. Lawrence and Malcolm Lowry, displayed some of their best work in the short-story form, and Virginia Woolf's early short stories for the Hogarth Press, especially 'Kew Gardens' (1919), are the first of her works to show her mature modernist style.

Like his novels, many of James's stories concern art and its form as well as its relation to society, and 'The Figure in the Carpet' (1896) has been taken as the quintessential self-reflexive modernist story, with its metaphor of hidden patterns in the weave of a carpet to stand for intricate design and for depth-reading. Another writer, much less often associated with modernism, whose late short stories suggest connections with modernist writing is Rudyard Kipling (1865–1936). If Kipling's work appears to owe more to Robert Louis Stevenson and H. G. Wells than James, this is because of his journalist's training and his ability, shared with Conrad, to tell 'a good yarn'. From the war onwards, several of Kipling's stories, such as 'Mary Postgate' (1917) or 'The Wish House' (1924), are as enigmatically allusive and symbolically dense as those of the canonical modernists, and some of his earlier pieces, such as 'Mrs Bathurst', have been read in terms of modernist techniques.

If we consider content, one rich vein of material mined by the modernist short story was that of sexuality, freed from the confines of Victorian morality into the open spaces of sensuous desire and erotic carnality directly addressed. For example, Wyndham Lewis's 'Cantleman's Spring-Mate' (1919) foregrounds sex in relation to essential nature and seasonal changes. The protagonist's name links the animal (cattle) to the human (man), and, in the story, nature is portrayed as human-made, industrial and scientific: 'strenuous fields, steam rising from them as though from an exertion, dissecting the daisies'. Animals' behaviour towards each other is characterised purely as a result of desire and devouring; and so are the attitudes of humans. In the story, a male bird sees a female bird as something 'from which certain satisfaction could be derived', and a sow, looking upon 'her hog', gives 'a sharp grunt of sex-hunger'. Cantleman similarly positions his mate in terms of her physical attributes: 'the animal fullness of the childbearing hips, with an eye as innocent as the bird or the beast'. Cantleman's Nietzschean will to power appears an assertion of sexual dominance masking an underlying knowledge that he is powerless. He must go to war with the possibility of not returning. His likening of women to animals: 'the way in which Stella's hips stood out, the solid blood-heated expanse on which his hand lay, had the amplitude and flatness of a mare', is a part of a fundamental animalism that suffuses his violent desires, and when he beats a German's brains out, it is with the same impartial malignity as animates his night with Stella, who he also refers to as a 'Hun'. Copulation and violence are simultaneously forces with which both to revel in and to defeat nature, yet Cantleman ultimately appears weak and out of control. He decides simply that what separates people from animals actually makes them worse because base lust and violence, and the will to power, are rationalised by humanity into noble ideas: 'human beings anywhere [are] the most ugly and offensive of the brutes because of the confusion caused by their consciousness'.

A second example is D. H. Lawrence's 'The Virgin and the Gipsy' (1930), which has much in common with his *Lady Chatterly's Lover* (1928), begun in the same year, and which is a text that also illustrates Lawrence's fondness for pivotal lower-class or 'alien' characters changing the lives of the rich or 'respectable', as in several of the short stories such as 'The Rocking-Horse Winner', together with his unprecedented interest in the effect of animals on human sexuality, as in 'The Fox' and 'St Mawr'. In Lawrence's title, the word 'virgin' connotes purity, chastity and innocence, while 'Gypsy' is a mysterious, enigmatic signifier associated with supernatural power and worldly passion. The virgin's name, Yvette, means little Eve and implies a questioning of conventional mythology, while the story's entire structure appears to rest on gendered binary oppositions of innocence and experience, reason and emotion, good and evil. This is replicated in the central metaphor of the Gypsy encampment opposed to Yvette's home at the conservative Vicarage, which is stable, regular, stagnant and ruled by a toad-like Mater who embodies authoritarianism. In many ways, the story adheres to a classic realist linear mode and rests somewhat heavily for its argument on a Victorian morality that maintains that if Yvette strays from her assigned subservient role she will become a ruined delinquent; a discourse Lawrence fails to subvert significantly. However, the story is modernist in many of its concerns: epistemological crisis; death of the old and birth of the new, since Mater and her 'will to power' are ceremoniously drowned in the flood; and overt sexual symbolism, evident in the cascading water and phallic chimneys. Accordingly, human identity is considered by Lawrence as unstable and fluid in opposition to the classic realist tradition which perceives it as essentially stable. Also, the narration is by an omniscient narrator, but the Gypsy's sexually attractive otherness is focalised from Yvette's perspective: 'A dandy, in his polished black boots, tight black trousers and tight dark-green jersey ... on his flexible hips, it seemed to her still that he was stronger than she was' and 'His bold eyes kept staring at Yvette, she could feel them on her cheek, on her neck and dared not look up'. The sense of visual communication characterises the power of the Gypsy, who is described repeatedly in physical terms but disempowered of dialogue until the end of the story. Where Lewis and Lawrence share the view that 'love' is not as far from animal sexuality as society claims to believe, Lewis's story exposes the similarity to show rapacious human blood-lust against the background of the war, while Lawrence's celebrates the common animality in terms of 'life'.

An example of a character coming to terms with desire and sexual repression is found in Katherine Mansfield's 'Bliss' (1918) from *Bliss and Other Stories* (1920). I will consider this story, and especially its opening, in more detail than the previous two in order to illustrate some of the approaches and techniques of modernism in general and, in particular, of the most important modernist author who wrote only short stories. Representative of modernist prose, at the beginning of Mansfield's stories the reader receives little orientation, and it is not unusual for her to start the narrative with a conjunction, suggesting that something has gone before. 'Bliss' opens with the word 'Although', just as her most well-known story 'The Garden Party' begins with 'And'. Both stories confront the reader with the characters without introductions or any descriptive preamble.

The initial usage of the word 'Bliss' is very much that of the heroine, Bertha Young, yet it is spoken by the third-person narrator. This is also typical of Mansfield's style, which employs a considerable amount of free indirect speech because her treatment of characterisation operates through a blend of third- and first-person narration. An interesting example occurs at the beginning of the second paragraph, which unusually moves into the second person, spoken by the narrator but with Bertha's words: 'What can you do if you are thirty and, turning the corner of your own street, you are overcome, suddenly, by a feeling of bliss'. The free indirect style allows the impression of access to Bertha's thoughts, combined with some detachment, to allow room for irony, ambiguity and

alternative meanings. The second paragraph of the story ends
with another of Mansfield's trademark devices: an ellipsis. Ellipses, which work by the suppression of words necessary to the full
form of a construction, are used by Mansfield as a method of
implicating the reader in the text, because the reader has to
supply the missing thoughts. This is, therefore, a 'writerly' text
in the Barthesian sense of the term discussed earlier (p. 83).
Three more ellipses occur together on two lines on the first
page, and here the hiatuses suggest that Bertha is searching for
the right word and that she is uncertain what 'divine' 'something' might 'happen'. All this seems an intimation of what is
to transpire later in the story, but if it is a premonition,
Bertha misreads its character, which she will find very upset-
ting. The rhetorical questions, ellipses and procrastinations that
infuse Bertha's thought show the repression that characterises
her life.

Bertha is, in many ways, childlike and naive, as the second
paragraph hints through its depiction of her innocent exuber-
ance. She feels younger than her thirty years, and both of her
names seem to suggest her immaturity. It is similarly significant
that her child, Little B, has the same name as Bertha. Bertha's
underdeveloped sexuality is first suggested in the story's third
paragraph, through the metaphor of the 'rare fiddle', an image
probably chosen because of its similarity in shape to the idealised
female body. The fourth paragraph illustrates Bertha's lack of
precision and also her forgetfulness. Bertha thinks that the fiddle
is 'not quite what I mean' and she cannot finish the thought, in
terms of explaining its inappropriateness or in terms of finding
an alternative. This matches with the several previous occasions
on which she has been unable to find the right word or to complete a thought. In the fourth paragraph, the reader also learns
that she has forgotten her key 'as usual', and the impression of
Bertha as muddled and dizzy is established, along with the
story's use of suggestive Freudian imagery. Bertha's incomplete
thoughts at this stage cannot be confidently completed by the
reader, but on a second reading their unspoken significance seems
greater. So, when Bertha thinks early on about the fiddle image
that 'It's not what I mean, because—', the reader can supply the

possible suppressed thought that Bertha does not use her body to express herself physically with her husband, and in that sense is posing the question to herself: 'Why be given a body if you have to keep it shut up in a case like a rare, rare fiddle?'

A last technique we should note in Mansfield's fiction is the way in which the prose style suits the content of the story. The opening sentence uses a repetitive form to imitate Bertha's restlessness:

> Although Bertha Young was thirty she still had moments like this when she wanted to run instead of walk, to take dancing steps on and off the pavement, to bowl a hoop, to throw something up in the air, and catch it again, or to stand still and laugh at – nothing – at nothing, simply.

The five-line sentence constitutes the whole of the opening paragraph, and its skip from clause to clause precisely mirrors in language Bertha's desire to run, dance, or even 'bowl a hoop'.

The story's title has several angles to it. On reaching the end of the narrative, the reader probably realises that one sense is that of 'Ignorance is bliss', because Bertha's inexplicable happiness has been based on a lie, as she discovers upon realising that her husband is having an affair. Additionally, the term refers to carnal pleasure, in a story of sexual awakening and disappointment, as Bertha uncovers her first feelings of physical desire for her husband, through her attraction to a dinner guest, Pearl Fulton, who is also Bertha's husband's mistress. More directly, the title refers to Bertha's 'shower of sparks': her straightforward, uncomplicated joy in her easy, contented, leisured lifestyle, with everything that society would say she ought to have in order to be extremely happy: husband, baby, sophisticated friends, servants and a large, smart home.

On entering this home, Bertha decides to arrange the fruit, and from here onwards the story's symbolism is enriched by the introduction of other keywords which will be repeated, like the title. The word 'cold' is reiterated on the first page and will be used in the story to symbolise both frigidity and emotional reserve, as well as the distant beauty of Pearl Fulton. On the word's first appearance, Bertha escapes 'the tight clasp' of her coat only to be chilled by the air on her arms, as she is later touched by Pearl's 'cool arm', giving the impression of someone caught between a need to escape and a fear of lonely exposure. The antithetical words 'bright' and 'dark' are also repeated in the first two pages to give a sense of Bertha trapped between opposites. Additionally, 'deeply' appears twice in succession on the first page, like 'rare' did earlier, and the reader begins to realise that this is a habit of Bertha's: the repetition of words seemingly to express her 'bliss' but also to cover her inarticulate incomprehension of her own life, which may be rooted in the repression of her sexuality. Other phrases used on the opening page will be significantly repeated later in the story: 'strange', 'something' and even 'idiotic civilisation'. All of these hint at Bertha's lack of engagement and suggest that she is someone who does not really understand the world around her. But it is the fruit itself which is the most potent symbol in the story, particularly the 'pears'. A reader's first thought might be that the similarity between 'pears' and 'Pearl' signals a connection. However, the story's central image is of a treasured 'pear tree' in Bertha's garden, which seems to symbolise her innocence (it is her 'lovely pear tree'), leading the reader to infer a reference to the Tree of Knowledge and to construe the pears in terms of the female body as well as the forbidden fruit of Eden. Indeed, many critics see the key revelation of the story to be Bertha's inkling of her latent homosexuality, which she displaces on to heterosexual feelings for her husband, making the pear(l) tree and its forbidden fruit a symbol of a love that is innocent in the sense that it 'dare not speak its name'. In terms of symbolism, colours are also important, and the early mention of 'white grapes covered with a silver bloom' presages Pearl's arrival later in the story, 'all in silver'. These details add up to one of the richest, most tightly structured and intricately arranged prose styles in twentieth-century writing. Mansfield, like Jane Austen, is often said to have narrowed her artistic range and limited her worth by concentrating on small social situations played out in almost plotless stories. Yet, in terms of textual density, there are few writers who will reward such close attention to the words and images used throughout their work. 'Bliss' proceeds in such a way that Bertha, who appears to have everything, proves to have nothing. Her home is run by servants, her baby is kept by the nanny, such that Bertha later wonders 'why have a baby if it has to be kept – not in a case like a rare, rare fiddle – but in another woman's arms', and her husband, it transpires, is also in another woman's arms. Bertha is left with nothing but her enigmatic but 'lovely, lovely' pear tree.

If we turn to consider the import of Mansfield's stories, it should be remembered that for a woman in the 1920s putting pen to paper was, consciously or not, a feminist act. Virginia Woolf illustrates this in her essay 'Professions for Women' (1931) when she argues that some 'phantom' stops her writing (1998: 58). Woolf concludes that she has internalised a particular patriarchal ideology and she calls this figure 'The Angel in the House', from Coventry Patmore's Victorian poem, which was widely used to show that men's and women's lives belonged in 'separate spheres': the man's was the world of business and politics and the woman's was the domestic and family world. In many of Mansfield's short stories, such as 'The Garden Party' and 'The Daughters of the Late Colonel', there are reworkings of the theme of the Angel in the House: how women ought to behave and what consequences such behaviour has for their inner selves as much as their social freedom. Though she was less overtly feminist than Woolf, Mansfield was more independent, and the images in her fiction of fruit, parturition, sexual repression and suppressed joy give the impression of female creativity struggling against male stereotyping. Mansfield explains that her stories are not just about the surface when she says: 'One tries to go deep – to speak to the secret self we all have'. Scraping the story's surface, 'Bliss' seems also to illustrate the dissociation of men's and women's lives, not just with Harry out at the office and Bertha at home but also emotionally – just as in 'The Garden Party' the Sheridan family live out the separation of spheres: father and son Laurie go to work in the city, while mother and daughters, like Bertha or Woolf's Clarissa Dalloway, prepare for their important social event. 'Bliss' is not a story about a simple, deceived housewife so much as a narrative about the deceptions of a decadent post-war society in the 1920s. In this way, Mansfield anticipates the coruscating satires of Evelyn Waugh, but her angle is enriched by her critique of gender relations, which reveals the vulnerability of a woman such as Bertha, an 'Angel in the House' whose model behaviour, including an extreme sexual innocence, cuts her off from the human beings around her.

To take a final example of a different author, at the edges of the modernist short story there are very different concerns under examination in the short stories of Samuel Beckett (1906–89). These range from shortened versions of his novels, as with 'First Love', to intensely repetitious, largely indecipherable experiments with phrases and extreme mental states, as in 'Ping' (1967). The title 'Ping' may refer to any of a number of things: life's soothing routines; the obsessions of memory; the sharpness of a sense of alienation; the carriage-return bell of a typewriter; or even the blip of a pulse on a hospital computer screen prior to death. But the title is not a clue to the story's meaning so much as another example of the many words and phrases that recur at irregular intervals in the 'story' – very few words appear only once. The reader is tempted to conclude that the narrative is meaningless, but the high degree of organisation suggests that there are patterns if not meanings to be uncovered. In this, the story, like much of Beckett's work, replicates the human experience of a world without God or purpose. Language has again broken down, and the signifier without a signified 'Ping' (in the original French 'Bing') stands as a speech act freed from a language system, a *parole* without a *langue* in which it can operate meaningfully. In other words, the reader struggles, probably in vain, to find a context or meaning for the title or the words in the text. It is arguable that something similar happened to the short story under modernist experimentation, as it changed from the slice-of-life realism of the mid-nineteenth century to the richly allusive and ambiguous prose meditations of the mid-twentieth.

## POETRY

The two most powerful foreign forces on modernist poetry in Britain came from France and the USA. The first brought symbolism and *vers libre*, the second a hybrid Anglo-American Imagism and the dry, contemplative, intellectual and allusive poetry of Ezra Pound (1885–1972) and T. S. Eliot (1888–1965). At the time of this steady increase in outside influence on literature up to the Great War, English poetry was at one of its lowest points, according to many critics. Prior to the changes in diction and subject matter achieved by the well-known war poets, such as Isaac Rosenberg, Wilfred Owen and Edward Thomas, many of whom were not highly regarded until the 1930s, poetry was deeply conservative and insular. A large number of the prominent names of the Edwardian period are now nearly forgotten: William Watson, W. E. Henley, Laurence Binyon and Alfred Austin (Poet Laureate from 1896 to 1913). Unless it is by the Romantic-turned-modernist W. B. Yeats, the poetry of the pre-war period most likely to be studied now was written by two independent-minded and highly individualistic poets better known to the public for their fiction: Thomas Hardy (1840–1928), whose influence on modern British poetry has been as great as anyone's, and Rudyard Kipling (1865–1936), probably the most popular literary writer of the period. Aside from these two mavericks, the avant-garde writers were those known as the Georgian poets, named after, but not fully represented by, Edward Marsh's five anthologies of *Georgian Poetry* from 1912 to 1922: Rupert Brooke, Lascelles Abercrombie, Gordon Bottomley, Wilfred Gibson, Walter de la Mare, W. H. Davies and John Masefield. The reputation of these poets, currently undergoing some revaluation, has largely been eclipsed by that of the modernists, to chart whose genealogy it is necessary to turn to France.

The French *symbolistes*, such as Arthur Rimbaud (1854–91), Stéphane Mallarmé (1842–98) and their precursor Charles Baudelaire, whose poem 'Correspondences' is especially important in this context, together with the critic and later poet Paul Valéry (1871–1945), were largely introduced to British writers by the decadent poet Arthur Symons (1865–1945) in his study of *The Symbolist Movement in Literature* (1899). Symons, through his poetry and criticism, greatly influenced Eliot, Yeats and Pound; indeed, Michael Bell has gone as far as to suggest that modernism was in many ways a second-generation *symbolisme* (Bell 1980: 16).

The *symbolistes*, who believed in indirect expression, reverie and inspiration, had much in common with the aesthetes and also viewed art as an escape from the grind of human reality, not a reflection of or on life but a step back from it. Symbolism is often seen as a reaction to both the systematising of Darwin and Marx and the exhaustion of realism, which, in the work of Zola in France, George Gissing in England and George Moore in Ireland, had hardened into a more austere naturalism. The idealist and aestheticist philosophy of the *symbolistes* insisted upon the autonomy of the poem together with the importance of the mystical and spiritual worlds they alluded to through symbols and phrases. They also advocated that the poet needed to revel in sensuality and in language, such that Pound and Eliot took from Mallarmé the belief that they should 'purify the dialect of the tribe'. Words and expressions should be chosen with precision for their intensity, the everyday transcended in the ideal, and linguistic profundity achieved by typographical experimentation and lexical accuracy; as Valéry expressed it, prose walks, in straight lines and even paces, but poetry should dance gracefully, with leaps, turns and pirouettes.

The 1890s witnessed a large-scale assimilation of French culture in Britain. Writers and artists served apprenticeships in Paris, while bohemianism, art nouveau and aestheticism, along with the many art movements discussed below, were exported across the channel to a cosmopolitan London society ready to change its clothes, furniture, manners and art. The decadent movement in England was the immediate fruit of this fertilisation, but the interest in individualism, form and stylistic beauty that characterised modernism after the turn of the century was also engendered by Mallarmé and Valéry. Paris directly produced George Moore's *Confessions of a Young Man* (1888), George du Maurier's Svengali in *Trilby* (1894) and Wyndham Lewis's *Tarr* (1918).

One key writer greatly influenced by symbolism, and particularly by the iconographic approach of Mallarmé, was W. B. Yeats (1885–1939), a poet who had steeped himself in mysticism and Celtic mythology. Yeats's early romantic work only appears modernist in that it represents an attempt to escape from urbanism and materialism into the Celtic Twilight of pre-industrial rural Ireland's folk tales and traditions. Yeats's verse evolved under several influences other than poetry: the advice of Ezra Pound, the political energy of the woman he considered his muse, Maud Gonne, his marriage in 1917, the patronage of Lady Gregory, in whose Coole Park estate in Galway Yeats took residence, and the changes in Ireland's fortunes in its struggle for independence from England. His poetry became more engaged with the modern world, if negatively, more characterised by dialectic and division, especially evident in the way Yeats adopted masks or personas, more complex in its twisting of traditional forms and syntax and more reliant on the abstractions of 'art' to find resolution and meaningful connections, as when dancer and dance are one at the end of 'Among School Children'. Most noticeably in his poems of the 1920s, in the volumes *Michael Robartes and the Dancer* (1921) and *The Tower* (1928), from 'Meditation in Time of Civil War' to 'The Second Coming', 'Nineteen Hundred and Nineteen' and 'Sailing to Byzantium', Yeats displays many of the characteristics of modernist disenchantment: scepticism towards the notion of 'truth', a sense of the individual's disorientation within modernity and a historically situated pessimism over contemporary life combined with an understanding that the modern world has become spiritually bankrupt and culturally fragmented. In ways that typify modernist historical disaffection and artistic recreation, Yeats turned to mythology for his structuring principles, submerged personality in multiple selves, championed the sheer energy of amoral and largely destructive or authoritarian Nietzschean forces and, like many novelists, fabricated a vast and dense symbolical mythopoetical world of his own.

In parallel with Yeats's largely separate development, modernism in Britain began with the movement known as imagism, which popularised free verse, reintroduced a hard classicism to poetry and sought to establish a new set of stylistic principles. What came to be called imagism began as a group in Soho led by T. E. Hulme in 1909, and ended with the last anthology published in New England in 1917. The creed of imagism has been expressed in polemical and prescriptive documents, but the poets' emphasis was always on precise and concrete presentation, without excess wordage. They disliked iambic metre and abstractions but favoured verse freed from metre while tied to accuracy and scientific principles. The idea of the 'image', influenced by the

Japanese haiku and *tanka* as well as French symbolist poetry, summed up the imagists' preference for concision and compression. As Pound wrote in his *Memoir* of 1916: 'The image ... is a radiant node or cluster; it is ... a VORTEX, from which, and through which, and into which, ideas are constantly rushing' (see Smith 1983: 3). 'Imagism' was named by Pound to describe the approach to poetry agreed upon by the members of a literary group he formed in London in 1912. In 1914 Pound was also to endorse vorticism, a movement most closely associated with the writing and painting of Wyndham Lewis. Pound had come to London in 1908, the year before Ford Madox Ford established *The English Review*. Spurred on by Ford, Pound set about the overhaul of what he saw as the continuing vogue for second-hand Romanticism and fourth-hand Elizabethan poetry. He was joined by T. E. Hulme and F. S. Flint in framing a new poetry with principles of precision, discipline, objectivity, lucidity and directness. Their manifestos were Flint's 'Imagisme' (1913) and Pound's 'A Few Don'ts for Imagistes' (1913), later incorporated in the much fuller discussion called 'A Retrospect' (1918). Their anthologies were Pound's *Des Imagistes* (1914) and Amy Lowell's three volumes of *Some Imagist Poets* (1915–17).

Imagism arguably marks the inception of English and American modernism while making real the desire of a new generation for a more precise and objective poetry developed from Hulme's 1909 group of impressionist poets who tried their hands at short concrete poems after Chinese and Japanese models. From the symbolists, imagism took an emphasis on pure poetry to the exclusion of all extrapoetic influence, as well as the practice of irregular verse while pioneering a poetry with affinities to the aims of sculpture: hardness, craft and directness.

From the start, imagism marked a classical revival (see Hulme 1924) and a return to principles and rules for composition, such as concrete visual metaphors. Romanticism was rejected as metaphysical, indulgent, sentimental, mannered and over-emotional, and its view of reality as inherently mysterious, while life for the new poets was to be glimpsed in definite visual flashes or images. The three founding imagists, Pound, H.D. (Hilda Doolittle) and Richard Aldington, agreed on three principles:

1  Direct treatment of the 'thing', whether subjective or objective.
2  To use absolutely no word that does not contribute to the presentation.
3  As regarding rhythm: to compose in the sequence of the musical phrase, not in sequence of a metronome.

Pound's additional catalogue of 'don'ts' for novice poets had the central idea that poetry needs to be studied in the same way as music: for many years and with the goal of technical mastery. Though he stated that the subject could be anything, Pound first defined an 'image' as 'an intellectual and emotional complex in an instant of time', which may work through metaphor, juxtaposition or fusion, as in his own 'In a Station of the Metro':

> The apparition of these faces in the crowd;
> Petals on a wet, black bough.

(1916)

Pound's greatest influence was, perhaps, on his fellow American expatriate T. S. Eliot, who he introduced in 1917 as Assistant Editor on *The Egoist*, a short-lived but extremely important experimental journal (Ross 1967: 60–70). It was Pound who nurtured Eliot's early work, indebted to the French decadent Laforgue, and edited the pre-eminent modernist poem *The Waste Land* (1922), a piece of work which encompassed many of the principles of the imagists but also expressed a horror at both the military and cultural barbarity of the early twentieth century. With Eliot's *The Waste Land*, for almost the first time in English poetry, a writer seemed to be getting to grips with the consequences of modernity. Eliot borrowed from Baudelaire, mythology, Shakespeare, Eastern religion, paganism, music hall and a host of literary predecessors in order to express contemporary life in a polyphony of cultured soundbites that he originally titled 'He Do the Police in Different Voices' (from Dickens's *Our Mutual Friend*).

While the poem draws in the First World War and the Russian Revolution, *The Waste Land*'s dissonances, sudden transitions, shifts in rhythm and characteristically modernist obsession with language have often been seen as indicative of an alienation from life and from history. Terry Eagleton writes that

> If objects and events in the real world are experienced as lifeless and alienated, if history seems to have lost direction and lapsed into chaos, it is always possible to put all of this 'in brackets' ... and take words as your object instead. Writing turns in on itself in a profound act of narcissism, but always troubled and overshadowed by the social guilt of its own uselessness.
>
> (Eagleton 1983: 140)

Eagleton sees *The Waste Land* as an example of literature and language in crisis. On the one hand, it exposes a need for the literary establishment to reassert its necessary elitism in the face of the disruption of the Great War and the beginnings of mass culture; on the other, it epitomises an attempt to free writing from its degradation as 'a mere instrument of science, commerce, advertising, and bureaucracy', hence Eliot's juxtaposition of ordinary language, such as that found in pub talk, popular music and commerce, with recondite literary allusions. What is revealed is a desire to break away from the idea that the artist writes about something for somebody in a literal or descriptive way. Instead, Eliot evinces a valorisation of erudition, mythology, symbol and elite culture.

In both criticism and poetry, Eliot sought discipline and structure. He disliked the tradition in art that promoted expressions of emotion and spontaneity, believing instead in a formulaic set of objects, events or situations which evokes a particular emotion; he famously called this 'finding an objective correlative' in his essay 'Hamlet and his Problems' (1919). In *The Waste Land*, as in Joyce's *Ulysses*, Eliot turned to a controlling and impersonal 'mythical method' to bring artistic order to the chaos of modern life. In a later famous essay on 'The Metaphysical Poets' (1921) he developed these ideas in relation to the history of poetry and identified what he called a 'dissociation of sensibility' in the seventeenth century. In the work of Donne and Shakespeare, Eliot found a unity of thought and feeling which was subsequently missing in poetry, which became increasingly vague and emotional by the nineteenth century. Eliot, with his 'objective correlative' and 'mythical method', thus attempted to reintroduce a combination of intelligence and wit to poetry, uniting feeling and thought once more.

In several ways, Eliot's earlier poem 'The Love Song of J. Alfred Prufrock' (from *Prufrock and Other Observations* [1917]) is more introspectively modernist, with thoughts that describe a melting pattern of conceptions, connected by inference or by some submerged principle of organisation working beneath consciousness. Prufrock's memory is iconic and draws on images from both life and culture. A model of the mind is implied in the structure of the poem, which, like the mind, is mood-driven and picks up on perceptions and cultural artefacts, reforming them into new meanings. Prufrock has intense feelings of inadequacy and is unable to find the right words to express himself. The title itself emphasises Prufrock's insecurity and contributes to a pervasive sense of bathos in the poem. Prufrock's preoccupation with himself is also representative of modernism. He spends the poem creating and recreating himself with various aliases or performative possibilities. In this way, the poem shows that the crisis over the self in modernist literature is also a crisis of discourse. In the search for oneself, 'in the search for sincere self expression', as Pound put it, 'one gropes, one finds some seeming verity, one says "I am this", that or the other, and with the words scarcely uttered one ceases to be that thing' ('Gaudier Brezeska: A Memoir', 1916). Eliot's poem repeatedly problematises the subject in relation to discourse. Prufrock is all too aware of the inadequacies and ambiguities of language: 'It is impossible to say just what I mean', he says, and his desire to identify himself through language is the same as his attempt to position himself in society. Prufrock's sense of himself is highly dependent on the gaze and opinions of others, the self is acutely conscious of itself, and of 'The eyes that fix you in a formulated phrase'. The lack of confirmation and affirmation of Prufrock's identity through social interaction with others places him in an untenable position within both language and society.

Prufrock's anxieties conjure up heroes from the past, and he sees himself as, for example, John the Baptist, the Christian hero crying in the wilderness. His alter egos, Lazarus and Hamlet, both fail to act and to say exactly what they mean. It is as though Prufrock doubts the viability of a love song that could offer meaning to an otherwise banal life and so disintegrates into self-absorption. And the shift in the poem from 'I' to 'we' to 'us' involves his dispersion and loss of identity in the crowd. In such ways, Prufrock appears as a split being, another instance of the fragmented modernist self cut off from society, caught in language, neuroses and psychological self-doubts. Thus, via French symbolism and Anglo-American imagism, the alienated, dazed and confused modernist subject appeared decisively in English poetry with 'Prufrock's' opening lines: 'Let us go then, you and I, / When the evening is spread out against the sky / Like a patient etherized upon a table'. After this point, the poet and poetry itself became in many ways etherised: anti-humanist, undermined by hidden desires, driven by the unconscious, lost in language, painfully self-conscious, apolitical and detached.

For all of Eliot's significance, however, if Anglo-American modernism could be thought to be initiated in prose by Henry James in his highly mannered, consciousness-obsessed late works such as *The Golden Bowl* (1904) that built on the naturalism of writers like Stephen Crane (1871–1900), innovative Anglo-American poetry was ignited by Pound, though the work of Walt Whitman (1819–92) would be a formative influence on later key American modernist poets such as Hart Crane (1899–1932), William Carlos Williams (1883–1963) and Wallace Stevens (1879–1955). As we've seen, 'imagism' was the term coined to describe the poetry of both American poets such as H.D. and British writers such as Richard Aldington; Pound, based in Europe, initially sent examples of their work to Harriet Monroe's *Poetry* journal in Chicago, making comparisons with Greek poetry and claiming imagism as 'direct', 'objective', 'straight talk' (American modernism even more than British thrived in such little magazines, including *The Little Review*, a revivified *The Dial* and *The Seven Arts*). This turn towards the concrete and direct was also supported by the American expatriate Eliot and the British writer-artist Wyndham Lewis, while the philosophical aspects of a hard neo-classicism were formulated by F. S. Flint and T. E. Hulme. The reintroduction of classicism into English writing that this new movement offered was a reaction to the tendency towards a verbose, florid romanticism of the kind perfected by Joyce in the closing section of 'The Dead', from *Dubliners*, and parodied at the end of Chapter 4 in *A Portrait of the Artist as a Young Man* when Stephen Dedalus swoons in an epiphany of ecstatic language. The spectrum of American modernist poetry, however, was far broader than an emphasis on Pound and imagism suggests, and is strongly characterised by innovation, collage, experimental verse forms and new techniques in poets such as Stein, Hart Crane, Marianne Moore (1887–1972) and Edna St Vincent Millay (1892–1950). While the Pennsylvania graduates, Pound, H.D. and William Carlos Williams, had studied Oriental literature, Wallace Stevens, Conrad Aiken (1889–1973) and T. S. Eliot at Harvard learnt the lessons of symbolism, and, before the Great War, Chicago was the foremost hub of innovative American poetic activity (Carl Sandburg [1878–1967], Edgar Lee Masters [1868–1950] and Vachel Lindsay [1879–1931]), complementing the distinctly New World architecture of Frank Lloyd Wright and Louis Sullivan.

Modernism is also notable for the large number of female poets of importance it can be said to include. These range from H.D., Amy Lowell, Edna St Vincent Millay and Marianne Moore in the USA to Nancy Cunard, Anna Wickham, Charlotte Mew and Edith Sitwell in Britain. Jane Dowson (2002) argues that while these female modernists were less stylistically experimental than many of the more well-known male poets, they were more radical with regard to personal politics, in terms of class as well as gender; and it is worth remembering that to readers in the 1920s Edith Sitwell, as much as any man, represented the literary avant-garde in the popular imagination.

## DRAMA

T. S. Eliot only turned to writing plays in the 1930s, and in a string of works he searched for a new religious drama using poetic language, from *Murder in the Cathedral* (1935) to *The Cocktail Party* (1949). However, Eliot's plays, like those of Terence

Rattigan and Noel Coward, came to stand for a tired old order which was enthusiastically overthrown in the 1950s by the new realism of works such as John Osborne's *Look Back in Anger* (1956). In the light of this, it is fair to say that modernism had less impact on writing for the theatre in Britain than on fiction and poetry, to the extent that Christopher Innes has wondered if its almost anti-modernist agenda might make a discussion of drama seem contradictory in a consideration of literary modernism (1999: 130–56). Yet, several European dramatists had a deep impact on modernist literature across the genres, even though their perceived radicalism was too great for contemporary theatre producers or audiences in London. Drama was written by several pre-eminent modernists in Britain, such as T. S. Eliot, W. B. Yeats, D. H. Lawrence and Wyndham Lewis, and was also evident across Europe in the movements better known for their fine art: most notably expressionism, Italian futurism, Dadaist cabaret and Antonin Artaud's surrealist 'Theatre of Cruelty' (for discussion of these, see Bradbury and McFarlane 1976).

Two Scandinavian writers were largely responsible for the pre-modernist style of naturalistic realism that came into vogue late in the nineteenth century. The Swedish dramatist August Strindberg (1849–1912) wrote three major plays in the late 1880s (*The Father* [1887], *Miss Julie* [1888] and *The Creditors* [1889]), all of which dealt contentiously with gender relations and portrayed characters in crisis, at odds with their world. His later dramas, such as *A Dream Play* (1902), are more important to modernism because they attempt to convey an inner reality, in a style that would come to be called expressionist, and anticipated the interior monologue of modernist fiction. Strindberg says of the characters in *Miss Julie* that since they are 'living in an age of transition more urgently hysterical at any rate than the age that preceded it, I have drawn them as split and vacillating ... conglomerations of past and present' (quoted in Bradbury and McFarlane 1976: 47), and he wrote in his note to *A Dream Play* that 'Everything can happen, everything is possible and probable. Time and space do not exist. ... The characters split, double, multiply, evaporate, condense, disperse, assemble. But a single consciousness holds sway over them all – that of the dreamer' (quoted in Levenson 1999: 139).

The Norwegian dramatist Henrik Ibsen (1828–1906) revolutionised European drama into the style of modern prose plays that dominated the twentieth century. While his later work when he returned to Norway veered towards symbolism (for example, *The Master Builder* [1892] and, especially, *When We Dead Awaken* [1899]), his most influential plays were social dramas written while he lived in Munich (for example, *A Doll's House* [1879], *Ghosts* [1881], *The Wild Duck* [1884] and *Hedda Gabler* [1890]). Ibsen was a great influence on the first Irish dramatist I want to touch on, George Bernard Shaw (1856–1950), whose socialist opinions permeated what have been termed plays of ideas, which comically and irreverently juxtapose conventional and paradoxical stances. Shaw was the most popular and respected dramatist of his time, but his work is less concerned with the modernist directions suggested by Ibsen and Chekhov than with the social debates which Wells favoured. Shaw's plays are principally interesting because they undermine accepted opinions of class, morality and gender. This is also true of another Irish dramatist whose subversive decadent style, more than his formal experimentation, prefigures the agenda of many twentieth-century writers. Influenced by John Ruskin's belief in the spiritual benefit of art and Walter Pater's emphasis on aesthetics, Oscar Wilde's *The Importance of Being Earnest* (1895) is a play that reaches towards modernism. A catalogue of inverted morality and plural identities, *The Importance of Being Earnest* advocates 'the importance of doing nothing' (part of the subtitle of Wilde's 'The Critic as Artist') and of *being* everything, in terms of appearance, dress, manners, gastronomy and wit. It is a play that, in the spirit of beauty, recommends pleasure in general. Indeed, in his essay 'The Critic as Artist', Wilde states that 'aesthetics are higher than ethics'. Wilde also repeats Baudelaire's idea of the city as a place of pleasure in contrast to the business of the country, attacks family and married life in the name of the individual and emphasises throughout his play the necessity for multiple masks. The theme of degeneracy mentioned in the previous chapter is parodied in Wilde's occasional depiction of almost all of the male characters as unwell. Bunbury is the key example, but Algernon's uncle has 'ailments', his and Jack's father suffered from 'the Indian climate' and 'indigestion', while Jack is 'so serious that [Cecily] think[s] he cannot be quite well' and even Algernon is putatively blighted with apoplexy or a severe chill as Jack's wicked brother Ernest. 'Health is the primary duty of life', insists Lady Bracknell, but all the men around her are, in a parody of the Victorian notion that homosexuality is a disease, unwell, just as, to facilitate their (sexual) pleasure, they all lead double lives.

Shaw and Wilde were Irish dramatists who took to the London stage and London society. Their plays are in many ways quintessentially English, but the Dublin theatre they left behind in Ireland was revolutionised far more radically than the conservative British drama at the turn of the century. Most decisive was the influence of Yeats, who wished to develop an Irish culture based on traditional and mythological themes, even though his Abbey Theatre thrived by staging the popular comedies his audiences preferred. Yeats's own plays, from *The Shadowy Waters* (1895) up to *The Death of Cuchulain* (1939), developed from an early symbolism to a more abstract, mythological form of presentation, influenced by anti-realist Japanese Noh theatre, which aspires to archetypes of music and dance rather than dramatic presentation. Much of Yeats's drama, and notably the best-known early plays *Cathleen Ni Houlihan* (1902) and *On Baile's Strand* (1904), was written as part of a nationalist attempt to develop both a national mythology and an Irish theatre in Dublin. Two other dramatists associated with the Abbey Theatre were J. M. Synge (1871–1909), a doyen of the Irish peasantry and of Gaelic folk culture, and Sean O'Casey (1880–1964). Plays by both of these authors led to theatre riots in Dublin over their representation of Irish society and politics, as when O'Casey depicted an Irish prostitute (supposedly none existed) in *The Plough and the Stars* (1926) or showed a suspected informer pragmatically and coldly assassinated by the IRA in *Juno and the Paycock* (1924). Many of their plays were parables of cultural nationalism, such as Synge's *Riders to the Sea* (1904), which depicted Irish life unsullied by English colonialism, or *The Playboy of the Western World* (1907), a call to young Ireland to overthrow the tyranny of an oppressive father, who represents the religious and cultural backwardness of the Irish orthodoxy.

If we move on a generation, the Irish dramatist who most fully espoused modernism in his plays lived mainly in Europe, like his mentor Joyce. Samuel Beckett shocked London in August 1955 with his play *Waiting for Godot*, 'in which nothing happens, twice', as one critic wrote. *Godot* depicted life as a purposeless if comic attendance on nothing but futile endeavours, hopeless philosophies and inevitable death. In a barren landscape, two friends called Vladimir and Estragon, usually played by tramps, wait for a message from a man who never comes. Their memories fail as they turn to reminiscences, pass the time in squabbles and speculations and seek refuge in talk (Didi/*dit,dit*) or action (Gogo/*go,go*) to stave off the boredom of waiting for something to happen, to give them some reason to think their lives are not utterly pointless. Their only distraction is a couple of travellers, Pozzo and Lucky, who, joined by a rope, represent the mutual degradation of master and slave, the only and worse alternative to living life amicably; they also represent the only alternative to Didi and Gogo's pointless stasis: pointless movement. Later works, such as *Happy Days* (1961) and *Endgame* (1957), add to the impression that, for Beckett, human existence lacked meaning, and his later works seemed, in increasing brevity, to represent life, individual and collective, nearing exhaustion, running out of spiritual sustenance or hope of rebirth.

In the early to mid-twentieth century, Continental European drama, more than Irish plays, which, like O'Casey's and Synge's, were broadly naturalistic if mythologically symbolic, had much more in common with modernism than its largely conservative British counterparts, by writers such as Arthur Pinero and H. A. Jones. Of note among the later dramatists are Eugène Ionesco (1909–94), Jean Genet (1910–86), Federico Lorca (1899–1936) and, particularly, the Italian Luigi Pirandello (1867–1936) and the German Bertolt Brecht (1898–1956). Pirandello's most famous play is *Six Characters in Search of an Author* (1921), a grotesque exploration of illusion and reality, masks and pretence, disguise and disorientation:

> Each one of us believes himself to be a single person. But it's not true.
> Each one of us is many persons ... according to all the possibilities

> of being that there are within us. With some people we are one
> person. With others we are somebody quite different. And all the
> time we are under the illusion of always being one and the same
> person for everybody. We believe that we are always this one person
> in whatever it is we may be doing. But it's not true! It's not true!

Above all, like writings by psychologists such as Freud and William
James and like many other modernist works, the play is concerned
with the question of identity and the plurality and discontinuity
of the individual ego as the real self moves through time, in
opposition to the stability of a fictional character which in its
written solidity is immutable, fixed, consistent and rooted in an
unchanging text. Pirandello's *Henry IV*, first performed in 1922,
pushes several of these questions still further and also offers a
radical dramatic investigation of other philosophical issues such
as narrative irony and the representation of temporality.

Bertolt Brecht was the most successful explicitly modernist
dramatist. A Marxist, he appropriately maintained that the purpose of art was not to reflect social conditions but to attempt to
change them, as I noted in the last chapter, and this could only
be done through the shock tactics of avant-garde modernist aesthetics. Real social conditions such as poverty and inequality should
not be shown as either fixed or acceptable, as suggested by their
plain depiction in most naturalistic writing, but as abhorrent,
outrageous and unjust. Brecht's approach in his own plays, which
intentionally alienated the audience from the characters and conditions they saw on stage, was, in many ways, the (formal but not
ideological) incarnation of the modernist desire to 'make it new'
or at least to make life *strange* to the audience – to de*naturalise*
the status quo. Brecht also felt that as social conditions changed,
as capitalist forces adjusted to and assimilated revolutionary
forms of art, those means of artistic representation had themselves constantly to change in order to force people to reappraise
society and their relation to it. Developing from his early
expressionist dramas, Brecht used simple staging, defamiliarisation, montage and non-linear discontinuous narrative in such
plays of social conditioning and shifting personality as *The Caucasian Chalk Circle* (1949) and *Mother Courage* (1941). He did this

in a style he named 'epic theatre', which required the audience *not* to suspend disbelief but to see the play as a performance with a message rather than as a true-to-life story. Despite the opinion of British dramatists and stage producers that modernism would not be popular, Brecht has become the most performed playwright in the world.

It is also true that American modernist drama was more challenging, innovative, strident and successful than the plays of British counterparts. Susan Glaspell (for example, *Suppressed Desires* [1914] and *Trifles* [1916]) and Eugene O'Neill (for example, the expressionism of *The Emperor Jones* [1920] and *Desire Under the Elms* [1924]) dissected issues of gender and the crisis of masculinity, race and sexuality, in ways that British theatre did not and probably could not, though the London Irish dramatists Wilde and Shaw had shown the possibilities for such socially delicate themes to be explored in Britain.

## ART MOVEMENTS

Before I discuss various styles and artists, it is worth, first of all, considering from a socio-cultural point of view why European art underwent a series of upheavals from the mid-nineteenth century. Three principal reasons come to the fore.

First, the Kodak camera had made it possible to do what the painter had often been asked to do, that is, to give a lifelike representation of any chosen object. As a consequence, artists needed to assert an alternative, non-representational approach that differed from that of the camera. Second, painting materials had become much cheaper since there had been major breakthroughs in chemistry, the most successful industry of the late nineteenth century. Painters did not need money or patronage as in the past, and so someone like Van Gogh could survive with little income and without selling his paintings. Cheap housing and food in the cities also meant that the Romantic idea of the struggling artist could become a commonplace reality. Third, particularly after the French Revolution confiscated the art of the rich, museums and art galleries opened to the public and, therefore, to aspiring artists. Because of either state funding or the legacy of private collectors, all people living in cities and those who were able to reach them on the new high-speed trains could, for the first time, see the history of art and understand the way it had evolved. Related to the increase in art galleries was the growing market for paintings; with the expansion of the mercantile middle classes and the arrival of dealers, art became an industry.

With these key changes in mind, I now want to focus on several art movements of the late nineteenth and early twentieth centuries alongside some corresponding approaches and techniques in literature.

## Impressionism and after

The last representational art movement was arguably impressionism, as practised by Renoir, Monet, Degas, Manet and Sisley. Most impressionists shared the general view that all life contained a vision of beauty: cafés, villages, boulevards, salons, bedrooms and theatres all expressed a joy of life, a wholeness and a radiance. Impressionism was, in many ways, the essence of realism because its aim was to paint a specific object at a specific moment, to capture the effect of light and colour at an instant in time. In theory, an impressionist painting would take no longer to paint than it took to look at an object, making the finished canvas akin to an early Kodak photograph but shot through with colour.

Impressionism's unit of colour was the brushstroke, which was challenged by Georges Seurat (1859–91). More concerned with how vision worked than with the broad impressions created by the effects of light on objects, Seurat wanted to paint the constituent blocks or atoms of seeing. As language could be stripped down to its letters and sounds, painting could also perhaps be reduced to its smallest elements: the molecule or dot. Seurat's views were based on scientific studies of colour and perception which had shown that local vision or perception has a halo, a haze of colour surrounding it; for example, when seen in the eye, orange might have a blue halo or red a green one, depending on the light and the colours surrounding it. Colour, this theory suggested, is 'mixed in the eye'. So, Seurat turned to a kind of 'pointillism' (because of its 'points' or dots) or 'divisionism', the name he preferred. His paintings are composed of discrete points of colour, but as the viewer stands further back, the eye fills in the gaps and mixes the colours to create a total image. The eye sees 'orange', for example, but looking closely there would be constellations of reds and yellows making up this impression. Though painting in the 1880s, Seurat has often been credited with anticipating the fractured, divided sensibilities of the modernist period, thus predicting the way that art would become more self-referential, more concerned with form. His holistic approach through the assembly of atoms in a fragmented world is reflected in much modernist writing, where individuals, like Woolf's heroine in *Mrs Dalloway*, compose their selves from many parts, while Ford Madox Ford seems to allude directly to Seurat's art in *The Good Soldier* when his narrator declares that 'the whole world for me is like spots of colour in an immense canvas' (Ford 1972: 20).

Seurat's subject matter was the same as that of the impressionists, but his aims were not. He painted formal figures, seeing the bourgeoisie in a similar light to courtly figures of the past, detached and aloof on the surface, concerned with the decorum and propriety of life, like Ford's characters in *The Good Soldier*. The year Seurat died, 1891, Monet exhibited for the first time in what can be called his post-impressionist style. He displayed fifteen views of two haystacks seen at different times of the day, and he tried to show through this series of studies the infinite variety of colour that different light could produce. He chose haystacks because they could be shown as simply swathes of colour with no intricate details: something seemingly bland and uniform that would have little interest for art, but through effects of light would show innumerable shades of colour (he similarly painted Waterloo bridge and the Houses of Parliament). Monet's paintings of Rouen Cathedral are also interesting because he paints the cathedral simply as a mass of colours, not as a holy building or an intricate piece of architecture.

What Monet and Seurat have in common, which is taken into modernist writing, is the idea that there is a mist or halo to what the individual perceives. Seurat saw a point surrounded by a halo of colour, Monet painted his views as though seen through fogs and mists. There is here a suggestion of Woolf's description above of consciousness as an 'incessant shower of innumerable atoms', a 'luminous halo' or 'semi-transparent envelope'. Conrad, sometimes considered an impressionist writer, also seems to render a parallel view of 'meaning' in *Heart of Darkness*:

> to [Marlow] the meaning of an episode was not inside like a kernel but outside, enveloping the tale which brought it out only as a glow brings out a haze, in the likeness of one of those misty halos that sometimes are made visible by the spectral illumination of moonshine.
>
> (Conrad 1973: 30)

A manifesto in this respect was Maurice Denis's book *The Definition of Neo-Traditionalism* of 1890. It begins: 'A picture, before being a warhorse, a nude woman, or some sort of anecdote – is essentially a surface covered with colours arranged in a certain order'. Denis, thus, stressed the attention to shape, surface and colour that was to obsess the modernists as artists. Art had to be about art before it could be about the world: either form before content, or form as content.

## Cubism

The decisive shift between representational and abstract forms, cubist paintings were nearly all still lifes, even though the cubists rarely used nature, preferring to paint humans or constructed objects. Previously to cubism, virtually all painting had obeyed the principle of 'one point perspective': seeing and painting an object from one position, as exemplified in the work of the impressionists. But this is perhaps not what we see in terms of either the subject or the object. In terms of the object, art is a two-dimensional medium, but it is usually trying to represent three-dimensional space and, in this, can never be fully faithful to reality. In terms of the subject: humans have bifocal vision; the eyes see depths; the individual can move around an object to see it from different directions; the point of focus and the centre of vision can move between foreground and background as a person's point of interest shifts while scanning over the object.

Consequently, in cubism, instead of one subject looking at and painting one object, there is a shift to a position of relativity and interaction. To an extent, as with writing, we can say that a large element of doubt enters the frame. Just as, again, Dowell is uncertain how to tell his story in *The Good Soldier*, many modernist artists felt the need to question their traditional methods of representation. Here, the basic tenets of abstract art arise. Paul Cézanne (1839–1906) and Seurat, the early post-impressionists, had already questioned what exactly it was that the eye saw. Seurat used points, while Cézanne used lines and colours rather than objects because he argued that it was the mind that arranged what the eye saw, colours separated by lines, into distinct objects such as trees and mountains or leaves and fruits. Cézanne, the foremost theorist of painting at the end of the nineteenth century, maintained that the artist should not paint an object, such as an apple, but should paint what he or she saw: mixed shades of green, red and yellow bounded by a round line.

The founding cubists, Pablo Picasso (1881–1973) and Georges Braque (1882–1963), took this another step further by trying to depict the three-dimensionality of the object in the two dimensions of the canvas. To do this, they showed several sides to the object, maybe from five or six angles, and, because they dispensed with a fixed perspective, the cubists did not paint to size either. The various sides might be seen from different distances and, therefore, vary in proportion. The resulting paintings are composite images and perhaps Picasso's most influential effect was to introduce collage techniques, which have since become a staple of artistic composition. Work prior to 1912 is called analytical cubism because forms were analysed down to their geometrical structures while colour was minimised. From 1912 onwards, however, when the Spanish painter Juan Gris was as important as Braque and Picasso, colour was used to a greater extent and shapes became more decorative in a synthetic cubism. This was when the cubists produced collages using such new features as stencilled letters or scraps of newspaper.

In the cubists' early compositions, it is still possible to reconstruct the objects from the painting. The observer can see part of a violin, or part of a newspaper in these works, but in Picasso's later cubist paintings, it becomes impossible to reconstruct objects in a naturalist manner. Consequently, the early paintings, which seemed to combine old representational and new abstract styles, often provoked more hostility from critics because there was a tension between ideas about perception and about mimesis, about how 'reality' is seen by the eye and made sense of by the mind.

Picasso, who painted a famous portrait of her, discussed several of his ideas with the American modernist writer Gertrude Stein, who wrote that

> Everything I have done has been influenced by Flaubert and Cézanne, and this gave me a new feeling about composition. Up to that time composition had consisted of a central idea, to which everything else was an accompaniment and separate but was not an end in itself, and Cézanne conceived the idea that in composition one thing was as important as another thing. Each part is as important as the whole, and that impressed me enormously, and it impressed me so much that I began to write *Three Lives* under this influence. ... I began to play with words then. I was a little obsessed by words of equal value. Picasso was painting my portrait at that time, and he and I used to talk this thing over endlessly. At this time he had just begun on cubism. And I felt that the thing I got from Cézanne was not the last composition. You had to recognise that words had lost their value in the Nineteenth Century, particularly towards the end, they had lost much of their variety, and I felt I that I could not go on, that I had to recapture the value of the individual word, find out what it meant and act within it.
>
> (Quoted in Scott 1990: 502–4)

Both artists and writers thus shared a desire to reappraise their fundamental materials, to redesign composition and remake form. Woolf attempts this in *To the Lighthouse* (1927), a novel that uses the example of Lily Briscoe's painting as an image of how art, which is, in many ways, opposed to reason, shapes chaos using form. For many modernists, what was painted and what was written about became in some ways less important, and how it was written or painted became the key question. Much of this, as Stein suggests, was part of a drive to move away from the devaluation of art and writing that modernists perceived to have taken place in the Victorian period. Cubism, or rather the ideas of collage and multiple perspective, suggested to writers new ways of constructing both narrative and 'character' as composites, as not singular but an assembly of fragments. For example, similarly trying to break away, this time from country, family and religion as much as aesthetic ties, Stephen Dedalus has been described by Dennis Brown (1989) as being, just prior to his departure from Dublin at the close of Joyce's *A Portrait of the Artist as a Young Man* (1916), 'portrayed' as a cubistic collage of miscellaneous impulses and awarenesses.

For his part, trying to escape the conventions of centuries of European painting, Picasso also borrowed from the styles of African art, most famously in his *Les Demoiselles d'Avignon* (1907). His inspiration came from the many collections of masks and sculptures brought back after the 'scramble for Africa' in the late nineteenth century. In writing, D. H. Lawrence also saw a regenerative beauty in African art that could reconnect Europeans with their animal nature:

> It was an ordinary London sitting-room in a flat, evidently taken furnished, rather common and ugly. But there were several negro statues, wood-carvings from West Africa, strange and disturbing, the carved statues looked almost like the foetus of a human being. One was a woman sitting naked in a strange posture, and looking tortured, her abdomen stuck out ... Conveying the suggestion of the extreme of physical sensation, beyond the limits of mental consciousness.
>
> (Lawrence 1986: 127)

Where Picasso saw the possibility of an intense study and analysis of form, Lawrence perceived African culture, in certain respects, as simply an opportunity to imitate a beautiful representation of the primitive, because it was thought that European society needed to return to the elemental sources of its unconscious desires. For Picasso, Africa represented the possibility of regeneration from outside; he once said to Stein, 'I do not care who it is that has or does influence me as long as it is not myself' (quoted in Scott 1990: 496). In turn, the move towards abstraction taken by Picasso influenced every other artist, and as a consequence European art underwent its greatest revolution since the Renaissance.

## Futurism

Largely an Italian movement, 'futurism' (a name chosen over 'dynamism' and 'electricity') was the invention of Filippo Tommaso Marinetti (1876–1944), who published the first 'Futurist Manifesto' in *Le Figaro* in 1909 as a preface to his volume of poems. In it he declared:

> we affirm that the world's magnificence has been enriched by a new beauty; the beauty of speed. A racing car whose hood is adorned by great pipes, like serpents of explosive breath – a roaring car that seems to run on shrapnel – is more beautiful than the Winged Victory of Samothrace [a famous Hellenistic sculpture in the Louvre]. We will glorify war – the world's only hygiene. ... We will sing of great crowds excited by work, by pleasure, and by riot; we will sing of the multicoloured, polyphonic tides of revolution in the modern capital.

Marinetti claimed that time and space had 'died' with the arrival of speed, in the form of the motor car, the airplane and the ocean liner. In proclaiming the future, he also asserted that all libraries should be burnt so that only memory and legend would survive, thus enabling the world to turn to the future. His writings, which eschewed traditional syntax and punctuation, were very influential across Europe. On the one hand, he thought technology was the solvent of all ills; on the other, he believed that it had created a new kind of individual, a class of machine visionaries such as himself. Consequently, every aspect of human life and behaviour could be seen as an art form in the sense that humans, whether walking, dreaming or eating, might function efficiently and dynamically like machines. At one point, Marinetti, who called himself the 'caffeine of Europe', proposed making a film to show how the futurist would do all of these things. But Marinetti was not alone in wanting to rethink the aims of art in order best to represent the impact of machinery, of high-speed transport, of all new ideas concerned with process and transformation. For example, Degas had earlier been interested by photography because for his paintings of racehorses he had wanted to understand how their legs moved at speed. Photography helped nineteenth-century painters like Degas, but the futurists were more intrigued by the possibilities for representation opened up by the later development of motion pictures, just as Turner had attempted to show motion in a single image in his earlier paintings of speeding steam engines. Unlike Degas, they did not want to see, for example, how a bird's wing would look if captured in one instant, but instead set themselves the problem of how to represent the movement and speed of the bird's wings on a single canvas, without using a series of pictures.

There were different schools of thought about the effects of technology but almost every modernist artist felt the need to represent the social changes effected by machinery and the fact that humanity was becoming more machine-like. Jacob Epstein, whose rock-drill sculpture depicted a worker as a combination of a human torso and a drilling machine, lamented that machinery represented the 'terrible Frankenstein's monster into which we have turned ourselves'.

Another futurist, Francis Picabia (1879–1953), proclaimed, like the Russian poet Vladimir Mayakovsky (1894–1930), who declared that all existing art should be destroyed, that all previous art was dead. Consequently, to demonstrate the evolutionary leap represented by new forms of art, he exhibited a stuffed monkey labelled: 'Portrait of Cézanne, Portrait of Rembrandt, Portrait of Renoir'. The futurists generally appeared to the world as fanatics, and that Marinetti espoused Fascism is less surprising given his desire to perceive people in terms of automated machines. While Wyndham Lewis abandoned futurism to create his own version of a world in flux, vorticism, and Lawrence attacked Marinetti's vision in *Women in Love*, a later writer who satirised the modernist desire for machine-living was Evelyn Waugh. In his first novel, *Decline and Fall* (1928), there is a futurist architect called Otto Silenus who pictures life as a big wheel at a fairground, full of 'scrambling and excitement and bumps and the effort to get to the middle'. Otto then declares that 'Instead of this absurd division into sexes they ought to class people as static and dynamic' (Waugh 1970: 209). In Waugh's next novel, *Vile Bodies* (1930), he continued playing with the distinction in another futurist metaphor:

> *real* cars ... become masters of men; those vital creations of metal who exist solely for their own propulsion through space, for whom their drivers, clinging precariously at the steering-wheel, are as important as his stenographer to his stockbroker. These are in perpetual flux; a vortex of combining and disintegrating units; like the confluence of traffic at some spot where many roads meet, streams of mechanism come together, mingle and separate again.
>
> (Waugh 1972: 161)

Though futurism as a style did not have much prominence in Britain other than through Wyndham Lewis's vorticist experiments, the idea of dynamism, of the importance of speed, flux and movement, was widely known, and Waugh's auto-anthropomorphism alongside a reification of the human expresses a common horror of being 'lost in the machine' (compare with Charlie Chaplin's film *Modern Times* [1936]), and a fascination over images of the fusion of metal and flesh which preceded cyberpunk fiction by over fifty years. Futurism's lasting influences have also been evident in popular culture's fascination with technology and machinery, especially in film and graphic art.

## Expressionism

Expressionism has many roots in the work of another post-impressionist, Vincent Van Gogh (1853–90). In Van Gogh's self-portraits, the self is always apparently trying to escape, to flee itself in search of a new way of expression. In this desire not to represent but (self-)express or project, Van Gogh anticipates the dark world of expressionism.

Perhaps the most well-known expressionist painter is Edvard Munch (1863–1944), who said in a phrase that encompasses the philosophy of expressionism: 'Nothing is small, nothing is great.

Inside us are worlds'. Munch did not want to depict the impression the world made on him in certain lights, like Monet. He wished to paint the way that the world or a situation made him feel, to portray emotions provoked by and projected onto the world. Like Freud, Munch saw the self as a battleground between desire and social constraint, between id and superego. If the pleasure-seeking id dominates the ego, Freud says, psychosis results; if the superego dominates the ego, neurosis results. Only if they are in balance is the individual well adjusted. Munch foregrounded kinds of maladjustment in nearly all his paintings, and he showed the world through the eyes of individuals in extreme conditions. For example, he has a series of paintings called 'By the Deathbed' that show a sickroom from the point of view of a dying girl. Everyone is pale and ghostly or colourless, and the room appears as in delirium.

Unlike the impressionists, expressionist painters concentrated more on shadows than light, on the sinister effects of shade and dark, the qualities of nightmare and alienation, in opposition to the celebration of incandescence and beauty found in the work of a painter such as Renoir. Where the impressionists showed the uniqueness of an object in a moment of time, the expressionists did the same with the human subject. This is why they are considered modernists and the impressionists are not; because painters like Munch projected an alienated self onto the environment, painting the way reality felt, not the way it looked.

Passages of Joyce's *Ulysses*, especially the 'Nighttown' section, and of Woolf's *The Waves* (1931) are reminiscent of expressionist techniques, but Franz Kafka (1883–1924) is the most famous European expressionist novelist. Wyndham Lewis is probably the best-known British writer and artist, but another author who began as a modernist and later used expressionist techniques to convey the feeling of the rise of the Third Reich is Christopher Isherwood (Germany is the country most associated with expressionism, in film, art and painting). For example, this passage from *Goodbye to Berlin* (1939) shows the feelings of threat and fear portrayed through perceptions of darkness and shadow:

> They all thronged round us for a moment in the little circle of light
> from the panting bus, their lit faces ghastly like ghosts against the

black stems of the pines. This was the climax of my dream: the image of nightmare in which it would end. I had an absurd pang of fear that they were going to attack us – a gang of terrifying soft muffled shapes – clawing us from our seats, dragging us hungrily down, in dead silence. But the moment passed. They drew back – harmless, after all, as mere ghosts – into the darkness, while our bus, with a great churning of its wheels, lurched forward towards the city, through the deep unseen snow.

(Isherwood 1989: 174)

While expressionism projected the individual's feelings and disquiet onto the world, a later art movement also transformed representation by externalising an inner reality; only in the case of surrealism, the source was not emotion but the unconscious.

## Surrealism

Art was changed by the war, but not always in obvious ways. One clear response was Dadaism, which had links with futurism and was a forerunner of surrealism. Nobody knows for certain where the name came from, but its repetition of the slavonic word for yes, *da da*, is one possible meaning or origin, as is the fact that 'Dada' means 'hobby horse' in French. The movement began in Zurich at the new Cabaret Voltaire set up in 1916. Its champion was a twenty-year-old poet called Sami Rosenstock, who wrote under the name Tristan Tzara. Repelled by the slaughter of the First World War, the Dadaists turned to art as a means to redirect humanity away from the war's madness. They emphasised the illogical and the absurd, together with the importance of chance in artistic creation. They also believed that art could reform the order of human experience and so alter the conditions of social life. Dadaists wanted to draw on spontaneity through childhood innocence and chance, hence Tzara's arbitrarily scrambled poems and Jean Arp's collages of randomly dropped scraps of paper, or, later, Max Ernst's photomontages. Several of Beckett's short stories, especially 'Ping', discussed earlier in this chapter, appear to have elements in common with Dadaist (lack of) form.

The surrealists, influenced by the late eighteenth-century paintings of Francisco Goya and Henry Fuseli, were led by the French poet, essayist and critic André Breton (1896–1966), who broke from the Dadaist movement early in the 1920s. Though sharing the Dadaist rejection of bourgeois values, the surrealists developed a far more positive philosophy derived from the theories of Freud. Breton had treated shell-shock victims during the war at a psychiatric centre, and this led to his idea that reality was subjective, was constructed by the self and influenced by the unconscious. Noting how shell-shocked patients projected visions from their unconscious onto the world, Breton considered that this creation of a reality could also be artistic. Where the expressionists projected conscious fears and feelings, the surrealists, who espoused 'automatic writing', as did Yeats, took their imagery from the unconscious and created a super- or sur- (meaning above or beyond) realism. Taking the new term from a review by Apollinaire, in his 1924 'First Manifesto of Surrealism', Breton said that he wanted to achieve 'the resolution of these two states, dream and reality, which are seemingly so contradictory, into a kind of absolute reality, a *surreality*' (quoted in Kolocotroni et al. 1998: 308).

The imagery of dreams was, of course, the source and instrument for much of this, but Breton, unlike Freud, who was primarily interested in treatment, saw the insane or shell-shocked as prophets or oracles, thereby giving access to hidden sides of the mind, to the inspiration and imagination that artists also used. With expressionist painting, shapes, colours and therefore reality are distorted, but with surrealist art, unnatural or illogical scenes are represented and bizarre images juxtaposed.

In the work of David Gascoyne and others, surrealist poetry flourished in Britain in the 1930s, but, *avant la lettre*, antecedents of surrealist imagery in English poetry can also be found in Eliot's poetry, for example in the images used in 'Morning at the Window'. In fiction, the 'Nighttown' or 'Circe' section of Joyce's *Ulysses* is probably the most well-known equivalent to surrealist writing, though, as it was written well before 1924, many critics prefer to describe it as expressionist, which raises the question of whether it is possible to decide conclusively whether imagery in art is taken from the conscious or unconscious mind. There are, however, many other examples of dream-like phantasmagoric fictional visions before Breton founded the movement in the mid-1920s, and even in Woolf's *Mrs Dalloway*, discussed at length in the next chapter, there is a kind of surreal expressionism in the way that the shell-shocked soldier Septimus Smith projects his paranoia onto the world. For example, in this disorienting extract from one on Septimus's hallucinations in Woolf's novel, as Breton found with his patients, a new grotesque reality is created:

> Diagrams, designs, little men and women brandishing sticks for arms, with wings – were they? – on their backs; circles traced round shillings and sixpences – the suns and stars; zigzagging precipices with mountaineers ascending roped together, exactly like knives and forks; sea pieces with little faces laughing out of what might perhaps be waves: the map of the world. Burn them! he cried. Now for his writings; how the dead sing behind rhododendron bushes; odes to Time; conversations with Shakespeare; Evans, Evans, Evans – his messages from the dead.
>
> (Woolf 1976: 131)

It is appropriate that Woolf's 'hysterical' shell-shocked soldier, petrified by the world and obsessed by his dead officer Evans, should produce the kind of decodable but 'nonsensical' images which Freud sought to analyse in *The Interpretation of Dreams* (1900), where he stated that 'the verbal malformations in dreams greatly resemble those which are familiar in paranoia but which are also present in hysteria and obsessions' (1991: 412). Septimus's 'messages from the dead' appear, after Freud's work, far more likely to be messages from the unconscious: chilling images of the sort that achieved potent visual expression in the work of the avant-garde European film-makers of the 1920s.

## FILM

By the 1920s, film, which itself drew both subject matter and techniques from fiction, was having an enormous cultural impact on Euro-American art and literature. Many of the modernist writers discussed in the next chapter were influenced by cinema as much as by art, and many more wrote in a cinematic style, especially Woolf, Joyce, Beckett, Lowry and Conrad. In the discussion below, I want to outline some of the features of surrealist film, of German expressionism and of the work of the Russian director Sergei Eisenstein, before illustrating ways in which filmic techniques are echoed in fiction.

Experiments with surrealism in film as well as on canvas were enormously influential, especially the work of the Spaniard Luis Buñuel (1900–83), who collaborated with his countryman the painter Salvador Dali (1904–89) on *Un Chien andalou* (1928) and *L'Age d'or* (1930). *Un Chien andalou* has been dubbed the proto- type of film surrealism; Buñuel called it 'a despairing passionate call to murder'. The film begins with a woman's eyeball slit with a razor, moves on to show a colony of ants emerging from a hole in a man's palm and contains a pair of harnessed priests dragging a piano adorned with the carcasses of two donkeys. If there is any dominant narrative theme, it is the sexual relationship between the two main, but psychologically inconsistent, characters. Anticipating Beckett's play *Happy Days*, the film ends with the lovers buried in sand up to their waists, motionless and apart. The story, which has no organising pattern, was putatively made by assembling bizarre, striking images and dream fragments. Perhaps the most significant repeated image is that of a severed or separated hand, cut loose. The range of meanings for a dis- embodied hand is enormous: from castration, through bodily fixation, to a fear of murder (by strangling or shooting). The film blurs the boundaries of the human form: sometimes cutting it up, sometimes allowing it to move impossibly through time and space, and making transformations such as when the leading man's mouth is replaced by the armpit hair of the principal woman. Space is handled in a non-linear way, as when the lead- ing woman walks out of her bedroom onto a seashore, or when the man shoots his *Doppelgänger* in their bedroom and then falls to the ground in a forest. In terms of time, the film has five main parts. These are titled: 'Once Upon a Time'; 'Eight Years Later'; 'Towards Three in the Morning'; 'Sixteen Years Before'; and 'In the Spring'. The titles seem random but also appear designed to suggest a range of narrative genres. 'Once Upon a Time' suggests a fairy story and that the audience should think of the events as akin to a folk tale. It also implies universality through its time-lessness. The two more common kinds of title are 'Eight Years Later' and 'Sixteen Years Before', which arrange the events in a different order for viewers from the one in which they see them, but which also seem completely irrelevant: the only connection they create is three scenarios, each separated by eight years. 'Towards Three in the Morning' is incongruously specific in comparison with all the other titles; and 'In the Spring' both seems metaphoric, suggesting love and sex, and also contrasts with the depressing scenes it prefaces. The ending of the film – just as much as the prologue – appears cut off from the rest of the story, like the severed hand. Only the leading woman appears throughout the film, while minor characters appear briefly, serve a specific function in terms of sex or violence and then disappear: the man at the start, who blinds the leading woman, is the director Buñuel, but he then does not feature again; the leading man shoots his own 'double' when he appears; an obsessed and daydreaming woman appears in the street, only to be run down by a car; and, lastly, a new lover appears towards the end of the film, only to be replaced again by the leading man. Most comi-cally, the music in the film plays on an opposition between two kinds of sexual love. There is the Romantic excess of Wagner's *Tristan and Isolde* and the physical rhythmic steps of Latin American music. For example, the leading man's attempt to seduce the main woman is satirised and made comical by placing it against the strident insistency of the tango, a dance associated with passion and death.

The film can be rationalised in multiple ways, perhaps most commonly and easily as a series of filmic metaphors for *amour fou*, but to do so would seem to undermine the experiment itself, and, in many ways, the audience's emotional response to the images displayed is of more importance than their intellectual one.

German expressionism created in film an equivalent to the nightmare visions portrayed in Franz Kafka's fiction, such as *The Castle* (1926), *The Trial* (1925), and 'Metamorphosis' (1916). Where Kafka often used a plainly described world of persecution in which one irrational element would be introduced to compel the narrative down an absurd path, many expressionist films turned far more to the supernatural and the Gothic or the futuristic. The key elements were disorientating camera angles, a distorted *mise-en-scène*, painted, looming and misshapen sets, shadow projections and melodramatic acting, in films such as *The Cabinet of Dr Caligari* (directed by Robert Wiene, 1919), *Nosferatu*, (directed by F. W. Murnau, 1922), and *Metropolis* (directed by Fritz Lang, 1926).

In expressionist films, as in modernist narratives, point of view is crucial. A roving camera that can move anywhere is used and can take the perspective of different actors so that the audience can understand their 'expression'. Not only are inner and outer worlds synchronised, but the type of treatment conveys the quality of the feelings involved. Similarly, action can be repeated or replayed in slow motion to suggest a subjective experience of time and a vividness or intensity of sensory perception. Many writers used expressionist film techniques, especially shadow and distortion, as a way of superimposing their inner complexes on the outside world, as in Lowry's *Under the Volcano*: 'Their shadows crawled before them in the dust, slid down white thirsty walls of houses, were caught violently for a moment in an elliptical shade, the turning wrenched wheel of a boy's bicycle. The spoked shadow of the wheel, enormous, insolent, swept away' (Lowry 1962: 281).

In a passage that conveys the expressionists' method of projecting an inner world, Virgina Woolf wrote of a 'tadpole-shaped' shadow from *The Cabinet of Dr Caligari* in her essay on 'The Cinema' (1926): 'For a moment it seemed to embody some monstrous diseased imagination of the lunatic's brain. For a moment it seemed as if thought could be conveyed by shape more effectively than words. The monstrous quivering tadpole seemed to be fear itself, and not the statement "I am afraid"' (quoted in Levenson 1999: 219).

To perhaps the most important director of the 1920s, *The Cabinet of Dr Caligari* was simply a 'barbaric carnival'. In films such as *Strike* (1924), *Battleship Potemkin* (1925) and *October (Ten Days That Shook the World)* (1928), Sergei Eisenstein honed the cinematic equivalent of carnivalesque subversion in the technique of montage: of juxtaposing, organising and splicing together images that by their assembly imply a fresh meaning or metaphor. Eisenstein's film *Que Viva Mexico!* was the greatest single influence on the subject matter of Lowry's *Under the Volcano*. In his book *The Film Sense*, Eisenstein explains the influence of cubism's use of multiple viewpoints on film, and the new techniques in art to alter perceptions and create ambiguity which were studied by Russian propagandists after the revolution alongside theories of perception. Like that of the German expressionist Ufa (Universum Film-Aktiengesellchaft) directors, Eisenstein's originality sprang from his desire to treat film as an art and, therefore, not to offer a *representation* of reality in his work but to use the medium's unique visual capabilities, such as montage, editing, exposure and splicing techniques, in order to establish a new *expression* of reality and to develop film's own aesthetic theory. In fiction, which often represents thought by overlaying images, something like montage can be seen in the closing pages of *Mrs Dalloway*, especially in the climax of the story as Clarissa's mind ranges over: her party, Septimus's death, a phrase from Shakespeare and her own actions and perceptions.

> It was fascinating to watch her, moving about, that old lady, crossing the room, coming to the room, coming to the window. Could she see her? It was fascinating, with people still laughing and shouting in the drawing-room, to watch that old woman, quite quietly, going to bed alone. She pulled the blind now. The clock began striking. The young man had killed himself; but she did not pity him; with the clock striking the hour, one, two, three, she did not pity him, with all this going on. There! The old lady had put out her light! The whole house was dark now with this going on, she repeated, and the words came to her, Fear no more the heat of the sun. She must go back to them. But what an extraordinary night! She felt somehow very like him – the young man who had killed himself. She felt glad that he had done it; thrown it away while they went on living. The clock was striking.
>
> (Woolf 1976: 165)

Images of ageing, suicide and passing time in the midst of a party combine to create the impression of death's involvement in life, of the inseparability of fear and mortality.

The visual depictions of innumerable numbers of authors ranging from Dickens to Conrad have suggested ways of using the camera to directors. Similarly, the camera's ability to move rapidly through space, to pan out, zoom in and focus in on, is evident in many novels, such as the opening to E. M. Forster's *A Passage to India*; and Isherwood begins *Goodbye to Berlin* by describing himself as a camera; 'quite passive, recording not thinking'. Beckett's work is indebted not just to Eisenstein, under whom he wished to study, but also to slapstick comedians such as Buster Keaton, for whom he wrote *Film*. Malcolm Lowry, who worked briefly in Hollywood, was as influenced by film as he was by fiction, especially the German expressionist Ufa directors such as Murnau. Many other writers from the 1920s onwards clearly use, wittingly or not, cinematic descriptions and techniques like montage, flashback and panning, from Wyndham Lewis and Virginia Woolf to Aldous Huxley and Jean Rhys, underlining again how writers from modernism onwards worked more and more in the context of art and culture than simply within literature.

# 3

---

# TEXTS, CONTEXTS, INTERTEXTS

By now, it is clear that the term 'modernism' is not a precise label but, instead, a way of referring to the efforts of many individuals across the arts who tried to move away from established modes of representation in formal or political terms. In fine art, this required a reappraisal of the basic elements of painting (line, colour and shape), plus its conceptual underpinnings concerning two-dimensional perspective. In literature, the push to new forms necessitated a reconsideration of the fundamentals of imaginative writing: theme, character, narration, plot, the presentation of time and space, imagery and, above all, language. For example, the depiction of time is fundamental to the working of fiction, and, because modernist writers favoured intensity of experience, it has often been commented upon how the typical unit of time for the modernist novel was the day (*Ulysses*, *Mrs Dalloway*, the four parts of *The Sound and the Fury*) whereas for the realist novel it was the year (*Emma*, *Under the Greenwood Tree*).

Taking into account the diversity of changes wrought upon literature by the modernists, I have divided the key areas and aspects of the many stylistic and thematic shifts into five sections.

Overall, the chapter considers texts by fifteen authors who represent, on the one hand, the modernists' central preoccupation with questions of form and, on the other, their concern with issues of subjectivity in relation to gender, history, language, social division and (mis)perceptions of reality. Each section is prefaced by short biographies of the three authors under discussion.

## 'THE STRUGGLE OF BECOMING': FREEDOM AND GENDER

### Charlotte Mew (1870–1928)

Mew was declared by both Thomas Hardy and Virgina Woolf to be the greatest living female poet. A distinctively original writer, she was largely ignored by critics up until the 1980s and has only recently been re-evaluated as a stylistic innovator. She wrote in a formal lyrical verse, which now seems striking for its sexual undertones, its criticism of Victorian attitudes and its political as well as erotic analysis of female subjectivity. Mew lived in London amid an oppressive family, had little education and committed suicide, by swallowing disinfectant, after her sister's death.

**Major works:** *The Farmer's Bride* (1916), *The Rambling Sailor* (1929).

### Katherine Mansfield (1888–1923)

Mansfield was born in New Zealand but studied in London and lived her adult life in Europe. A bohemian by temperament, she lived an eventful if short life, and interest in her biography has often eclipsed discussion of her stories: she left her first husband three weeks after she first met him, soon after had a miscarriage and later married the writer and critic John Middleton Murry; she contracted tuberculosis, which led to her early death. A writer of stories which relied on feeling and style more than plot for their shape and meaning, she added to the modernist development of both a stream-of-consciousness technique and the use of multiple perspectives.

**Major works:** *In a German Pension* (1911), *Bliss and Other Stories* (1920), *The Garden Party and Other Stories* (1922).

## D. H. Lawrence (1885–1930)

Lawrence was born in Nottinghamshire, the son of a genteel, middle-class mother and a coal miner between whom there were many tensions. He was a school teacher, like his mother, before he became a novelist. In 1911, after the death of his mother, the success of his first novel, *The White Peacock*, and the worsening of his health, he turned to writing full time. The following year, he met and then eloped with and later married Frieda Weekley (*née* von Richtofen), the wife of his former college tutor. Travelling in Italy and Germany, Lawrence worked on the novels that made his name, even though several were censored during his lifetime. In 1919, the Lawrences' disillusionment with England caused them to leave the country for good. At the age of forty-four, Lawrence died of the tuberculosis that had overhung most of his life. Lawrence is chiefly remembered for his frank treatment of sexuality, and nearly all his work deals with tensions between passion and convention. Much of his finest work is contained in his poetry, short stories, plays and essays.

**Major works:** *Sons and Lovers* (1913), *The Rainbow* (1915), *Women in Love* (1920), *Lady Chatterley's Lover* (1928).

Changes away from realist representations of character and Victorian discourses of gender are evident in several canonical male modernist writers, such as Joyce, James and Lawrence. Each of these novelists shifted understandings of identity by evolving a distinctive and, to different degrees, controversial use of language which challenged the externally focused portrayals of Wells, Bennett and Galsworthy. Additionally and alternatively, the work of Mansfield, Mew, Woolf, and Rebecca West shows how avant-garde women writers were concerned in different ways to problematise or subvert not just gender stereotypes but also orthodoxies of sexuality and class. To deepen traditional views of modernist identity, there have been a number of studies in recent years of the relationship between modernism, feminism and gender, such as Janet Wolff's essay on 'Feminism and Modernism' (1990) and Bonnie Kime Scott's *Gender and Modernism* (1990). While, on the one hand, critics have frequently noted how books by Lawrence, Lewis, Ford and others are marked by femme fatales, sexually alluring but also active and independent women who provoke feelings of anxiety and vulnerability in male protagonists, other critics have suggested that there is a distinct 'tradition' of a separate female aesthetics within modernism.

Many women were excluded from the modernist canon until the 1980s and even the 1990s. Before then, writers such as May Sinclair (1863–1946), Mina Loy (1882–1966), Rose Macaulay (1881–1958), Jean Rhys (1890–1979), Sylvia Townsend Warner (1893–1978), Edith Sitwell (1887–1964), Anna Wickham (1884–1947) and Charlotte Mew were consigned to minor roles in literary history as lacking the qualities required in either fine and important or original and experimental writing. Before considering one in more detail, Charlotte Mew, I would like to outline in a sentence or two the significance of each of these figures, to give a brief idea of several writers largely excluded from studies and syllabuses until recently. Nearly all of these women writers can be read about further in Bonnie Kime Scott's edited collection *The Gender of Modernism*.

May Sinclair was a student of philosophy, mysticism and psychology and a painstaking champion of many modernist writers, particularly Dorothy Richardson. It was Sinclair who first applied the term 'stream of consciousness', coined by William James to describe the activity of the mind, to Richardson's prose technique in 1918. In her own writing, she was preoccupied with identity and the category of the individual, especially in her own stream-of-consciousness novels *Mary Olivier* (1919) and *The Life and Death of Harriett Frean* (1922).

Mina Loy studied painting and exhibited her work in Paris from 1903 to 1907, and only later turned to criticism and writing, her first published work being 'Aphorisms on Futurism' (1914). Her experimental poetry was published alongside Ezra Pound's and inspired by the work of Gertrude Stein.

Rose Macaulay is principally important here for her war novels (*Non-Combatants and Others* [1916] and *Told by an Idiot* [1923]), which express a 'female' modernism in which the relationship between gender and literary style is a dominant theme.

Jean Rhys is now most well known for her 1966 novel *Wide Sargasso Sea*, but in the 1920s and 1930s she published a series of metropolitan books, concerned with the passage of time, polyphony and fragmented consciousnesses, the best of which is the last, *Good Morning, Midnight* (1939). Through a variety of styles, including interior monologue, Rhys's early novels unremittingly explore the role of woman as victim within male fantasies. Sylvia Townsend Warner wrote seven novels, nine volumes of poetry, ten short-story collections and much more; she was a radical feminist writer whose concern with difference, Marxism and history meant that in many ways she reached beyond the dominant concerns of the modernist period. Her novel *Lolly Willowes* (1926) has been called 'feminist fantastic realism, a direct forerunner of Angela Carter' (Jane Marcus in Scott 1990: 531). Edith Sitwell, critic, promoter and editor of the important experimental magazine *Wheels*, was also a significant poet herself, influenced by the French symbolists. Her sequence of poems *Façade*, set to music by William Walton, was an experimental tour de force which subsumed sense to sound and so was greeted at its premiere in 1922, like *Ulysses* and *The Waste Land*, with hostile incomprehension.

Anna Wickham was a class-conscious feminist and pacifist. She wrote poems about marital reform, the shortcomings of the Catholic Church and her own sense of exile as an Australian in England. Though extremely popular at the time, it is also fair to say that Wickham was far less experimental than her contemporary Charlotte Mew, who, in her longer poems, was an innovative and original writer whose exclusion from discussions of modernism can be understood in terms of gender but only excused in terms of her few publications.

Mew's first collection of poems, *The Farmer's Bride*, was published in 1916 by Harold Monro's Poetry Bookshop and reissued in an expanded edition in 1921. The poems focus on lost love and emotional denial, quite possibly because Mew was fearful of the hereditary mental instability in her family or because she was caught between her sense of propriety and her lesbianism; her most well-known poem, 'The Farmer's Bride', ends with a man's overpowering desire for his newly returned runaway wife, who

sleeps above him in the attic. Mew renounced marriage and children, and her poems frequently deal not with family life but with
such subjects as pedlars, changelings and asylums (see Fitzgerald
1984).

Her longest early poem, over 200 lines, is the contemplative
meditation 'Madeleine in Church', in which Mew experiments
with the length and indentation of lines within a complex verse
structure. On the one hand a religious reverie of ecstasy, the
poem discusses female pleasure apart from men and can be taken
as being concerned with lesbianism and autoeroticism as well as
with religious suffering or sacrifice. On the other hand, as a
dramatic monologue, the poem's style uses variations in rhyme
scheme and in rhythm, while the narration leans towards the
stream-of-consciousness technique employed by Richardson and
less famously by May Sinclair, then Mew's close friend. The
verses of 'Madeleine in Church' vary in many respects, including
length, appearance and arrangement, but usually in ways that
echo the tenor of the woman's thoughts as her mind falls in and
out of imagined dialogue with others and with herself, often on
the thought of self-sacrifice:

> I think my body was my soul,
> And when we are made thus
> Who shall control
> Our hands, our eyes, the wandering passion of our feet,
> Who shall teach us
> To thrust the world out of our heart; to say, till perhaps in death,
> When the race is run,
> And it is forced from us with our last breath
> 'Thy will be done'?

Such lines question the constraints that Victorian notions of
religion and patriarchy placed upon women and their allotted
role as virtuous, passive sufferers. Mew's revisionary Magdalen
kneels in a side chapel away from Christ, unsure what and whether she believes. Ultimately Mew's Madeleine places faith only
in her senses and recollections, while her thoughts consistently
dwell on the past, the war and her own love affairs, including

marriage and divorce. Like much modernist writing, the poem is an uneasy meditation in fragments of memory and yearnings for the return of youth, and it is also one which opposes the comforts offered by Christ with the isolation of the individual: 'What can You know, what can You really see / Of this dark ditch, the soul of me!'

As a general reflection on loss, the poem considers the separation of the physical and the spiritual worlds and the difficulty of faith without revelation; all Mew's poetry is suffused with images of suffering, punishment and denial, reinforcing the general impression that she found the male literary scene intense, sorrowful and, at her suicide, finally overwhelming. Her participation in the creation of a lesbian aesthetic, alongside writers such as Radclyffe Hall and in America Djuna Barnes, can now be considered an important aspect to modernism's assault on accepted notions of sexual identity.

Where, in terms of content, Mew's poem evinces a preoccupation with the restraints on sexuality and of religion, Katherine Mansfield's short stories frequently coalesce around the theme of the constraints on silenced or muted women within society and patriarchy. In terms of form, Mansfield's work is characterised by obliquity and hiatus, such that what is not said in her stories is as important as what is. To create the effect of unspoken meaning, Mansfield uses symbolism, unfinished questions, indirect expression and partial revelation in a narration filtered through the partial understanding of principal characters who are often marginalised figures: children, spinsters, women subservient to fathers, brothers and husbands. Many of the stories therefore concern the gradual coming to awareness of an individual excluded from power or knowledge and thus appear plotless in a traditional sense but involve a development of self-understanding and a concomitant disillusion, confusion or frustration.

The socialisation of children observing the adult world is one theme of 'The Garden Party' (1921), Mansfield's most famous story. Children of both sexes in the Sheridan family accept their roles within a patriarchal system of interpellated identities (allotted roles), with the potential exception of the main character Laura, who is largely puzzled by patterns of behaviour conditioned by gender and class. The sense of mystery surrounding Laura's initiation into the adult world, with its unspoken laws and rules of behaviour, comes across in the gaps and breaks in the dialogue, represented in the text by hyphens, ellipses and the occasional 'awkward little silence' (Mansfield 1951: 82). Laura finds that when she speaks like her mother she sounds 'affected' and is even 'ashamed' (Mansfield 1951: 66). It is clear that she senses the dishonesty and denial of herself implicit in imitating her mother and she isn't prepared at the story's outset to fall in with her family's plans for her or easily to accept their values. Her idea of what is correct also goes against the opinion of the adults when they learn of the death of a local worker. Instinctively and impulsively, Laura is prepared to cancel the Sheridans' party out of respect for the neighbouring family whose father has died.

On hearing news of the carter's death and having rejected Laura's original suggestion of calling the party off, her mother invests Laura with the responsibility of carrying scraps of food and some arum lilies to the dead man's cottage:

> 'People of that class are so impressed by arum lilies.'
> 'The stems will ruin her lace frock', said practical Jose.
> So they would. Just in time. 'Only the basket, then. And, Laura!' – her mother followed her out of the marquee – 'don't on any account—'
> 'What mother?'
> No, better not put such ideas into the child's head! 'Nothing! Run along.'
>
> (Mansfield 1951: 83)

The saving of Laura's dress 'just in time' from the red stems has obvious sexual and social connotations of staining, or at least of contamination. Her white lace dress, like a bridal gown, positions her on the border of innocence and experience, leading to an inevitable loss of childhood 'purity' in a story which has many echoes of fairy tales, especially 'Little Red Riding Hood'.

What she is being told not to do on any account is a thought contained in unspoken words which the reader has to work out. Laura is presumably not to stay and talk to the working people or perhaps not to see the man's corpse. The dramatic withdrawal of the warning 'don't on any account—' symbolises a perceived need to withhold information from girls, in a society in which they are kept subordinate. Laura, unlike her mother, is young enough to be largely free from certain ideological constraints, in a state of innocence, and might, therefore, recognise her society's innate injustices for what they are; hence her mother's decision not to 'put such ideas into the child's head'. Laura's mother fears encouraging her daughter to question the social order, symbolised in the story by tokens of vanity such as the 'big hat' that her mother places on Laura's head.

This is the self Laura sees reflected in the mirror and also in the figure of her mother, in opposition to the self she constructs when she thinks independently: 'the first thing she saw was this charming girl in the mirror, in her black hat trimmed with gold daisies and a long black velvet ribbon. Never had she imagined she could look like that. Is mother right? she thought. And now she hoped her mother was right' (Mansfield 1951: 79–80).

It is made more explicit that she has fallen into self-concern and a preoccupation with appearances when her brother's compliment on her dress specifically prevents her from asking him if he thinks she is absurd for wanting to call off the party. She 'smiled up at Laurie, and didn't tell him after all' (Mansfield 1951: 80).

In the story, Mansfield questions the allotted role of women and the strictures of class. Working-class families are, literally as well as symbolically, at the bottom of the hill, while the Sheridans live at the top. The latter carry on their party while the working class mourn their dead, and this expresses the gulf between them. We might note, for example, the symbolic difference between the smoke from the respective chimneys: 'The very smoke coming out of their chimneys was poverty-stricken. Little rags and shreds of smoke, so unlike the great silvery plumes that uncurled from the Sheridans' chimneys' (Mansfield 1951: 77).

One of Mansfield's innovations was to hone the style of the 'plotless story'. So, in 'The Daughters of the Late Colonel' in *The Garden Party and Other Stories*, to take a different example also from 1921, in terms of incident almost nothing happens. Two daughters, Josephine and Constantia, carry on with their lives after the death of their tyrannical father. They are cocooned after the colonel's death and are marooned in what almost amounts to illness. Superficially, the story appears to be an upper-class domestic comedy of manners, an aesthetics of boredom. On further reflection, it can be seen instead as an articulation of the crises exposed by the First World War, foregrounding restrictive Edwardian social and cultural mores. Scenes alternate between the present and the past with occasional intimations of an empty future, while Mansfield's time-shift technique intensifies the protagonists' vagueness and indecision.

The apparently artless beginning is pivotal to the rest of the text. The opening appears to deal with two children in bed, thus disorienting the reader, who soon realises that the daughters are not young but quite old. Then there is a change in point of view from the sisters to the maid, which places the 'daughters' in a different aspect, building up the reader's impression of them slowly: 'And proud young Kate, the enchanted princess, came in to see what the old tabbies wanted now' (Mansfield 1951: 93). Rhetorical questions, unfinished sentences, hesitancies and procrastinations show the fear and desolation of the daughters now outside their father's jurisdiction. The colonel himself is presented as an amusing caricature of a leftover colonial who, in old age and decrepitude, returned home to oversee his household with an authoritarianism akin to imperial rule; he had a cycloptic stare, suggesting monocular views, and an inability to hear well that symbolises a self-opinionated interpretation of the world, unheeding of the views of others. The daughters appear to have fallen into the trap of accepting their father's many pronouncements to the point where after his death they have become their own oppressors, while their frequent absurd interchanges represent a crisis of selfhood and identity.

Some critics see in the sisters a sense of female rebirth, of a slow transition into a new existence. The death of the colonel is a metaphorical statement about the imminent demise of the bigoted and abusive face of patriarchal power in the light of women's emancipation. Yet, Mansfield presents not the liberated New Woman but two dominated, oppressed and repressed daughters of the colonial upper middle classes.

Overall, the story reveals that the daughters have replaced an awareness of life with fantasy and daydream. Their guilt at having buried their father 'without his permission' expresses not only fear but a deep psychological desire, in that they have probably secretly wished him dead for a long time. The sisters' apprehension over their own liberation and Mansfield's writing of 'The Daughters of the Late Colonel' shortly after women won the vote for the first time, suggests a wider social message. The story, in twelve parts, evinces a fascination with time and, therefore, change versus stasis, while the cluster of symbols in the story (such as cats, the moon and a statue of the Buddha) militates against easy interpretation. For example, the figure of the Buddha that appears at the end of the story might represent male authority or signify the need for a contemplative withdrawal from life. Yet, Buddhist theories can provide direct ways of linking the idol in the sisters' house to the assault on the stable ego mounted by modernism; for example,

> The Buddha teaches that what we call the ego, self, soul, personality etc, are merely conventional terms not referring to any real independent entity. And he teaches that there is only to be found this psychophysical process of existence changing from moment to moment. This doctrine of the egolessness of existence forms the essence of the Buddha's doctrine of emancipation.
>
> (Collins 1982: 155)

In addition to the ambiguity of symbols, both 'The Garden Party' and 'The Daughters of the Late Colonel' have similarly enigmatic endings, and one of Mansfield's most representative modernist devices is to leave things unsaid. This was not a trait shared by D. H. Lawrence, who was most definite in his assault on 'the old stable ego' and who had his two principal novels, in which Mansfield is the prototype for one of 'The Sisters', suppressed for obscenities several years before *Lady Chatterley's Lover* was banned.

Lawrence's candour over sex was only a part of his conviction that much-needed change could only happen through the genuine desire to forge honest relationships and to have the courage to risk the certainties of the past when gambling on the uncertainties of the future:

> Are you willing to be sponged out, erased, cancelled, made nothing?
> Are you willing to be made nothing?
> dipped into oblivion?
> If not, you will never really change.

('Phoenix', 1932)

For Lawrence, the freedom of the new, of change and renewal, could only come through an awareness of the individual's multiplicity and versatility. In an essay from *Reflections on the Death of a Porcupine* (1925) called 'Love Was Once a Little Boy' he argues: 'Instead of the Greek "Know Thyself" we shall have to say to every man, "Be Thyself". "Be Thyself" does not mean "Assert Thy Ego" ... individualism makes the mistake of considering an individual as a fixed entity'. In another of the remarkable poems he wrote in the months before his death, 'God is Born', Lawrence asserts that 'The history of the cosmos / is the history of the struggle of becoming', and much of his work is concerned with this need to attain self-understanding not through knowledge but through 'life', as I mentioned in the last chapter. In a famous letter of 5 June 1914 to Edward Garnett he explained:

> You mustn't look in my novel for the old stable *ego* – of the character. There is another *ego*, according to whose actions the individual is unrecognisable and passes through, as it were, allotropic states which it needs a deeper sense than we've been used to exercise, to discover are states of the same single radically unchanged element.

When he wrote this, Lawrence was working on his two early novels, *The Rainbow* and *Women in Love*. Together, they were intended as a thousand-page tour de force originally projected as one novel to be called 'The Sisters'. According to Lawrence, in another letter to his mentor Garnett, on 22 April 1914, they concentrate most fully on the theme of 'woman becoming individual, self-responsible, taking her own initiative' and 'the establishment of a new relation ... between man and woman'. The two books concern the Brangwen family over three generations from around the mid-nineteenth century to the First World War. *Women in Love* focuses on Ursula and Gudrun Brangwen and their relationships, particularly with 'soldier, explorer and Napoleon of Industry' Gerald Crich, son of the local colliery owner and the Lawrentian artist Rupert Birkin, two men who also embark upon their own, alternative, manly physical relationship. Unlike its companion novel, *Women in Love* proceeds through counterpointed dramatic action, not chronological progress, in which the relationships of characters develop a rhythm over several separate scenes, accumulating history, antagonisms, desires and oppositions. The book ends pessimistically, conditioned by Lawrence's horror at the war and at the modern misuse of will, but there are many pronouncements on the kinds of individual and individual relationships Lawrence believed to be transcendent, progressive and liberating.

First, there is the ambivalent love between Gerald and Birkin. Developing from their fundamental lack of awareness ('They had not the faintest belief in deep relationships between men and men, and their disbelief prevented any development of their powerful but suppressed friendliness' [Lawrence 1986: 83]), Birkin and Gerald debate a newspaper columnist's 'cant' that there 'must arise a man who will give new values to things, give us new truths, a new attitude to life' (Lawrence 1986: 105), and begin to forge a deeper attachment to one another. This culminates in Birkin's offer of love to Gerald:

> 'You've got to take down the love-and-marriage ideal from its pedestal. We want something broader. – I believe in the *additional* perfect relationship between man and man – additional to marriage'.
> 'I can never see how they can be the same', said Gerald.
> 'Not the same – but equally important, equally creative, equally sacred, if you like'.
> Gerald moved uneasily. – 'You know, I can't feel that', said he. 'Surely there can never be anything as strong between man and man as sex love is between man and woman. Nature doesn't provide the basis'.

> 'Well, of course, I think she does. And I don't think we shall ever be happy till we establish ourselves on this basis. You've got to be rid of the *exclusiveness* of married love. And you've got to admit the unadmitted love of man for man. It makes for a greater freedom for everybody, a greater power of individuality both in men and women'.
>
> (Lawrence 1986: 439–40)

Birkin says that he wants with Gerald 'an impersonal union that leaves one free', and this is expressed in the idea of *Blutbrüderschaft*, of strongly individual men who might still fight, as Gerald and Birkin do semi-playfully, but who remain joined in an oath of blood-brotherhood.

The second kind of love-attachment theorised by Birkin, while Gerald is 'willing to condemn himself in marriage' to Gudrun, is the nearly 'perfect and complete relationship' (Lawrence 1986: 452) he has with Ursula (who desires a 'worship of perfect possession' [1986: 271]), which is primarily undermined by its being in tension with Birkin's other desires:

> [Ursula] believed in an absolute surrender to love. She believed that love far surpassed the individual. [Birkin] said the individual was *more* than love, or than any relationship. For him the bright, single soul accepted love as one of its conditions, a condition of its own equilibrium. She believed that love was *everything*. Man must render himself up to her.
>
> (Lawrence 1986: 343)

Birkin finds this concept of love claustrophobic, while Ursula believes it is the ultimate of self-expression. Birkin argues instead for balanced singleness, not the 'broken halves' of a conventional couple:

> he wanted to be single in himself, the woman single in herself. He wanted sex to revert to the level of the other appetites, to be regarded as a functional process, not as a fulfilment. He believed in sex marriage. But beyond this, he wanted a further conjunction, where man had being and woman had being, two pure beings, each constituting the

freedom of the other, balancing each other like two poles of one force.

(Lawrence 1986: 269–70)

Birkin asks Ursula to meet him 'not in the emotional, loving plane – but there beyond, where ... we are two stark, unknown beings ... responsible for nothing, asked for nothing, giving nothing, only each taking according to the primal desire' (Lawrence 1986: 208–9). Through Birkin, Lawrence asserts the idea, radical then but commonplace today, that men and women should live both in complete singleness and mutually sustaining union. By contrast, Lawrence's pessimism about European civilisation at the time of the war is also expressed by Birkin: 'Humanity is less, far less than the individual, because the individual may sometimes be capable of truth, and humanity is a tree of lies. – And they say that love is the greatest thing; they persist in *saying* this, the foul liars, and just look at what they do!' (Lawrence 1986: 187). The individual, but not humanity, can have integrity, the 'value behind values in *Women in Love*' according to Michael Levenson (1991: 145).

As in *The Rainbow*, Lawrence argues for a recognition that would now be discussed in terms of 'difference', or an understanding of the 'otherness' of people in all relationships: 'One man isn't any better than another, not because they are equal, but because they are intrinsically *other*, that there is no term of comparison' (1986: 161). As a frank exploration of modes of love and friendship, the book was deeply shocking despite its somewhat vague recommendations for new ways of living. But, as a mythologically inflected and symbolically rich text written in an original idiom, *Women in Love*, together with *The Rainbow*, represented the first concerted attempt by an English modernist to reassess and remake as well as, in Nietzsche's term, 'revalue' human relationships. Here Lawrence was consciously building on the elements of social critique and proto-modernist experimentation in Hardy's equally reviled late novels of stifled sexual emancipation and unequal power conflicts between classes, generations and genders. Where Mansfield had considered the often painful and frustrated social and personal release of women from the ties of Victorian attitudes, Lawrence championed deeply problematic but liberating sexual and spiritual aspirations towards new relations, self-responsibility and the emergence of a free individuality rooted in a recognition of otherness.

## 'IT SEEMS TO ME I AM TRYING TO TELL YOU A DREAM': EPISTEMOLOGY AND NARRATION

### Joseph Conrad (1857–1924)

Conrad was born Józef Teodor Konrad Korzeniowski in Russian Poland. His father was exiled from the Ukraine for political activities in 1861, and the family moved to northern Russia; his mother died when he was seven, his father when he was eleven. From an early age, Conrad was enthralled by the sea, and he joined the French merchant navy in 1874, later switching to an English ship and years afterwards becoming a British subject in 1886. In his career at sea, he visited South America, Central Africa and the Far East. He started writing around 1886, but his first novel was not published until a decade later. Conrad is noted for his complex narratives alongside his depiction of imperialism and colonialism, in the Malay Archipelago in *Almayer's Folly* (1895) and *An Outcast of the Islands* (1896), in the Belgian Congo in *Heart of Darkness*, and in South America in *Nostromo*. His political novels *The Secret Agent*, which revolves around an anarchist plot to bomb Greenwich Observatory, and *Under Western Eyes* (1911), which focuses on revolutionaries in Russia and in exile, are also much studied, as is the first novel of his mature phase, *Lord Jim*, a story of honour and the codes of the sea narrated by Conrad's surrogate, Marlow.

**Major works:** *Heart of Darkness* (1899), *Lord Jim* (1900), *Nostromo* (1904), *The Secret Agent* (1907).

### Henry James (1943–1916)

James, an American with a high regard for European culture, settled in England in 1876. His experiments, following the lead of Flaubert, with the mind as an 'active reflector' of life, with the representation of consciousness, and with symbolism, caused his work to appear to move from the realism of his early novels to an enormously influential if commercially unsuccessful nascent modernism by the turn of the century. Born in New York, his father was a well-known theologian and lecturer and his brother an eminent philosopher and psychologist who coined the term 'stream of consciousness'. Henry James's novels have been said to fall into three phases: those dealing with the interrelation between American and European civilisation, followed by those in the 1890s concerned with English life, and the final modernist works which revert to transatlantic subjects and attitudes. He is also important for his essays, short stories and critical introductions to his own novels.

**Major works:** *What Maisie Knew* (1897), *The Wings of a Dove* (1902), *The Ambassadors* (1903), *The Golden Bowl* (1904).

## Ford Madox Ford (1873–1939)

Ford, an eccentric Catholic born in Kent and brought up in the pre-Raphaelite movement, was a prolific writer who published over seventy books in his lifetime, including fiction, poetry, essays and criticism. A Francophile of German heritage, Ford represents the internationalist aspect of modernism, and he lived much of his later life in America. He influenced almost every major British experimental writer of the early twentieth century and set about updating the English novel, in line with the French, to take account of formal considerations. He collaborated with Joseph Conrad on two novels, played a part in the formation of the imagist movement, edited the *English Review*, founded the *Transatlantic Review* and wrote what many critics consider to be the finest fiction on the First World War in his *Parade's End* tetralogy.

**Major works:** *The Good Soldier* (1915), *Parade's End* (or the *Tietjens Quartet*): *Some Do Not ...* (1924), *No More Parades* (1925), *A Man Could Stand Up* (1926) and *Last Post* (1928).

Appreciative of the influence of the writers discussed in Chapter 1, and especially the work of Freud and Nietzsche, several critics have argued that the modernist novel is characterised by its obsession with epistemology, by a search for knowledge. For example, in Conrad's *Heart of Darkness*, discussed below, Marlow is constantly trying to find the key to understanding Kurtz, and, more generally, to comprehend the 'darkness' he believes to be inside all human beings. In relating his narrative, Marlow foregrounds the fact that he doesn't understand his own story. Again, in Ford's *The Good Soldier*, considered below, the narrator John Dowell attempts, unsuccessfully, to understand reality, to fit a rational pattern of explanation onto the world. But he soon finds that modern existence won't fit any system, and he slips into repeatedly telling the reader, 'I don't know' or 'you sort it out'. Ford, here, expresses a shift from nineteenth-century certainty to modernist disorientation through Dowell's inept narration and constant doubt. Dowell tries to tell the story with the competency and omniscience of a third-person realist narrator, but he is forced to admit his limitations, his incomplete knowledge and understanding. There is, consequently, no authority in the novel, mimicking the absence of certainty in the larger world. Dowell makes mistakes about dates and names, changes his mind, contradicts himself, forgets things and gets events in the wrong order. He tries to find some basic certainty, some Cartesian *cogito* that he can be sure of and build the truth from but keeps coming back to the opinion that he knows nothing for certain. Dowell remains trapped in his subjectivity and cannot even rest any faith in himself, deciding, with Freud, that he doesn't even understand his own mind. Dowell attempts to resolve his epistemological problems and self-doubt through identification. He repeatedly says that he is like Edward Ashburnham, when he is patently dissimilar to him in every way. To fantasise that he is akin to his friend allows Dowell to picture for himself the personal certainty of a romantic hero of the British Empire and the social certainty of a respectable landlord and 'good soldier'. But this is then shattered by the very narrative that Dowell relates.

A search for knowledge arguably sits at the core of modernism's concerns alongside the struggle to convey through the strained medium of language the heterogeneity of modern life. As Eliot's Prufrock puts it: 'It is impossible to say just what I mean!' The authors I will be looking at in this section, Conrad, James and Ford, were all innovators in their representation of character and in their construction of dense narratives notable for shifting spatial arrangements, temporal complexity and radical ambiguity.

The example I want to use of Conrad's concern with narration and epistemology is arguably his first extended modernist work and also his most studied, *Heart of Darkness*. In this text, Conrad uses the conventions of oral storytelling, and so the novella begins with a group sitting in semi-darkness listening to each other take turns to tell stories to pass the time as they wait for the tide to turn on the Thames. Like James in *The Turn of the Screw,* discussed below, Conrad does this to mimic the archetypal scene of a story told around the village fire at night as well as to reflect the practice of sailors' yarns, linking his concern with Africa and the (male) microcosm of society constituted by a ship's crew. On board the boat at the beginning, the *Nellie,* Conrad uses an all-male cast of businessmen known only as the accountant, the lawyer and the Director to emphasise something about colonialism. The story was written in the 1890s, when colonialism in Africa was no longer the prerogative of entrepreneurial explorers and missionaries like David Livingstone but had become a business, a commercial concern. The decisive change here was the Berlin Conference of 1885. At this, the European powers carved up the continent to try to prevent further colonial wars between them. No Africans were present. The fate of the Congo, where most of Conrad's story is set, was to be formally recognised as the personal property of the King of Belgium, Leopold II. For Conrad, the Belgian Congo was the worst example he had seen of colonial exploitation, the political theme of *Heart of Darkness*. He wrote to the editors at Blackwood's magazine, where the story was serialised, that he thought 'The criminality of inefficiency and pure selfishness when tackling the civilising work in Africa is a justifiable idea' (quoted in Trodd 1991: 20). Thus, on the one hand, *Heart of Darkness* is clearly a piece of imperial adventure fiction. But, on the other hand, it was first offered to Blackwood's as a documentary, an account of Conrad's own experiences on the Congo a decade earlier in 1890.

The outline of the story as told by Marlow traces his appeal to his aunt to secure him a position, his trip to Brussels and his journey along the Congo on a small steamboat, all taken from Conrad's own travels in Africa.

*Heart of Darkness* is often seen as a text that stresses the notion that 'civilisation' only provides the modern urban individual with a veneer of eloquence, restraint and sophistication to cover the true 'primitive' nature at the heart of every person. Marlow credits 'civilisation' with the apparatus of the police force and the abattoir to prevent individuals reverting to a less enlightened state, just like the crews of the *Erebus* and the *Terror* (Conrad 1973: 7) who turned to cannibalism when their ships became stranded near the pole. His conclusion is that the colonialists are 'going at it blind' (Conrad 1973: 10), that they are themselves tainted by 'darkness' and that the 'light' from the 'sacred flame' of European learning is bright enough to blind its possessor. This is despite the colonialists' 'idea at the back of it' (Conrad 1973: 10), that light *is* civilisation *is* Western progress *is* good. A moral superiority, as of travelling back through time to observe his ancestors' shortcomings, attends Marlow's journey, and his first thought is that his most distant kin are of the same blood as he, and, therefore, he will find himself behaving like a 'savage' if he succumbs to the influence of 'primitive' Africa. All that the colonialists can produce to shield them from this atavism or reversion is their 'civilisation', which Marlow and the man he travels to meet, Kurtz, take with them in the form of culture and oratory to envelop the darkness, proclaiming the coming of 'civilisation' to Africa like John the Baptist's voice in the wilderness announcing the advent of Christ. However, the novella is itself a disrobing of Kurtz's 'magnificent eloquence' (Conrad 1973: 83) which leaves him naked in the African 'darkness', bereft of a rhetoric which has nothing underneath, a 'hollow' man. Marlow's own downfall following his involvement in the colonial project is to tell a lie, the thing he hates most in the world, to Kurtz's 'Intended'.

In this, the book is concerned with the ability of language to deceive, to persuade and dissemble, to obscure knowledge. For example, the associations which become attached to the words 'dark' and 'light' in *Heart of Darkness* leave the terms themselves empty and hollow, signifiers which have slipped from signified to signified so often that they can no longer serve as images or metaphors for anything but each other. And this is the end of the novel's epistemological journey, yet it has arrived here only from an assumption of superiority, of enlightened European self-knowledge over 'dark' African otherness. Once Marlow returns to Brussels at the end of the story, he begins to readjust. He still knows the animality that is in his own 'heart', but he also believes that only extreme situations and 'primitive' places like Africa will release the recidivistic darkness which European civilisation has hidden behind institutionalised restraints. Back in London, recounting his story, the actual experience of his journey along the Congo now strikes him as unreal, and it has faded into the background like the memory of a nightmare, such that, Marlow concludes, 'It seems to me I am trying to tell you a dream' (Conrad 1973: 57).

Conventional wisdom in the 1890s deemed Africa a darkness awaiting 'civilisation', which to Marlow amounts to 'external checks' (Conrad 1973: 31) on the traits that lie buried in the European: barbarity, idol-worship and rejection of the work ethic. In his own terms, Marlow is anti-colonialist, and, though the African voice is so muted that it can constitute no positive force, he thinks he is aware of a restraint in the actions of the Africans which focuses the book's major criticism of *fin-de-siècle* European civilisation. Conrad, in this way, appears to make a virtue out of his omission of the Africans' language and society. However, it is because African society is alien to Eurocentric apprehensions of civilisation that Conrad is able to depict Kurtz and Marlow as 'wanderers on a prehistoric earth'. Conrad's thesis is that, in removing the need for 'savagery', by providing the policeman and the butcher, Europe has obviated the need for self-restraint also. Hence, Marlow's indictment of the 'civilised' African helmsman: 'He had no restraint, no restraint – just like Kurtz' (Conrad 1973: 73).

This is the price of Western civilisation in *Heart of Darkness*, a loss of self-restraint. It is pointed up by the distinction between the crews of the *Erebus* and *Terror* and a cannibal who, to Marlow's amazement, has had almost no food for days and yet resists the temptations of human flesh on the Congo steamer (Conrad 1973: 58). Despite this, Marlow's assumption that Africans are inferior to Europeans in terms of evolution is maintained: the Africans 'still belonged to the beginnings of time − had no inherited experience to teach them as it were' (Conrad 1973: 58). Marlow can feel a 'distant kinship' with some of the Africans and knows the connection is only buried by history because, despite its progress at the end of the nineteenth century, London 'used to be' one of the dark places of the world before the Romans brought their painful light of progress to Britain. The most useful image here is Kurtz's painting at the Central Station of a blindfolded woman carrying a lighted torch (Conrad 1973: 36). Through its fusion of Liberty and Justice, it implies that for the European in Africa's 'darkness' Liberty is blind to her own light and Justice is deprived of her scales of judgement. Africa, there-fore, becomes the 'other' which keeps Europe thankful for the thick veneer of its juridical, humanitarian and egalitarian mechanisms. In brief, European knowledge and language, epito-mised and championed by the social and cultural progress of the Enlightenment, have become weapons alongside military strength for the Western individual to wield superiority over the colonies and assert a significant difference between humans across the continents, when, for Conrad, their chief importance is to blind the colonialists both to their own basic drives and to the primitive desires shared by all people.

In 1982, the African novelist and critic Chinua Achebe alter-natively summarised Conrad's message thus: 'If Europe, advan-cing in civilisation, could cast a backward glance periodically at Africa trapped in primordial barbarity it could say with faith and feeling: There go I but for the grace of God' (see Achebe 1988). The central point that Achebe makes is not that Conrad was more of a racist than other Europeans at the turn of the century, but that in *Heart of Darkness* there is an implicit assumption throughout that Europeans and their culture are of more impor-tance and interest than Africans and theirs. The British critic Cedric Watts has written a reply to this argument, but he is unable to deny Achebe's fundamental contention (1983). Watts's argument is that writers such as Conrad were subject to the beliefs and theories of their day, including racism and anti-Semitism in particular, but that their best work 'seems to transcend such prejudices'. Whether this is to be accepted or not, it appears both that the prejudices are there and that Conrad was more concerned with revealing European barbarism and its coverings than African civilisation.

Above all, in *Heart of Darkness*, as Marlow constructs and reconstructs 'reality' through his narration, Conrad exemplifies the modernist suspicion that knowledge is a function of culture and language, and in this he anticipates, as Watts argues elsewhere, Wittgenstein's conviction that 'our language determines our view of reality, because we see things through it' (1982: 125). While Marlow recounts his story, the listeners on the *Nellie* are slowly engulfed in darkness, making Marlow as difficult for them to perceive as his story, mimicking the reader's difficulty unravelling the meanings of such an enigmatic text.

The question of the relationship between language, narration, perception and knowledge is also at the 'mysterious heart' of a novella of similar length published in the year before Conrad's and which is similarly preoccupied with ambiguity, mystery and obscurity. Henry James's *The Turn of the Screw* (1898) is, like many modernist stories, including *Heart of Darkness* and Forster's *A Passage to India*, a text which has an enigma at its centre. In what on the surface appears to be a simple ghost story about a governess appointed to take sole care of two children at a remote country house, specific questions such as what happens to the children, Miles and Flora, or whether the governess sees anything supernatural can only be decided upon by readers who are determined to resolve for themselves. James's text itself is inconclusive and relies heavily on ambiguity and openness to underscore the complexity and uncertainty of representation, perception, knowledge and even sanity. In the story, there are questions over the difference between what is seen and what is known, running parallel with the reader's experience of an unclear and untrustworthy narration. Both the narrative of the novella and the reader's understanding of it are concerned with the question of the 'right' interpretation of what is happening. The reader has only the narrator's word to rely upon, just as the governess in the story has only her fallible senses to guide her. In even most unreliable narrations, this is less problematic than it is in James's novella because *The Turn of the Screw* is a story that raises issues of the Freudian 'uncanny'. Such works of art provoke feelings of unease, dread or horror as well as the relative probabilities of ghosts, wishful thinking, hallucinations and delusions. Language is all the reader has to go on, but, as the story progresses, it seems to become a less and less secure entity, just as in *Heart of Darkness* the reader also comes to distrust the meaning of the most simple words. This is well illustrated by the fact that the reader looks for a sign that the governess's visions are shared by other characters, but no confirmation is ever given.

*The Turn of the Screw* was published just after the inception of psychoanalysis as well as at the beginnings of what we now call modernism. Freud's key theoretical concerns at this time were with issues also brought up by James's novella: hysteria, fantasy, children's sexuality, repression and projected desires. The publication of Freud's and Breuer's *Studies in Hysteria* in 1895 is often seen to mark the beginning of psychoanalysis and the notion of the 'talking cure': therapy based on expressing repressed memories and feelings in words. In this light, the governess's act of writing her manuscript can be considered as an attempt to expel the very psychic trauma the reader perceives in her story.

Layers of destabilising narrative also act as a hindrance to the reader's understanding: an unnamed narrator frames the story (like *Heart of Darkness*, *The Time Machine* and other novellas from this time), which he has heard read by a second narrator, Douglas, who presented the autobiographical manuscript as that of the governess, a third narrator, whose sanity is in question. Here, an oral tale is traced at the opening to a written text, unread for many years, deposited in a locked drawer. The story we actually read is supposed to be a transcript of the governess's faded manuscript owned by Douglas, adding layer upon layer of distance, expressed in terms of time, space and narrative, between the reader and the story's 'origin'. The governess's narrative itself is obscure or enigmatic, impressing its feeling more than its fact upon the reader from the start: 'I remember the whole beginning as a succession of flights and drops, a little see-saw of the right throbs and the wrong' (James 1969: 14). Such lines hint at the questions of ambiguity and epistemology which preoccupied modernist writers who retreated from the comparatively easy use of 'facts' and 'knowledge' which had characterised their predecessors.

So, James's novella is preoccupied with interpretation, meaning and the act of 'comprehending', with parallels between seeing and reading. Much of the dialogue, like that in Mansfield's stories, is full of gaps, unfinished sentences and ambiguous words. As a ghost or horror story, *The Turn of the Screw* appears concerned with whether or not there is such a thing as the supernatural, but, unlike in most ghost stories, that question is embedded in the text's incidents, narration, structure and language. The issue of the story's meaning is finally undecidable because its precise events are indeterminable, its narrative multi-layered and its language, inevitably, problematical (see Felman 1982 for a detailed discussion).

A useful concept when considering modernist fiction such as *Heart of Darkness* or *The Turn of the Screw* was expounded in an essay by Joseph Frank on 'spatial reading' (1963). Frank coined this term from an idea of the critic Wylie Sypher's that modern art is pervaded by a philosophical formalism that amounts to a 'style' which requires the reader to be more 'active' and also highly self-conscious. This is mainly because of the complex construction of modernist texts, which militates against drawing conclusions from any part of the book before its end is reached. A parallel example is with land surveying, which is impossible from low ground and needs to take place from an elevated position from which all of the land can be seen at one time. The idea of spatial reading largely derives from cubism, which argues that a three-dimensional object, or an event, needs to be analysed from multiple angles and not just one. So, to take a different example in Ford Madox Ford's *The Good Soldier*, the narrator John Dowell returns again and again to relate the same events from different angles. Modernist approaches also mean that the reader often cannot fully understand events when first encountering them. For instance, there are many references to 'the girl' early on in *The Good Soldier*, but it is only much later that the reader finds out that this is a character called Nancy Rufford. Ford also employs this technique because Dowell is trying to record how events struck him at particular times, when he was often only in partial possession of the 'facts'. Through this technique, Ford suggests the often-made point in the novel that we can never fully know other people. All we see is their external show. In the text, Dowell says of his relation to the 'good soldier' of the title that 'it is very difficult to give an all-round impression of any man. I wonder how far I have succeeded with Edward Ashburnham' (Ford 1972: 140). His attempt, however clouded by Dowell's unconventional narration, is to lay out all the sides to Ashburnham so that when readers finish the text they can see his whole character. Spatial reading additionally addresses the problem of linearity in fiction: Dowell knows that events are really too multi-dimensional to be told in one straight line, moving from clue to clue like a simple detective story, even though writing automatically gives temporal precedence to whatever is narrated first in a number of synchronous events. Dowell says at one point: 'it is so difficult to keep all these people going. I tell you about Leonora and bring her up to date; then about Edward, who has fallen behind. And then the girl gets hopelessly left behind' (Ford 1972: 200). When the story is narrated in such a cubist or many-sided way, where every statement is provisional and partial, the reader is required to adopt a spatial reading of the text in order to survey any part of it adequately.

*The Good Soldier*, whose preferred title for Ford was 'the saddest story', is told by John Dowell, a rich Philadelphian Quaker (Ford 1972: 40), who has no occupation. He recounts the events of his life in an effort to understand what has happened to him and to those around him. The people he is principally interested in are his dead wife, Florence, and his close friends Edward and Leonora Ashburnham. The four of them seem to be happy, monied, leisured couples. They have every opportunity in life, and they see their principal task in society to be setting a good standard. The novel explores the surface conventions and the private passions and hypocrisies of these putative models of social behaviour. The most significant event of the first half of the novel is the affair between Florence and Edward. The major consideration of the second half is the relationship between Edward and a young woman, the 'girl' Nancy Rufford. *The Good Soldier* is subtitled 'A

Tale of Passion' and it could be described as a narrative based around the infidelities of its discredited hero, Ashburnham. It is narrated over two years in all; Dowell writes initially for half a year, then there is an eighteen-month gap before he continues.

It is clear that the various fractures of *The Good Soldier* mirror the uncertainty of the pre-war period. The novel is littered with new or rare terms like 'breakdown', 'unconscious', 'hysteric' and 'pathological'. Dowell reveals himself to be unable to reconcile his conscious beliefs and conventional wisdom with his own unconscious desires and fears. The society he discusses is similarly split between a surface rationality and propriety and a deeper aggression and passion. Nothing on the surface is true; it is the unconscious of Edwardian society that drives and motivates the characters. In this way, the book describes a struggle between superego and id, convention and passion, or public and private worlds. The public world is dominated by the upper-class land-owning elite which tries to perpetuate its standards and manners, while the novel's private world operates along entirely different lines; for example, Edward and Leonora Ashburnham do not even speak to each other in private. The characters have idle lives, with little employment, no family and only an outmoded social or economic role alongside the rising commercial classes. Dowell, the narrator, having nothing better to do, even counts his own footsteps (Ford 1972: 27). Above all, despite their private affairs, it is seemingly the public façade that matters with these characters: Dowell says they have a dread of scenes, scandals, publicity or open confrontations (Ford 1972: 61).

Thematically, the novel is concerned with weak hearts and heart conditions to express the characters' irresponsibility and their imminent demise as a class. It is, therefore, a book about 'heart failure' in its medical and metaphorical senses. The narrative appears to be written as Dowell's enquiry into 'what went wrong' for these sophisticated, privileged and wealthy people. This is on a personal level, but Ford's themes of naivety, deception, credulity and callousness are easy to generalise over the western hemisphere at this time. The staged, artificial quality of the characters' lives seems appropriate to the pointless waste of the coming war, a perspective signalled by the constant repetition in the novel of 4 August, the date the war will begin.

The only character fully taken in by the veneer of this polished world of manners, Dowell is a narrator from the 'New World' of America, but he is the novel's prime exponent of an old *European* social mythology. He embodies the ideals of Victorian morality when he says, 'I will vouch for the cleanliness of my thoughts and the absolute chastity of my life' (Ford 1972: 18). Dowell admires 'manly' virtue, is condescending and dismissive of his black servant and gently patronising to all women. Consequently, he also believes his wife Florence to be the ideal Victorian woman, delicate, virtuous and in need of protection from all excitement because of the strain it would put on her weak heart. However, after many years' experience of European fine society, Dowell's conclusion is brief. He says: 'I think that it would have been better in the eyes of God if they had all attempted to gouge out each other's eyes with carving knives. But they were "good people"' (Ford 1972: 223). 'Good' is a word in the novel which is stripped of its usual worth and linked with a feudal morality and an anachronistic code of honour associated with the aristocracy before the war.

In *The Good Soldier*'s cast of representative characters, the consequences of European hypocrisy expressed in the brutality and madness of the war are embodied in Nancy, the Ashburnhams' ward. At the end of the novel, she retreats into herself, as though shell shocked. Dowell remarks on how her outward calm and normality mask her inner vacancy and seeming insanity. This appears as a comment on the behaviour of the other characters. Their destructive effect on Nancy is a judgement on the irresponsibility of their lives. *Her* effect on them is to bring about Edward Ashburnham's suicide, Leonora Ashburnham's breakdown and moral capitulation, Florence Dowell's suicide and John Dowell's miserable loneliness.

The shambles of the world is exposed by the mess that the characters make of their lives. For example, there is this typical paragraph from Dowell near the end of the book:

> not one of us has got what he really wanted. Leonora wanted Edward and has got Rodney Bayham, pleasant enough sort of sheep. Florence wanted [the house at] Branshaw, and it is I who have bought it

from Leonora. I didn't really want it; what I wanted mostly was to cease being a nurse-attendant. Well, I am a nurse-attendant. Edward wanted Nancy Rufford, and I have got her. Only she is mad.

(Ford 1972: 213)

The comic absurdity of this state of affairs is the result of the debasing of old values and the frustration or perversion of emergent, new ones. The main characters, by the end, have nothing left to believe in, and only Nancy, in her madness, retains faith by declaring over and over that she believes in an omnipotent deity. Unable to cope with history and society, she unquestioningly places her trust in the certainties of religion.

The novel uses a peculiar time scheme, moving between past and present. In terms of space, it also moves from location to location, from Nauheim, to the cruise ship, to the country house and so on. There are few points of stability, and the narrative jumps around to suggest Dowell's confusion and also to reflect the characters' nomadic lifestyle. The two couples, the Ashburnhams and the Dowells, are consequently represented as adrift, or homeless. Dowell says at one point, 'we are almost always in one place with our minds somewhere quite other'. Modernism is noted for shifting emphases from the external world to the internal, and *The Good Soldier*, like *Heart of Darkness* and *The Turn of the Screw*, has much more to do with how the world is perceived by an individual mind than with how the individual functions within society. In a way quite different from the first-person narration in a nineteenth-century novel, say *Jane Eyre* or *Great Expectations*, Dowell's perceptions do not simply mediate the story; to a large extent they *are* the story.

Dowell's narration proceeds in a piecemeal fashion, and there is little attempt to tell events chronologically, or in accordance with any other principle of order. The story is primarily told through memories and is arranged by association not causality. This reflects Dowell's inability to comprehend what has happened around him. His style is solipsistic and introverted, so the story is disjointed, with few scenes lasting more than one page. Dialogue is minimal, and Dowell rarely quotes more than two sentences, largely because, in his confusion, he cannot remember accurately what was said. There is also no attempt to create traditional narrative suspense and tension: early on, Dowell exposes events that are going to happen later in the story, like Florence's death, as though these were trivial details. Ultimately, everything he says draws attention to the fact that Dowell is reconstructing a painful story and is having a great amount of difficulty in doing so. Accordingly, the narrative does not end with a formal 'closure'. The conclusion of the novel does not coincide with the end of the story. In other words, Ford rejects suspense and historical development for the relativity of subjective impressionism, concentrating on the observer, not the event, which in this case is a dislocated individual's fragmented memories of an alienating world he does not understand. As he starts his narrative of 'the saddest story' he has ever *heard*, he confesses to the reader his own personal epistemological crisis: 'I know nothing – nothing in the world – of the hearts of men. I only know that I am alone – horribly alone' (Ford 1972: 14). A last point to note, which adds some credence to this declaration by Dowell that he knows nothing, is that the version of events related in his narrative is not actually his. Most of it is told to him by Leonora, some by Edward. Consequently, in many ways the story is based on Leonora's understanding and perception, even though it is told from Dowell's perspective, and, in this way, foregrounding once more the difficulties of interpretation and knowledge, Dowell's search for the truth, like Marlow's and the governess's, in many respects stands as a metaphor for the reader's encounter with the novel, as both struggle for the truth of 'what happened'.

## 'THESE FRAGMENTS I HAVE SHORED AGAINST MY RUINS': IDENTITY AND WAR

### Virginia Woolf (1882–1941)

Woolf was born in London into a famous family and was educated at home. Her father was the critic and scholar Leslie Stephen and her sister was the painter Vanessa Bell. In 1904, after her father's death, her family moved to Bloomsbury and was the centre of the influential 'Bloomsbury Group' of philosophers, writers and artists. She married Leonard Woolf in 1912, and, together they formed the Hogarth Press in 1917. She began publishing novels in 1915, but her modernist style only fully began with *Jacob's Room* in 1922. Alongside Joyce, she is often regarded as the exemplary British modernist novelist because of her use of interior monologue, recurrent motifs, fragmented time and intense lyricism. Woolf, who had suffered serious bouts of depression for much of her life and who had attempted suicide in 1913, died by drowning herself in the River Ouse near her home in Sussex.

**Major works:** *Mrs Dalloway* (1925), *To the Lighthouse* (1927), *A Room of One's Own* (1929), *The Waves* (1931).

## Rebecca West (1892–1983)

West was born in London and passed much of her early life in Edinburgh (her mother's city) but had two older sisters who had been born in Australia. West was a socialist, anti-imperialist and feminist. She turned from acting to journalism and wrote for the *Freewoman*, *The Clarion* and *The New Statesman* amongst other journals and newspapers. In 1912, when she began writing for the *Freewoman*, she changed her name from Cicily Fairfield to Rebecca West, the name of the heroine in Ibsen's *Rosmersholm*. Her writing career spans many decades and styles, but her novels from the Great War into the 1920s can be considered in terms of modernism: *The Return of the Soldier*, *The Judge* (1922) and *Harriet Hume* (1929). For our purposes, perhaps the most significant personal event of West's early adult life was her affair with H. G. Wells, by whom she had a son in 1914. Wells was married at the time and had met West through her bitter attack on the institution as represented in his novel entitled *Marriage*. Wells became a great influence on her writing, and *The Return of the Soldier* contains a number of private references. Lastly, it is worth noting that Woolf uses West in *A Room of One's Own* as her example of the kind of feminist writer who drew hostility from contemporary patriarchs simply because she wrote about the equality of the sexes (Woolf 1973: 35).

**Major works:** *The Return of the Soldier* (1918), *Black Lamb and Grey Falcon: A Journey through Yugoslavia:* (1941), *The Birds Fall Down* (1966).

## T. S. Eliot (1888–1965)

Eliot was born in St Louis, Missouri, but lived most of his life in England and became a naturalised British subject in 1927. He was first and foremost a poet, who wrote several of the most famous and studied poems of the twentieth century, from 'The Love Song of J. Alfred Prufrock' (1915), through *The Waste Land* (1922) to *Four Quartets* (1944). In his later life, he turned to drama, beginning with *Murder in the Cathedral* (1935). He was also a respected editor: he worked on *The Egoist* from 1915 to 1917 and established one of the most celebrated literary journals of the century, *The Criterion*, in 1922. He later became poetry editor at Faber and Faber. His literary studies, from *The Sacred Wood* (1920) on, and his more general works on society and civilisation, such as *Notes towards a Definition of Culture* (1948), have contributed to making him one of the twentieth century's most influential figures in criticism as well as literature.

**Major works:** *Prufrock and Other Observations* (1917), *The Waste Land* (1922), *Four Quartets* (1935–42).

In the Introduction, I mentioned Matthew Arnold's 1857 delineation of the 'The Modern Element in Literature' as repose, confidence, tolerance, free activity of the mind, reason and universals. Half a century later, modernism developed a series of art practices that stressed the opposite: alienation, plight, chaos, unreason, depression and disenchantment with culture. Such disruption was epitomised by the war and the literary responses to it. Psychological and social disruption was encoded in modernist texts in a variety of ways, from the impressionistic devices of Ford's multi-layered *The Good Soldier* through to the plea for regeneration in Eliot's *The Waste Land*. The breakdown of the war was reflected in an aesthetic of fragmentation in art, but also in distressing criticisms of society, from analyses of shell shock, cowardice and psychiatry, to discussions of cultural crises and social upheaval.

Shell shock posed the greatest questions to British psychiatry in the 1920s. The expression was first used by C. S. Myers in 1915, and the term's popularity with doctors may well have had something to do with its contrast to the identical word 'hysteria', usually then reserved for women. According to a book on social history published in the Second World War, shell shock was

> a condition of alternate moods of apathy and high excitement, with very quick reaction to sudden emergencies but no capacity for concentrated thinking. ... Its effects passed off very gradually. In most cases the blood was not running pure again for four or five years; and in numerous cases men who had managed to avoid a nervous breakdown during the war collapsed badly in 1921 or 1922.
>
> (Quoted in Dowling 1991: 87)

Over the course of the war, medical officers treated 80,000 shell-shocked soldiers, and in the 1920s there were 114,000 pension applications related to war trauma. By 1932, psychiatric casualties accounted for 36 per cent of veterans receiving disability pensions (Dowling 1991: 89). The early responses of military doctors were extreme; for example, it was suggested that in wartime if no actual physical injury could be detected, then the soldier should be shot. Shell shock was, for many physicians, synonymous with cowardice or disobeying orders. However, doctors gradually started to utilise Freud's ideas of neurosis and the unconscious, and it was partly because of shell shock that Freudian analysis gained acceptability in England. In *Mrs Dalloway*, the disturbance to the conscious mind of shell shock is linked with sexuality as Septimus Smith represses his desire for his officer Evans and cannot contemplate sex with his wife, while she dreams of children. It is ironic that Septimus, who is supposedly a coward who fears death, takes his own life. We are told that 'he did not want to die', but it is his only way of defeating the world represented by William Bradshaw, his respected but authoritarian psychiatrist. Septimus also feels as though the world has been clamouring at him to 'kill yourself for our sakes', which is both the situation of war and the way in which Woolf turns Septimus into a martyr. This world, which demands his death, is the masculine culture surrounding him in war memories, doctors and politicians.

In this light, we can begin to consider Woolf's notion of 'androgyny' important in several of her novels. Woolf most fully discusses this, from Samuel Taylor Coleridge's idea of the great mind as androgynous, in her book *A Room of One's Own*. In these lectures, first given at Cambridge in 1928, Woolf wonders

> whether there are two sexes in the mind corresponding to the two sexes in the body and whether they also require to be united in order to get complete satisfaction and happiness ... in each of us two powers reside, one male and one female. ... It is fatal to be a man or woman pure and simple; one must be woman-manly or man-womanly.
>
> (Woolf 1973: 93)

Woolf's androgyny has been further defined by the critic Elaine Showalter as 'full balance and command of an emotional range that includes male and female elements' (1985: 263). While many more recent theorists have opposed themselves to all constructions of masculinity and femininity, of male or female behaviour, Woolf's strategy appears to be to fuse them, to argue for a hybrid identity that is both male and female, like the central character of the novel she published in 1928, *Orlando*.

To see how this view of human identity operates in her novels, it is necessary to know something of Woolf's unique method of constructing character. In her diaries, during the writing of *Mrs Dalloway,* Woolf called this technique 'tunnelling'. By this, she meant she would burrow into the characters' past in order to unearth their history. Her characters are then revealed to the reader as split beings who are living in the past and present. It is their current thoughts that tell us who they are, but only their memories of the past that explain them, that reveal how they came to be who they are.

To explore the notion of androgyny through the method of tunnelling, Woolf in *Mrs Dalloway* proposes a number of sexual possibilities for Clarissa Dalloway, but they are situated in the past. The narrative returns repeatedly to her youth at Bourton and to Clarissa's choice of either Sally Seton, Peter Walsh or

Richard Dalloway. These represent the possibilities for Clarissa of love with another woman, with a man who is not 'manly' (which is what we are told of Peter Walsh [Woolf 1976: 138]) and a man who epitomises masculinity in the society Woolf is discussing (Richard Dalloway is a Tory MP and sportsman).

But Clarissa is only one of the two main figures of the novel. The other is the shell-shocked soldier Septimus Smith. For several critics, Septimus's admiration for his officer Evans should be seen as an erotic homosexual love and the unresolved sexual attachment that is the cause of Septimus's apparent impotence with his wife Lucrezia. In Clarissa's love for Sally and Septimus's hero-worshipping of Evans, we are arguably seeing different aspects of their androgynous personalities: rather than reject the labels themselves, Woolf asserts that Clarissa has a 'manly' side and Septimus a 'womanly' side. This becomes more important when discussing society's positioning of Septimus as a 'coward', as a soldier lacking 'manly' courage, because of his experience of neurasthenia. If we take this as a depiction of 'madness' or hysteria, then, again, this is something that society has associated with women. Indeed, in the 1920s, both women and mad*men* would have been thought of as in some sense 'controlled' by the moon and as emotionally unbalanced. The War Office Committee that investigated shell shock in 1922 was reluctant to admit the term at all because it suggested that war was responsible for the soldiers' breakdown rather than a weakness in the men themselves; but 'shell shock' was preferred to 'hysteria' because of that term's suggestion of effeminacy. The recommended treatment for shell shock in 1922 was coercion and more violence, a kind of bullying therapy to cure what was assumed to be a lack of courage. What is most at stake here is the notion of 'self', which Woolf sees as many-sided and fragmentary but which the Harley Street doctors in the novel, Holmes and Bradshaw, and the War Office Committee see as essentially whole and unified. So Woolf gives us the epitome of social masculinity, a soldier, and concentrates on that side of him that Western culture perceives as both aberrant and feminine. Consequently, in the novel, Septimus himself believes, by contrast, that men and their institutions should become more feminine, holistic and nurturing.

Also, by linking Clarissa and Septimus together, emotionally and symbolically but never physically, Woolf presents to the reader an androgynous composite figure. She both compromises definitions of madness and cowardice and uses the gender that society applies to such concepts to undermine sexual identity.

If we return to the options in Clarissa's past (Sally, Richard or Peter), these three signify possibilities of sexual expression. Sally brings out what Woolf calls Clarissa's 'masculine' side; Richard Dalloway brings out her 'feminine' side; and Peter represents a different possibility because he is androgynous. To support this, David Dowling quotes one of the descriptions of Peter Walsh: 'he was not altogether manly. ... He was ... the perfect gentleman ... He could not keep out of smoking-rooms, liked colonels, liked golf, liked bridge, and above all women's society' (Dowling 1991: 122, quoting Woolf 1976: 140–1).

In terms of modernist experimentation, the sexual duality in the mind that Woolf terms 'androgyny' can be seen as actually just one part of her wider assault on the coherence and stability of unitary consciousness. She writes in *A Room of One's Own*:

> what does one mean by 'the unity of the mind'? I pondered, for clearly the mind has so great a power of concentrating at any point at any moment that it seems to have no single state of being. It can separate itself from the people in the street, for example, and think of itself as apart from them. ... if one is a woman one is often surprised by a sudden splitting off of consciousness, say in walking down Whitehall, when from being the natural inheritor of that civilisation, she becomes, on the contrary, outside it, alien, critical. Clearly the mind is always altering its focus, and bringing the world into different perspectives.
>
> (Woolf 1973: 92–3)

Consequently, Clarissa can be both perfectly conventional in her role as drawing-room hostess and, at the same time, a misfit in the order, proportion and classification of imperial patriarchy. The rationalist, masculinist hegemony in the novel is epitomised by the psychiatrists, Holmes and Bradshaw, who are seen to attempt to colonise Septimus's mind, to cure him of the 'cowardice' that

Woolf considers a love of life and an expression of his androgyny. With respect to Clarissa, *she* agonises over the fact that she is still divided in her mind over a choice apparently completed a generation before. The importance of her decision to follow social custom, abandon Peter and Sally and marry Richard, is revealed in the celebratory way she responds to the death of Septimus. Both Clarissa and Septimus have submerged their sexuality in the social convention of marriage and neither has sex with their spouse. As a consequence, through an inability to express androgyny, both have effectively chosen celibacy.

Woolf's writing has also been seen in terms of an attempt to blend style and gender, to subvert social norms through the less oppositional strategy of reinventing form rather than content, which is symptomatic of the general modernist strategy to change society through the reconstruction of self not system, individual rather than social reality.

Toril Moi writes in *Sexual/Textual Politics*:

> Kristeva has argued that the modernist poetry of Lautreamont and Mallarmé and others constitutes a 'revolutionary' form of writing. The modernist poem, with its abrupt shifts, ellipses, breaks and apparent lack of logical construction is a kind of writing in which the rhythms of the body and the unconscious have managed to break through the strict rational defences of conventional social meaning. Since Kristeva sees such conventional meaning as the structure that sustains the whole of the symbolic order – that is, all human social and cultural institutions – the fragmentation of symbolic language in modernist poetry comes for her to parallel and prefigure a total *social* revolution. For Kristeva, that is to say, there is a *specific practice of writing* that is itself 'revolutionary', analogous to sexual and political transformation, and that by its very existence testifies to the possibility of transforming the symbolic order of orthodox society *from the inside*. One might argue in this light that Woolf's refusal to commit herself in her essays to a so-called rational or logical form of writing, free from fictional techniques, indicates a similar break with symbolic language, as of course do many of the techniques she deploys in her novels.

(Moi 1985: 11)

So, as with her depiction of sexuality, Woolf's fictional method attempts to 'transform the symbolic order of orthodox society from the inside'. Probably the key way in which she does this is in her transformation of the representation of self and consciousness, which I will now say something about.

Where Joyce has the 'epiphany', an intense experience or an insight, Woolf has what she calls 'moments of being' or simply 'the moment', a word that is used some seventy times in *Mrs Dalloway*. 'Epiphany' and 'moment' have often been equated, but Woolf's term describes far more of a physical feeling than Joyce's spiritual insight, as demonstrated here in *Mrs Dalloway* when Clarissa thinks she sometimes feels for women as men are supposed to:

> it was a sudden revelation, a tinge like a blush which one tried to check and then, as it spread, one yielded to its expansion, and rushed to the farthest verge and there quivered and felt the world come closer, swollen with some astonishing significance, some pressure of rapture, which split its thin skin and gushed and poured with an extraordinary alleviation over the cracks and sores. Then, for that moment, she had seen an illumination; a match burning in a crocus; an inner meaning almost expressed. But the close withdrew; the hard softened. It was over – the moment.

> (Woolf 1976: 30)

This spreading emotional orgasm is expressed in such vivid sensual detail that its suggestive physical imagery, like 'a match burning in a crocus', can link all the minds in the text, uniting them in an androgynous sexuality open to both sexes. 'The moment' is primarily a connecting force – an expression of common, heightened, intense feeling – and this is something Woolf's depiction of thought also aims to include.

Joyce and Woolf are similarly often compared on their use of a stream-of-consciousness style, and yet their methods are different. The term itself originates with William James's observation that the mind proceeds like a river or stream rather than in blocks or units like speech. So, thought is fluid, fast-flowing, associative rather than structured, and, though built from words, it is not wholly grammatical. Joyce is probably the most well-known user of stream of consciousness, notably in Molly Bloom's soliloquy at the end of *Ulysses*, but in her fiction of the 1920s Woolf more often employed 'interior monologue' to render the thoughts of her characters. Her practice differs from Joyce's in at least three key ways. First, she uses many more tags, such as 'he thought' or 'she wondered'. Second, the style of Woolf's interior monologue is similar from character to character; sentences, syntax and vocabulary do not alter as much as they do in Joyce's prose, and this helps to connect characters. Third, Woolf always uses the past tense for interior monologues, to stress the importance of personal history. Overall, Woolf uses numerous metaphors and similes for the way the mind functions, and, in some of her fiction, images of thought are as common as the thoughts themselves. The effect of this is important in a book such as *Mrs Dalloway* because it allows the narrative to skip from character to narrator to character without seeming to make abrupt shifts. In this way, Woolf conveys what she calls 'life'; that is, the narrative can slide between different consciousnesses for purposes of comparison and connection, evoking the idea of many minds operating individually but similarly.

This technique is made more complex by Woolf's use of time. Throughout the novel, she contrasts public with private time. So, she may start to describe a character's thoughts when a clock begins striking the hour, report those thoughts for several pages and then return to the character's awareness of the clock finishing striking. In public time, only a few seconds have passed, but in the character's mind, it may be nearer to several minutes. Woolf's technique here is indebted to the work of Bergson and other psychologists and philosophers who distinguished between temporal duration in the mind and chronological common time in the world, once more asserting the importance of the individual against the social.

In all her mature novels, Woolf handles time in idiosyncratic ways. In *Mrs Dalloway*, it is superficially structured around the divisions of the clock. The novel was originally called 'The Hours', and the intrusions and oppression of public time are used to associate the characters. For example, time intrudes on their consciousnesses through the sounding of Big Ben, which breaks up the novel into hours and sections. In this way, the internal mental time of the characters, the duration that is timed according to the memories and preconscious thoughts that are recalled to the mind's surface reality, is interrupted by a shared time. Yet, time also links characters because the narrative uses the distribution of the clock chimes in the air to form links across space: different places can be connected by a common chronology, which must always be public, external, shared. So, because Clarissa and Septimus both hear the striking of the clock, the narrative can move between them; for example, 'twelve o'clock struck as Clarissa Dalloway laid her green dress on the bed, and the Warren Smiths walked down Harley Street' (Woolf 1976: 84).

This propensity of time to intrude and oppress as well as to connect is construed in gender terms also. Men are seen dividing and women connecting, and this seems to be part of what Woolf means by the 'masculine' and 'feminine' aspects of androgyny. The easiest example of this to take is that of the clocks: 'the sound of Big Ben striking the half-hour struck out between them with extraordinary vigour, as if a young man, strong, indifferent, inconsiderate, were swinging dumbbells this way and that' (Woolf 1976: 44). Similarly male are the clocks on the street of the authoritarian doctors in the book: 'shredding and slicing, dividing and subdividing, the clocks of Harley street nibbled at the June day, counselled submission, upheld authority and pointed out in chorus the supreme advantages of a sense of proportion' (Woolf 1976: 91). However, another clock is in contrast to these, and it connects like a hostess at a party; it is seen in terms of what Woolf perceives as a feminine role or ability to connect:

> Ah, said St Margarets, like a hostess who comes into her drawing-room on the very stroke of the hour and finds her guests there already. I am not late. No, it is precisely half-past eleven, she says. Yet, though she is perfectly right, her voice, being the voice of the hostess, is reluctant to inflict its individuality.
>
> (Woolf 1976: 45)

I ought to add that ascribing a sex to everyday objects is important to Woolf, who wrote in her drafts of *Mrs Dalloway* that 'it is impossible to have anything to do with inanimate objects without giving them [a] sex'.

So, Septimus and Clarissa are linked by their marginal position in patriarchal society: she as a woman, he as a shell-shocked soldier. Woolf shows their similarity in her portrayal of their alienated minds. The thoughts of each are often apparently disjointed, seemingly random but actually associative. The difference between the two characters is that Clarissa retains the ability to draw her fragments together while Septimus cannot. In this, Woolf, who had suffered mental breakdowns on the deaths of each of her parents, gives her definition of 'madness' or trauma. Clarissa considers the facets to her personality in terms of the sides of a diamond, aspects she can compose or bring together in order to communicate with others. Septimus cannot perform this drawing together, and, therefore, when he hears the birds, he thinks they are singing directly to him. He is unable to bring the internal and external aspects of his experience together, to form a whole self. In this distinction between Clarissa and Septimus, Woolf is not arguing for a unified ego but suggesting that the difference between the balanced and the unbalanced is the ability to mould the fragments of self into a whole for the purposes of social interaction. In society, individuals are required to answer for themselves, account for their actions, as rational, responsible stable identities. This is why the social dimension, the party, which is a collection of different identities, is a gathering at the climax of the novel. This bringing together of things is Woolf's metaphor for everyday, shared social life, for reality. This is why Septimus, petrified of the reality of war, is also so scared of drawing life together, as the reader finds on the very first occasion he appears:

> everyone looked at the motor car. Septimus looked. Boys on bicycles sprang off. Traffic accumulated. And there the motor car stood, with drawn blinds, and upon them a curious pattern like a tree, Septimus thought, and this gradual drawing together of everything to one centre before his eyes, as if some horror had come almost to the surface and was about to burst into flames, terrified him.
>
> (Woolf 1976: 15)

Therefore, for Woolf, the self, sexually and mentally, is an integration of facets. The clearest exposition of this in the novel is when Clarissa struggles to assemble herself, and posits or (mis)recognises an illusory wholeness in the mirror before her:

> she pursed her lips when she looked in the glass. It was to give her face point. That was her self – pointed; dart-like; definite. That was her self when some effort, some call on her to be her self, drew the parts together, she alone knew how different, how incompatible and composed so for the world only into one centre, one diamond, one woman who sat in her drawing-room and made a meeting-point . . .
>
> (Woolf 1976: 34–5)

Unlike Septimus, who has seemingly reverted to a stage prior to the Lacanian 'mirror phase', in which he is unable to recognise a coherent identity for himself, Clarissa is able to distinguish what is herself from what is not in the chaos of sense-perceptions and images, and so she enters the alienating London world, which for Woolf is gendered male, by assembling those pieces into a concentrated single image. Much of the rest of the time, she withdraws from this masculine world and exists in her 'attic room', the 'room of her own' that Woolf laid such stress on for a woman. In this attic room, two images of Clarissa are presented, the nun and the child, sexually innocent figures reflecting her lack of desire for Richard or her celibacy. However, these might also be read as images of characters free from the male world, withdrawn into the female worlds of the convent or the nursery.

With respect to the construction of self, Woolf writes in *A Room of One's Own* of women's given roles as 'connectors' or 'reflectors':

> women have served all these centuries as looking-glasses possessing the magic and delicious power of reflecting the figure of man at twice its natural size. Without that power probably the earth would be swamp and jungle. How is he to go on giving judgment . . . unless he can see himself at breakfast and at dinner at least twice the size he really is?
>
> (Woolf 1973: (35–6)

Thus, Clarissa, before the mirror, reconstructs her self as a mirror too, which she will take to the party she is throwing for the doctors, politicians and urban aristocracy, in order to flatter them.

In conclusion, Woolf presents a multi-planar, non-linear view of reality in order to represent the complexity of the modern world, and much of this was to do with the structural dislocation of the First World War. Gertrude Stein once wrote:

> really the composition of the war, 1914–18, was not the composition of all previous wars, the composition was not a composition in which there was one man in the centre surrounded by a lot of other men but a composition that had neither a beginning nor an end, a composition of which one corner was as important as another corner, in fact the composition of cubism.
>
> (Quoted in Bhabha 1990: 266)

The same could be said of much modernist prose writing in which an attempt was made not to describe one narrow individual, a stable ego or Victorian realist character, but as many sides as possible to what Woolf early in *Mrs Dalloway* calls 'life; London; this moment in June' (1976: 6).

In her study of sex and the social construction of madness, *The Female Malady*, Elaine Showalter claims that 'Woolf was the first woman writer to connect the shell-shocked veteran with the repressed woman of the man-governed world through their common enemy, the nerve specialist ... [Septimus's] grief and introspection, emotions consigned to the feminine, belong to Clarissa's world' (1986: 172) However, Rebecca West, nearly ten years before *Mrs Dalloway* in *The Return of the Soldier*, portrayed some of the links between the repressed woman and the feminised shell-shock victim who has to be rescued from his incompleteness by a society with taboos on sexual identity. Many ex-servicemen after the war displayed symptoms which made psychiatric institutions rethink the 'female malady' of hysteria.

An important difference between Woolf's Septimus Smith and West's Chris Ellis in *The Return of the Soldier* is class. Officers like Chris were treated differently from enlisted men like Septimus, a volunteer. Treatment for shell-shocked officers entailed talking-and-writing therapy to bring about catharsis. Enlisted men by contrast were cajoled back into action, routinely accused of cowardice and given electric shock treatment.

As I will discuss below, to complement the introduction of a shell-shocked soldier into their lives, West has the three women in her story assume, in different guises, the role of nurse. In the First World War, nursing, like shell shock, both reinforced stereotypes and challenged them. From a traditional perspective, women were the carers, the mother figures who looked after the men. However, on a larger scale than ever before, men were taking the position of children, establishing a role reversal in which women were active and in control, while men were supine, passive and vulnerable. The nurse's evolution into an active, autonomous, transcendent subject is, therefore, associated with the patient's devolution into dependent, immanent medical object. This is clear in a number of war texts by men such as D. H. Lawrence and the American novelist Ernest Hemingway, where nurses are portrayed with a sinister power. According to Sandra Gilbert, for the nurses, the role reversal brought about a release of female libidinal energies, as well as a liberation of female anger, which men usually found anxiety-inducing and women often found exhilarating (1989: 295). The war, to which so many men had gone in the hope of becoming heroes, ended up emasculating them, depriving them of autonomy, confining them as closely as Victorian women had been restricted. As if in acknowledgement of this, doctors noted the symptoms of shell shock were precisely the same as those of the most common hysterical disorders of peacetime, and the soldiers' condition acquired dramatic names like 'the burial-alive neurosis', 'soldier's heart' and 'hysterical sympathy with the enemy'. In brief, what had been predominantly a 'disease' of women before the war became one of men in combat (see Ouditt 1994).

One way of reading the title of West's book is in terms of the attempt to restore a shell-shocked man's masculinity, to cure him of his loss of memory and so achieve *The Return of the Soldier*. Set in 1916, West's story commences with a woman, Margaret Allington, receiving a letter from the front sent to her by Chris Ellis, a man she knew fifteen years earlier when she was living at her father's inn. She is now married. Meanwhile, Chris's wife Kitty and his cousin Jenny are making preparations at Baldry Court for his return. When Chris arrives, however, it becomes clear to them, as Margaret discovered from the letter she received, that Chris has forgotten completely that he has a wife and a house. The pre-war part of his life operates in a symbolic landscape entirely at odds with the cultured chill of his marital home. Kitty appropriately laments that with his loss of memory comes her and Jenny's loss of him too: 'he isn't ours any longer' (West 1982: 31). Chris has 'returned', in the title's word play, to a youth uncontaminated by the war, by his business projects and by his marriage; to his world at age twenty-one, which Kitty had no part in and which pre-dates his own life-altering decisions and loss of innocence. Only Margaret is important here. To Chris, she represents a warm sensual nature and a passion of the soul, traits which have been 'educated out' of him. To restore the soldier to 'normality', Margaret comes to form with Jenny and Kitty an alliance of convenience fraught with jealousy. A psychiatrist, Dr Anderson, offers little hope, but eventually Chris's 'recovery' is achieved when Margaret gets him to familiarise himself with the toys of his infant son who died five years previously.

In traditional terms, *The Return of the Soldier* appears a story about salvation through unselfish love. However, it operates through a number of binaries, which it also interrogates: new wife Kitty/old love Margaret; Baldry Court and society/Monkey island and nature; married/unmarried; men/women; sanity/insanity; superficial regard for beauty/deep love; external/internal; happiness/truth (the dilemma faced by the women at the end). The other key binary is between upper and lower class. Margaret is from Wealdstone, 'the red suburban stain which fouls the fields three miles nearer London' (West 1982: 22), and, consequently, Jenny hates her 'as the rich hate the poor, as insect things that will struggle out of the crannies which are their decent home, and introduce ugliness to the light of day' (West 1982: 27).

West's novel chiefly strikes the reader as modernist because of its use of medical psychology to explore the hidden motivations of human behaviour. In fact, West was one of the first novelists to make full use of the psychological realism of Henry James, on whom she had already written a book. However, the novel also uses a complex modernist narrator who mediates between the reader and the story. Jenny is not entirely reliable in that she never acknowledges the sexual feelings she evidently has for her cousin. The reader comprehends her desire only through her expression of jealousy for the power that Margaret holds over Chris. The focus of the story is on her reactions to him and on the relationship between the four central characters. West's novel is also modernist in its preoccupation with gender relations. Initially, the story appears as a study of the psychology of shell shock but, more importantly, it involves a study of the psychology of Kitty and Jenny and the socially unacceptable love between Margaret and Chris across classes. The narrative's interest lies far less in Chris's condition than in the relationships between the three women, particularly in terms of the motivations and desires behind their different efforts to rehabilitate him into society and restore him to Kitty.

In its presentation of Kitty, who appears porcelain and doll-like, *The Return of the Soldier* contains an explicit attack on the figure of the 'Angel in the House', mentioned in the last chapter: 'I saw that her golden hair was all about her shoulders and that she wore over her frock a little silken jacket trimmed with rose-buds. She looked so like a girl on a magazine cover that one expected to find a large "7d" somewhere attached to her person' (West 1982: 16). The novel also implicitly parodies the 'Angel in the House' ideal embodied in Kitty by presenting the lower-middle-class Margaret as the repository of genuine values. Elaine Showalter argues in *The Female Malady* that the concept of the 'Angel in the House' was a particularly corrosive one employed to infantilise women. In the late Victorian period, the internalisation of this figure led many women to a sense of their own deviance, resulting in a high incidence of neurasthenia, of debilitating nervous conditions. Doctors argued that 'uterine instability' needed a 'rest cure', such that the prescribed treatment was to isolate patients and to withdraw intellectual stimuli. To some critics, therefore, Chris's mental instability could be considered a displacement of the symptoms likely to result from the directionless life led by Kitty and Jenny.

Margaret, who was loved by Chris fifteen years earlier, has married someone else after a jealous quarrel and has since had a child, who died at the age of two. Kitty and Chris have also had a child who died at the same age. Both children died five years before the main action of the novel begins. Hence, the removal of some psychological block, through his handling of a child's toys and clothes, is portrayed as essential if Chris is to regain his memory. The child's death is evidently the painful event in his marriage that has led Chris to react to the war by blotting out all the time he has known Kitty. This stands in distinction from Kitty's earlier failed attempt to bring back his memory by dressing like a bride again, in white satin and with necklaces of pearls and diamonds. The events at the end of the story are notable less for their credibility as a cure for mental illness than for illustrating that West is one of the first English novelists to exploit psychoanalytical theory as a narrative device.

Overall, *The Return of the Soldier* implies that the worst force behind the war is class. Like an enemy, from the minute she walks in with 'her deplorable umbrella, her unpardonable rain-coat', Margaret represents opposition. Margaret's entry into the lives of the inhabitants of Baldry Court seems improper to them, and they intend to dispose of her quickly; her worst aspect is her lower class, and she becomes for them, like Wealdstone, 'a spreading stain on the fabric of our life' (West 1982: 30). Though figured here in terms of soiling, she symbolises a world uncontaminated by the war. In distinction from Kitty, Margaret represents inner values which have nothing to do with appearances. By contrast, Kitty and Jenny find it hard to believe that after their decorative influence Chris could possibly be interested in Margaret – 'that dowd' (West 1982: 45).

However, Margaret is described in terms that emphasise her maternal qualities rather than her sexuality, and so she becomes a kind of earth mother, who, in certain respects, symbolises an alternative stereotype of idealised femininity. Chris praises her warmth and humanity: 'When she picks up facts she kind of gives them a motherly hug. She's charity and love itself' (West 1982: 51). Jenny is forcibly struck by Margaret's healing powers when she sees her with Chris beyond the cultivated boundaries of the estate: 'It means that the woman has gathered the soul of the man into her soul and is keeping it warm in love and peace so that his body can rest quiet for a little time. That is a great thing for a woman to do' (West 1982: 87). Margaret thus appears to represent protection from the horrors of war that Jenny experiences in her dreams. Jenny concludes that 'While [Margaret's] spell endured they could not send him back into the hell of war. This wonderful kind woman held his body as surely as she held his soul' (West 1982: 89). The happiness her position represents, however, is the happiness of innocence. This cannot be integrated into existing social structures, and the novel ends with class divisions intact. The process of distinguishing reality from romance is seen as being crucial to mental health even if it involves a brutal return to the barbarities of war. Yet bringing Chris back to that world of commerce, warfare and a loveless marriage may mean breaking his heart again and possibly sending him to his death in France. In several ways, Jenny recognises, the spiritual world he occupies in his shell-shocked condition transcends the real world: 'It was our particular shame that he had rejected us when he had attained to something saner than sanity. His loss of memory was a triumph over the limitations of language which prevent the mass of men from making explicit statements about their spiritual relationships' (West 1982: 81–2).

Chris ends the story no better off, but Jenny gains significantly from her relationship with Margaret: 'We kissed, not as women, but as lovers do: I think we each embraced that part of Chris the other had absorbed by her love' (West 1982: 109). This recognition, at the book's close, of her love for Chris and of the values that Baldry Court glosses over, forces her to renegotiate her own identity. If the predominant cultural values have not been changed, they have at least been exposed. In losing Chris, Jenny can embrace Margaret. If, at this point, we bring to mind again West's feminist agenda, this acceptance of a woman of another class has implications for a female solidarity which, in a different way from Woolf's *Mrs Dalloway*, challenge the male order at a time when the suffrage movement had suspended its activity to help in the war effort.

The two novels I have looked at above consider the destruction of the war in terms of personal identity, but a wider dimension, less often stressed in modernist works, is also found in depictions of social crisis, especially in the linguistic and cultural 'fragments' that Eliot's narrator in *The Waste Land* says that he has 'shored against my ruins'. From Baudelaire onwards, avant-garde writers focused on the city in a new way, and modernism is often considered to be the first literature to deal directly with urban existence. Novelists of the nineteenth century, such as Gaskell, George Eliot, Hardy and even Dickens, understood metropolitan society in opposition to life in the country, perceiving the city primarily as a place of conflict, poverty and industrialisation. However, after considerable technological changes, the modernists had to confront a new urban environment, with offices and traffic, advertising and shopping: the entire metropolitan utopia/dystopia of a fast and compact social and cultural existence that is not contrasted with provincial life but is divorced from and supersedes it. The modernists felt they had to write about the crowds, apartment blocks, mass entertainment, cars and concrete cityscapes that were celebrated in the architect Le Corbusier's 1924 manifesto *L'Urbanisme* (translated as *The City of Tomorrow*). For the twentieth-century writer, this is the reality that has to be expressed, along with the new experiences of anonymity, of being lonely in a crowd, of being surrounded and isolated.

Eliot's *The Waste Land* is, in this respect, a very modern poem in 1922: it talks of gramophones, trams, typists and insurance clerks, the brown fog of London, horns and motor cars, sandwich wrappers and empty bottles. The rhythms of industry and the city are mirrored in the constant repetitions the poem foregrounds in the behaviour of its characters. Ceremony and ritual have been overtaken by habit and compulsion, by individuals no longer purposeful but, as Freud was arguing, driven by irrational forces and strong desires outside of their conscious control. This is representative of the general confusion of motives, meanings and references in *The Waste Land*, a poem which also comments on the reader's uncertainty when faced with the act of interpretation: 'You cannot say, or guess, for you know only / A heap of broken images'. At the close of Part I, 'The Burial of the Dead', the reader is co-opted into the poem's analysis of the modern world through a quotation from Baudelaire that is far removed from the 'dear reader' of *Jane Eyre*: 'You! *hypocrite lecteur! – mon semblable, – mon frère!*'

While Eliot has been accused of turning away from history, *The Waste Land* has also been called a war poem. Its (dis-) arrangement and fragmentation echo the bewildering experience of the war in that the poem's allusions to events of the previous ten years and its disjointed narration could be that of a shell-shocked soldier. Everything, from East and West, past and present, the world of the war and its aftermath, becomes fused in the poem's linguistic eclecticism, its teasing quotations, snatches of song, snippets of conversation, multiple languages, half-thoughts, nursery rhymes, monologues and myths. There is, here, a clear tension between unity and disunity: the narrative ends with fragments and ruins; but, of course, the poem itself remains whole. The form of the verse aims to piece together or reconcile the jigsaw of the myriad references, half-lines, non-sequiturs and quotations; and all kinds of peripheral machinery is put in place around the poem as though to try to hold in the chaos: the endnotes, replete with their claim that all the personages in the poem are united, the Greek epigraph, the dedication, the redirection to James Frazer's *Golden Bough* and Jessie Weston's *From Ritual to Romance*, all bounding the five-section structure which assembles itself like the acts of a tragedy. But this is at loggerheads with the reader's experience of the text and with the lives of the figures depicted in the poem. In Part III, 'The Fire Sermon', the narrator says, 'On Margate sands / I can connect / Nothing with nothing', lines Eliot wrote while sitting in a shelter on the beach front at Margate. Yet for Eliot, the very act of writing these lines into the poem connected them, through comparison, contrast and association, with all the other ideas and images. While history, reason and logic had failed the modern world as organising principles, aesthetics had not. Using mythology and pre- to early modern culture, from the Fisher King and the Holy Grail through to Dante and Shakespeare, Eliot creates a form in the poem which aims both to master the content and to patch together all the many scraps of experience contained in the five parts.

To discuss the poem in this way is, in fact, also an example of modernist critical reading, which Eliot himself promoted, emphasising unity and wholeness amid the seeming chaos. Consequently, despite its fragmentation, different arguments for the poem's totality have been put forward. The influential British critic F. R. Leavis thought its unity came from its 'inclusive consciousness', from the mind behind the poem. Ezra Pound, who edited the poem and reduced its length considerably, thought it had an 'emotional unity'. Others have said that the justification for its form lies in the poem's many repetitions, parallel situations and allusions. For example, the idea of fragmentation is signalled in, and therefore made meaningful by, the epigraph: the Sibyl of Cumae was a prophetess required to answer any questions put to her. The way she replied was to write letters on leaves and then throw the leaves in handfuls to her questioner. However, half the leaves would blow away, and so the jumbled, disarranged message would be incomplete. This was her riddle. Eliot in this gloss to the poem is making another point about culture, that in modern life it is transmitted to us in fragments: with regard to literature, for every one person who reads *Hamlet* there are thousands more who know 'To be or not to be'; with regard to history, the Great War is best known through images of poppy fields, trenches and bayonet-charges. The modern individual's knowledge of the past is built from disconnected pieces, and Eliot makes the same point about modern cities, which are built on top of old cities, assembled together from new and old architecture. For one critic, those 'pieces' make the poem appear like a museum, such that *The Waste Land*'s relation to history and art is that of a treasure house; it stores/shores an immense heap of valuable materials torn from their original setting and displays them for the interested individual to contemplate and to contrast with modern discourses, heard in the pub or the music hall, on the gramophone or the tram (Moretti 1988: 303). The poem lays out its classical and literary references like the Sibyl's leaves or like cards full of meaning and warning on Madame Sosostris's table. (For an in-depth study of the poem see, Childs 1999, Chapter 3.)

Lastly, alongside its piecemeal treatment of history, the poem, like *Mrs Dalloway,* evinces a typically modernist preoccupation with time. In particular, it emphasises a distinction between the cyclical rhythms of nature and a contemporary indifference to the seasons in the face of regularised, mechanised clock time. In the poem, time performs many functions, such that it connects life and death; links memory and desire; divides the modern world from the organic order of the past (note the change of tense in a line such as 'And still she cried, and still the world pursues'); is a dimension across which characters move or see (Tiresias, Madame Sosostris, the Sibyl); and has come to an end: 'Hurry Up please, it's time'. It is characteristic of modernism that this interest in time is apparently unrelated to history and society. In *The Waste Land*, Eliot deals predominantly with a destroyed post-war Europe but the references to war are oblique, and social change only takes place within a mythological framework. The poem represses history and politics, which is itself a significant historical effect inasmuch as it exposes a contemporary disillusionment with the possibilities for collective action and social change at a time when Weber, Durkheim, Pareto and others had laid the grounds of modern sociology on not individual but group behaviour patterns.

Eliot's poem is representative of much modernist art produced during and after the First World War to the extent that it records an emotional aspect of a Western crisis, characterised by despair, hopelessness, paralysis, angst and a sense of meaninglessness shown on a spiritual, cultural and personal level.

## 'WHO'S PASSING FOR WHO?': SEXUAL AND RACIAL DIVISIONS

### Gertrude Stein (1874–1946)

A lesbian feminist intellectual, Stein was a pupil under William James at Radcliffe and enrolled at Johns Hopkins Medical School before giving up her studies and moving to Paris in 1903. She lived in the city until her death and established a famous salon on the left bank, to which American and European writers came to view her extensive art collection as well as make literary and artistic acquaintances (she coined the expression 'Lost Generation' to describe many of the expatriate American writers who visited her). For ten years, she lived with her brother Leo, but, after his departure in 1913, she was accompanied by Alice B. Toklas, her lifetime companion, whom she had met in Paris in 1907. In Paris, where Picasso was one of her closest friends, she was a mentor to many writers, from Hemingway to Paul Bowles, but she also became a prolific writer in diverse genres. All her work is characterised by fierce experimentation and an unwavering commitment to avant-garde principles.

**Major works:** *Three Lives* (1909), *Tender Buttons: Objects, Food, Rooms* (1914), *The Making of Americans* (written 1906–11, published 1925), *Four Saints in Three Acts* (1928), *The Autobiography of Alice B. Toklas* (1933), *The Geographical History of America* (1935), *Ida: A Novel* (1941).

## Nella Larsen (1891–1964)

Born in Chicago to a Danish mother and West Indian father, Larsen lived in Denmark for several years as a child before attending the all-black Fisk university in Nashville. After leaving Fisk prematurely, she lived in Denmark for four years and then trained as a nurse at Lincoln Hospital in New York. She worked in Tuskegee, Alabama, where she became familiar with Booker T. Washington's educational work, but soon moved back to New York and then changed careers to become a librarian. She married in 1919 and started work at a children's library in Manhattan on the Lower East Side in 1923, where she made friends with prominent members of the 'Negro Awakening' that evolved into the Harlem Renaissance. In 1926, she gave up library work for writing, publishing shortly afterwards the two well-received novellas for which she is best known. She received a Guggenheim Fellowship in 1930 and travelled in Europe for several years to do research on a third novel but never published long fiction again.

**Major works:** *Quicksand* (1928), *Passing* (1929).

## William Faulkner (1897–62)

Born in New Albany, Mississippi, Faulkner spent most of his life in the state and set many of his short stories and novels in the fictional Mississippi area of Yoknapatawpha County, whose life he based on his observations and experiences of southern living. Faulkner served in the First World War in the Canadian Royal Air Force. He married in the late 1920s and published his first novel, *Soldiers' Pay*, mid-decade, under the influence of writers like his new friend Sherwood Anderson, having earlier tried to make himself a poet in the style of Swinburne and Housman. Faulkner's mature work is famous for presenting a depiction and dissection of the post-bellum South, focused in particular on sexuality, violence, race relations and the decline of traditional southern culture. He worked on and off as a scriptwriter in Hollywood for three decades, beginning in the 1930s, and was awarded the Nobel Prize for Literature in 1949, which revived his flagging reputation and brought him wide recognition.

**Major works:** *The Sound and the Fury* (1929), *As I Lay Dying* (1930), *Light in August* (1932), *Absalom, Absalom!* (1936).

As I will mention again at the start of the next section, Gertrude Stein was an author who some critics thought aspired to aphasiac writing. Contemporary reviewers of her first major publication thought her style was characterised by 'a detailed showing of the repeated thoughts in the brain' and 'repetitions, false starts, and general circularity' (Stein 2006: 251–4). Born into a rich family, Stein published *Three Lives* privately in 1909. The central story 'Melanctha' was the last written of the three lives but was an adaptation of an earlier work *Q.E.D.* (not published until 1950, under the title *Things as They Are*). In her 1926 essay 'Composition as Explanation', Stein explained her writing in *Three Lives*:

> In beginning writing I wrote a book called *Three Lives* this was written in 1905. I wrote a negro story called *Melanctha*. In that there was a constant recurring and beginning there was a marked direction in the direction of being in the present although naturally I had been accustomed to past present and future, and why, because the composition forming around me was a prolonged present. a composition of a prolonged present is a natural composition in the world as it has been these thirty years it was more and more a prolonged present. I

created than a prolonged present naturally I knew nothing of a continuous present but it came naturally to me to make one, it was simple it was clear to me and nobody knew it was done like that, I did not myself although naturally to me it was natural.

(Quoted in Rainey 2005: 409)

Stein was influenced at this time by Cézanne, whose attention to detail and whose faux naïf approach to art allowed her to begin *Three Lives* as a new kind of writing, indebted to repetition and digression. Her 'continuous present' is one in which, in keeping with Bergsonian duration and Jamesian stream of consciousness, there is no linear progression through time in the narrative but, instead, a succession of moments that surround consciousness. Marianne DeKoven writes that this 'stylization of the prose surface' is often seen as a 'beginning of Stein's progress toward an abstract, self-contained, plastic, autonomous literature, whose only concern is its articulation of formal features of language' (Stein 2006: 324).

*Three Lives* was understood to be for a minority readership on publication, its style offering rewards to persevering readers, of whom it was not expected there would be many because the stories 'utterly lack construction and focus but give the sense of urgent life' (Stein 2006: 252). The *Chicago Record Herald* wrote that 'the slow, broken rhythm of the prose corresponds to the rhythm of the "lives" and to the reader's rhythmic comprehension; and that by this very token it is artistically justified, crudely inartistic as it may at first seem' (Stein 2006: 253). Equally challenging to bourgeois readers was the concentration on the thoughts, lives and deaths of three undistinguished women, all of whom are servants.

The counter-conventional aspect to modernism is particularly well represented by the central and most interesting story, 'Melanctha', with its linguistic experimentation, narrative obtuseness or indeterminacy, queer undercurrent and African-American heroine. One critic, writing in the early 1950s, Donald Sutherland, even pronounced that '*Three Lives*, more radically than any other work of the time in English, brought the language back to life' (Stein 2006: 276). Sutherland held this view because he thought Stein was using characters with no link to literary heritage in order to reinvent the language of fiction in a superficially simple, almost perfunctory style that bore little relation to any other and used a new syntax and little punctuation to break up the direct expression.

In terms of content, all three women are ethnic outsiders who live frustrated and unfulfilled lives leading to unhappy deaths. The book's epigraph (supposedly from the French symbolist Laforgue) underlines its portrayal of lives of suffering brought about by natural inclination: 'So I am an unhappy person and this is neither my fault nor life's'. Anna's goodness, Lena's gentleness and something unnamed in Melanctha are the cause of their unhappy lives and eventual deaths. Melanctha's unhappiness appears to be linked to her divided self and her desire, which Stein portrays in terms of both sexuality and ethnicity. The narrative is largely structured around Melanctha's relationship with Jeff Campbell, a doctor attending her mother, and moves through the psychological meetings between the two before showing Melanctha abandoning the relationship for service and respectability with Rose Johnson, for whom she seems to hold an unrequited and largely sublimated love. 'Melanctha' is, thus, the story that has drawn most critical attention because it is the most formally experimental, shaping its prose according to the character's mental processes but also because of its repeated sexual imagery and innuendo combined with its imaginative if problematic engagement with issues of ethnicity. Though the unprecedented patchwork style drew most of the attention of early critics, the aspect of Stein's work concerned with ethnicity in 'Melanctha' has attracted more recent comment, as pointed up by Michael North and quoted earlier (p. 28):

> Writers as far from Harlem as T. S. Eliot and Gertrude Stein re-imagined themselves as black, spoke in a black voice, and used that voice to transform the literature of their time. In fact, three of the accepted landmarks of literary modernism in English depend on racial ventriloquism of this kind: Conrad's *Nigger of the 'Narcissus'*, Stein's 'Melanctha' and Eliot's *The Waste Land*. If the racial status of these works is taken at all seriously, it seems that linguistic mimicry and racial masquerade were not just shallow fads but strategies without which modernism could not have arisen.
>
> (North 1994, Preface)

Like Picasso's use of African masks, the adoption, or appropriation, of a black mask allowed Stein in 'Melanctha' to flout the styles and conventions she wished to escape in order to represent fully both her life and a new twentieth-century form of writing. For Corinne Blackmer, Stein's

> deployment of the mask as a metaphor for modern culture relates to the affinity Stein perceived between American and Spanish cultures, both of which combined features of African, Latin, Anglo and Jewish cultural traditions, and whose forms and language tended toward "elemental abstraction" because of their racially, verbally, and visually "composite" or "mulatto" character.
>
> (Blackmer, quoted in Stein 2006: 418)

However, the expression of black female desire and the deployment of the Caucasian mask as an aspect of chromatic passing surface in two powerful texts, the only novels written by Nella Larsen, who was one of the prominent women writers of the Harlem Renaissance. Of the synchronicity of Anglo-American and African-American modernism, Michael North writes:

> Thus two different modernisms, tightly linked by their different stakes in the same language, emerge between 1922 and 1927. Houston Baker Jr., has argued that Anglo-American modernism is dangerously irrelevant to the movement that was born at about the same time in Harlem. In another sense, Anglo-American modernism is dangerous in its very relevance to the Harlem Renaissance because its strategies of linguistic rebellion depended so heavily on a kind of language that writers like [James Weldon] Johnson rejected. For this reason, however, it is impossible to understand either modernism without reference to the other, without reference to the language they so uncomfortably shared, and to the political and cultural forces that were constricting the language at the very moment modern writers of both races were attempting in dramatically different ways to free it.
>
> (North 1994: 11)

Larsen was one of the leading women writers of the Renaissance who found a home in Harlem, along with Jessie Fauset and Zora

Neale Hurston. As texts that concern a pivotal time in which African-Americans were finding new social and artistic urban lives, Larsen's novels are distinctive in their portrayal of sexuality and ethnicity in relation to the figure of the New Woman among the emerging black bourgeoisie.

In *Quicksand*, Helga Crane is a sophisticated and intelligent woman who marries a preacher and is brought low by the stifling atmosphere of the southern church parish and repeated child-births. The novel critiques the hold that stereotypes have on Helga's self-perception and -presentation. Uncertain about the nature of her desires, she fears her own sexuality and her relation to discourses of primitivism, with which many other modernist works are complicit (see Barkan and Bush 1995). Trying to come to terms with her identity as the child of parents of mixed ethnicities, like Larsen's own, Helga seeks an escape from her repression in Denmark where she falls into the trap of another racial stereotype: presented as the exotic Other in fine clothes, she is paraded by her wealthy relatives in Scandinavian society. Rejecting a marriage proposal in Denmark accompanies her feeling of alienation within white commodification, and she flees to Harlem, identifying now with her father's culture. However, as the novel's title suggests, this is another stage in Helga's descent as she buries her sexual desires in the production line of childbirth and sacrifices herself to the roles of dutiful wife and mother in Alabama. Helga is caught between the choices of social condemnation of her stereotyped black female sexuality and enslavement within a legitimated suffocating marriage. The book charts her decline and disappointment as she moves from her academic home in the black college at Naxos, which encourages conformity to an Anglo-Saxon norm, through Chicago, where she finds rejection and anonymity in the white north, Harlem, where she perceives a narrow-minded black essentialism in a community for whom race is the only subject, and Denmark, where she is a conversation-piece curiosity, to Alabama, where religion, marriage and family both comfort and oppress the black population.

Larsen's work is modernist in its presentation of both a new identity and identity in crisis; it concerns searches for an inner self amid feelings of duality in the intoxicating while alienating intensity of urban experience. *Quicksand* is open to a simple structuralist reading as it presents itself in terms of unresolved binaries (rich/poor, white/black, USA/Europe, individual/group, virtuous/promiscuous, sexual/religious ecstasy, north/south), but it is a more complex novel than this suggests, and its exploration of female sexual experience alongside its analysis of ethnic stereotypes and hybridity makes it a compelling account of inter-war double-consciousness.

With *Passing*, Larsen seems to develop Helga's good/bad, spiritual/physical, repressed/expressed split selves into the two characters of Irene and Clare. The 'passing' woman can also be understood in terms of a new urban possibility provided by the anonymity of the city, combining a conservative respectability with a sexual freedom outside traditional boundaries of family, patriarchy and close community living, as Stephen Dedalus understood the need to flee the nets of Ireland. In the case of Clare in *Passing*, however, it is a melodramatic death that closes her story, suggesting either a censure of her ethnic ambiguity or a critique of the duplicity she adopts in a racist society. Clare is the friend from Irene's past who now reappears as a white woman. Clare has to suppress her sexuality out of fear of conceiving a dark-skinned child with her white husband, and she represents the fear of her black identity that Helga struggled with in *Quicksand*. But it is Irene on whom the narrative focuses, and it is largely through her perceptions that the reader has to appraise. The novel's suggestions of dualism and, to a degree, lesbianism, mean that Clare's death at the end of the novel presents her as a secret sharer or, indeed, as a doppelganger who Irene secretly wishes to die because Clare represents the logical but unacceptable face of Irene's own desire: to be a wealthy, privileged, white bourgeois.

Irene's work is supposedly devoted to raising racial consciousness and to the 'uplift' program, but most of her energy and activity appears to promote herself among the white liberal community, whose society she courts through cocktail parties, fundraisers and charity events. Clare's death at the Christmas party at the end underlines her sacrifice by Irene, who has increasingly referred to Clare's attractiveness to her after early speculations on Clare's heterosexual love life.

Clare, thus, appears a Hyde figure that Irene kills in order to preserve her sanitised sense of her identity, allowing her racial, sexual and liberal conscience to survive at the expense of murdering her deeper self. This can be read as radical social critique or as a failed attempt to break free from social norms because in *Passing*, as in *Quicksand*, the sexualised black woman falls to her death.

Larsen died in the 1960s having published no more long fiction and, at her death, was accorded little recognition. The narrow focus of modernism into the 1980s meant that discussion centred on a coterie of white, male writers who vied to be the centre of attention. Consequently, as Michael North explains,

> a canonized version of modernism ... was ripe for the repudiation it received from postmodernism, feminism and African American literary studies. ... [T]he repair work necessary to bring African American literature and literature by Anglo-American women back into the canon had to begin with the demolition of a certain view of modernism. Houston Baker insisted in *Modernism and the Harlem Renaissance* that 'the very *histories* that are assumed in the chronologies of British, Anglo-American and Irish modernism are radically opposed to any adequate and accurate account of Afro-American modernism'. It now seems that Baker's emphasis was very justly placed, for it was the histories of modernism that were so thoroughly insulated and not the Anglo-American modernism itself.
>
> (North 1999: 10)

Modernism is, thus, a conflicted literary term in black studies, since it is complicit with a late imperial racism and a fetishisation of 'the primitive' but at the same time a formal mode that has contained possibilities for breaking free from historical narratives encoded in realism. Modernism's expression of alternatives, in language and in society, has thus presented an appealing possibility to many writers whose concern has been with various kinds of liberation.

Simon Gikandi writes that there is

a sense in which modernism came to be read, especially by colonised black writers, as a mode of liberation of race itself. In other words, in spite of what appears to have been sustained (mis)use of black subjects in modernism, the movement had a wide appeal to black writers in both Africa and the Americas: it was responsible for a major transformation in black writing in these regions, and it was to become the justification for various movements of cultural renaissance in places as diverse as Harlem in New York City and Haiti in the Caribbean.

(Gikandi 1997: 159)

Arguably, modernism becomes, or contains, the subversive possibilities of a kind of passing in which an appropriation takes place of white sensibilities, and a new ethnic agenda is activated by *signifying* (playing subversively) on its call to newness and reinvention. The 'poet of Harlem', Langston Hughes, tells a story of

shocking our white friends with tales of how many Negroes there were passing for white all over America. We were determined to *épater le bourgeois* real good via this white couple we had cornered, when the woman leaned over the table in the midst of our dissertations and said, 'listen, gentlemen, you needn't spread the word, but me and my husband aren't white either. We've just been *passing* for white for the last fifteen years'.

Everyone in Hughes's story laughs along with this and then starts to act naturally until, at the end of the evening, the woman reverses her story and declares that she and her husband were just passing as people who were passing. Hughes's narrator wonders: 'Were they really white – passing for colored? Or colored – passing for white?' (Hughes 1958: 33) The reinvents of identity and the dualities of modernism encourage such questions to be asked, but the answers are more complex. As Gikandi goes on to explain, the use of modernist approaches could not be uncomplicated for many black writers, and the aesthetic debates between writers from Achebe and Ngũgĩ in Africa to Walcott and Naipaul in the Caribbean have long roots:

what are now considered to be the foundational texts of modern black writing – W. E. B. DuBois's *The Souls of Black Folk* and Aimé Césaire's *Cahier d'un retour au pays natal* (*Notebook of a Return to the Native Land*), to mention two of the most prominent texts in this tradition – were written either as part of the modernist reconfiguration of industrial culture (DuBois) or under the influence of its radical break-up of traditional linguistic forms (Césaire). Three questions arise from this claim of affinity between modernism and modern black writing: how could the project of black liberation (the motivating factor behind black writing in the early twentieth century) be reconciled to modernism's imprisonment of the black subject as its radical other; how did black writers deal with the tremendous baggage of racist thought inherent in the modernist return to the *volk* or primitivism; and what was to be canonised as high modernism.

(Gikandi 1997: 159)

A continuing representative of that high modernism at the present time is William Faulkner, but that was not always the case. At the end of the Second World War, all Faulkner's novels were out of print and he, like Larsen, might have sunk without a trace. Faulkner is, thus, an interesting case of the double encoding of modernism. It is true that many writers of the 'high' period were aware that they were attempting to reinvent literature, from Pound and Eliot to Ford and Woolf. However, many writers, including Woolf and Ford, for example, have fallen on critical hard times, and it has required the efforts of many others to rework the modernist 'canon' to include them. This is to say that modernism will remain a contested term, and which authors and texts fall into its ambit varies over time: each generation reinvents modernism in its own image.

Faulkner is another writer whose works have given rise to discussion of ethnicity. His novels are full of admiration for African-American characters, particularly in terms of their endurance and forbearance, but these are patriarchal sentiments underlined by Faulkner's own views, which supported state colour segregation, for example. In respect of Faulkner's literary output, James Baldwin has argued that he was not a progressive writer in terms of race, and his attempts to map modes of classical tragedy onto his decayed white southern families obscured more momentous contemporary issues of the pre-Civil Rights USA, while, for Toni Morrison, Faulkner was the only white writer of his period who took blacks seriously.

*The Sound and the Fury* is a complex tour de force of modernist writing, if not a defining one, separated into four parts. Preceding an anonymised third-person final quarter, the first three are told by the Compson brothers, Benjy, Quentin and Jason, with each part serving as a revelation of style and character and contributing to a graphic depiction of a southern family in decline, pointed up by the disappearance of Caddy, the brothers' sister, whose sexual behaviour exercises much of their thoughts. The Compsons have sold their pasture so that Caddy can marry and Quentin can go to study at Harvard, and, at the time of the novel, twenty years later, the land has been turned into a golf course, which the Compsons can stand upon their remaining land and look upon from the other side of a dividing fence. The first part is 'told by an idiot', Benjy, a Christ-compared thirty-three-year-old who has no concept of time. His narrative consists of an interior monologue that arcs forwards and back with few orienting pointers, bar a change to italics in the text, while he mooches by the dividing fence, drawn by the golfers' cries of 'caddie', which recall to him the missing centre of his life. Benjy is locked into his memories and cannot distinguish past from present, serving as a metaphor for the plight of the South since the Civil War. The second part is narrated by Quentin and precedes his suicide by drowning eighteen years earlier in 1910, mocking the family's sale of their land to educate him. On his last day, Quentin is obsessed by the loss of Caddy's virginity and is filled with guilt over his incestuous desire for her. The third part belongs to the bigoted and violent hardware-store clerk Jason, who is angered by what he sees as his selfish and irresponsible relatives but also jealous and grudging of Caddy because he thinks she has escaped the family's fate (she has left behind her illegitimate daughter, also called Quentin). Jason's narrative takes place on Good Friday, the day before Benjy's narration, while the final part is set the day after, on Easter Sunday. This section reveals the Compsons' distorted values and degenerate lifestyle through its focus on their servant Dilsey and her grandson Luster.

Faulkner claimed the four parts of *The Sound and the Fury* were failed attempts to tell the same story in different ways. Yet, the novel displays a characteristic prose, in Faulkner's long snaking measured sentences that mix archaic and arcane terms with oratory and colloquialism. The style has been called southern Gothic and bristles with grotesqueries, melodrama, excess and bizarre imagery. The rivalry and intensity of relationships between men and women, blacks and whites, neighbours and relatives adds a mythic quality to Faulkner's stories, but they are also marked by a concern for the marginalised and downtrodden. This resonates with all the novel's characters as the defeated post-bellum members of southern white aristocracy like the Compsons have declined through the after-effects of the failed war, which was waged by the American South to defend slavery and segregation, the legacy of which brings its own guilt. A counterpoint to this is the Compsons' sexual obsession with Caddy, which invokes fears of miscegenation and of the consequences thought to follow from mixing races, which, again, contrast with the other taboo of incest, which is another shadow that hangs over the Compson family and their fortunes.

It is the fourth section of the novel that provides a different voice from that of the Compsons and offers alternative characterisations of African-Americans as Faulkner's third-person narrator takes up the story. For example, the Reverend Shegog appears as a figure 'passing' for a white preacher in his use of language, but his speech changes into black dialect as the minister warms to his theme. He is repeatedly presented as a wizened 'small, aged monkey', and he starts to speak to the church congregation 'like a white man' but as he fills with more passion about the power and glory of Christ on Easter Sunday he is pictured differently: 'his monkey face lifted and his whole attitude that of a serene, tortured crucifix that transcended its shabbiness and insignificance' (Faulkner 1964: 260–1). Soon the congregation are united with one voice as the minister draws them into identification with Christ's suffering through the emotive and transformative power of an authentic language. With its focus on Dilsey and Luster, the fourth part, or final gospel, of Faulkner's novel allows a reimagination of the significance of the book's various motifs that have led to it being read as an allegory of the South, as a sardonic treatment of Christ's agony and as a protracted philosophical meditation on memory, change and time, in which the change to third-person narration needs to be read not simply as an example or allegory of black disenfranchisement but in the context of the previous three narrators' agonised states of mind. Those *states* of mind also suggest the South's problems with the colour line, in which Benjy's narration, for example, knows nothing of the racial divisions that govern his society, forcing readers to establish the place and significance of ethnicity, discrimination and skin colour for themselves. Benjy is a mute, and when he travels/descends with Dilsey and the others to 'Nigger Hollow', he is both unable to report on what he finds and (some critics see him as a Christ figure) privileged as the only white who can cross the colour line. Benjy is also castrated, which is something that Quentin wishes on himself; Quentin is also at times mistaken both for 'a woman' and for 'a coloured man', challenging the divisions of gender and race that the Compsons' society relies upon, a fact compounded by Caddy's decision to name her daughter after her brother.

It is said of the curiously named minister Shegog that 'his intonation, his pronunciation, became negroid' but that no one notices in the congregation when this happens. They all become one when 'he was nothing, and they were nothing and there was not even a voice but instead their hearts were speaking to one another in chanting measures beyond the need for words' (Faulkner 1964: 261). It is a vision of union in communion that goes beyond the language of division that has striated the narrative. However, despite the symbolism contained in the Easter Day call-and-response African-American gospel sermon, in which Benjy and perhaps also Faulkner cross the colour line and, if not pass, at least participate, the reality of salvation and redemption remains far distant.

## 'HISTORY IS A NIGHTMARE': SYMBOLISM AND LANGUAGE

### E. M. Forster (1879–1971)

Forster was principally an Edwardian novelist concerned with the restrictions placed on personal freedom by English sensibilities, but his later work, especially his last novel *A Passage to India*, can be called modernist in its use of symbolism and its style of repetition-with-variation (which Forster called 'rhythm'). A free thinker by conviction and inclination, Forster was associated with the Bloomsbury Group and lived much of his life at King's College, Cambridge. He was a lifelong member of the Labour Party, an agnostic and also an avowed liberal humanist who believed strongly in personal relationships: he famously wrote in 1939 that he would sooner betray his country than his friend. His early novels and stories use Italy and to a lesser extent Greece as a vibrant, life-affirming antithesis to the stultifying repression of England. His homosexual novel *Maurice*, written in 1913–14, was only published posthumously.

**Major works:** *A Room with a View* (1908), *Howards End* (1910), *A Passage to India* (1924), *Aspects of the Novel* (1927).


## W. B. Yeats (1865–1939)

Yeats was born into an Anglo-Irish Protestant minority in Dublin. His father was a painter (like Yeats's brother Jack) and a lawyer, and his mother came from a prosperous Sligo ship-owning family. In 1883, Yeats refused to go to Trinity College and took up art and poetry instead. In 1887, he met Maud Gonne, an active nationalist campaigner who was to become the subject of nearly all his love poems. Yeats joined the Theosophical Society and the Order of the Golden Dawn, founded the Irish Literary Society and served as an active member of the Irish Republican Brotherhood from 1896 to 1900. For the fifteen years after his 1893 collection of folk stories *The Celtic Twilight*, Yeats attempted to instigate a new Irish poetry, a national theatre and a unifying Celtic mythology: amounting to a National Literary Revival. In 1896 he met Lady Gregory, who became a patron and invited Yeats to spend his summers at Coole Park. In 1916, after the formation of military groups such as the Irish Citizens' Army and the Ulster Volunteer Force, the Easter Rising in Dublin revived Yeats's interest in Irish nationalism, and he became a senator of the Irish Free State from 1922 to 1928. The influences that shaped his poetry after 1916 can be summarised as follows: the nationalist cause, Irish identity, the Protestant aristocracy, civil war, his love for Maud Gonne and her daughter Iseult, his marriage to Georgie Hyde-Lees and the revelations he perceived in automatic writing and mysticism. During this time, he composed many of the poems that make up his principal modernist works between the wars.

**Major works:** *The Wild Swans at Coole* (1919), *Michael Robartes and the Dancer* (1921), *The Tower* (1928), *The Winding Stair and Other Poems* (1933).

## James Joyce (1882–1941)

The eldest of ten children, Joyce was born into a prosperous but soon-to-be impoverished Catholic family in Dublin. He was educated at a Jesuit boarding school and University College. During a brief attempt to study medicine in Paris, he took up writing poetry and prose sketches. After returning home to visit his dying mother and meeting his future wife, a young woman from Galway called Nora Barnacle, Joyce lived on the continent in Pola, Trieste, Rome, Zurich and Paris. Despite this self-enforced 'exile', all his fiction is set in Dublin. Joyce's first major publication was the short-story cycle *Dubliners*, soon followed by the semi-autobiographical novel *A Portrait of the Artist as a Young Man*, which charts Stephen Dedalus's development from a child to a university student who decides to become an artist. His next book, *Ulysses*, is set on one day in Dublin in 1904 and uses Homer's *Odyssey* as a template to explore the modern urban individual with unprecedented detail and candour. Though Joyce also published three volumes of poetry and one play, *Exiles* (1918), his only other novel was published seventeen years after *Ulysses*: *Finnegans Wake*, the story of one night, but also in a sense of everything, told through the dream language of a publican's unconscious mind.

**Major works:** *Dubliners* (1914), *A Portrait of the Artist as a Young Man* (1916), *Ulysses* (1922), *Finnegans Wake* (1939).

In his article 'Modernism, Anti-Modernism and Postmodernism', and at length in his book *The Modes of Modern Writing: Metaphor, Metonymy and the Typology of Modern Literature* (1977), David Lodge advances the theory that modern literature swings between two dominant poles of symbolism. He takes his lead from an essay by the Russian formalist Roman Jakobson, which, through his study of aphasia (language disorder), argues that the two types of figurative imagery, metaphor and metonymy, play with language in significantly different ways. Lodge goes further to argue that some modern writers, such as Beckett and Stein, aspire 'to the condition of aphasia', to a loss of the ability to communicate. Metaphor works by analogously describing one thing in terms of another to which it is not literally related but has some resemblance ('window' for 'eye'). By contrast, metonymy works by contiguity and association and replaces an object with its attribute ('greens' for 'vegetables'). Just as metaphor encompasses simile, metonymy is often considered also to include synecdoche, which substitutes the part for the whole ('motor' for 'car') or the whole for the part ('England played hockey yesterday').

For Jakobson, the distinction between metaphor and metonymy can explain numerous differences: films are metonymic, drama metaphoric; prose and the epic are metonymic, poetry and the lyric metaphoric. Similarly, Freud's interpretation of dreams refers to the metonymic aspects of dreamwork (condensation and displacement) and to metaphoric aspects (identification and symbolism). For Lodge, the value in Jakobson's theory lies in its explanatory power when considering literary shifts over time. Nineteenth-century Romanticism, he argues, was characterised by metaphor in its representation of individuals and their imaginative life in reaction to eighteenth-century classicism's metonymic imagery used to describe the social. Realism was metonymic, while modernism swung the pendulum in the opposite direction again. In the twentieth century, the process appears accelerated. The socially aware political writers of the 1930s favoured metonymy, while the late modernists, such as Beckett, Lowry and Lawrence Durrell, staged a recovery for metaphor before the down-to-earth post-war authors (such as Philip Larkin, Kingsley Amis and John Wain) once more championed a realist style. Finally, postmodernism witnesses a resurgence of metaphoric writing, in its use of the fantasy mode, in its radical dismantling of character and plot and, particularly, in its experiments with language.

The most important distinction to arrest our attention here is that between the primarily metonymic style of realism and the metaphoric mode of modernism. This can be demonstrated at the level of titles: *David Copperfield*, *Middlemarch*, *Mary Barton* and *Northanger Abbey* are indicative of realist writers' penchant for the representative, the social and the use of the part to represent the whole (the individual or town representing the populace or the country); *Heart of Darkness*, *To the Lighthouse*, *The Waste Land* and *The Rainbow* operate not through association but through symbolic resonance. Similarly, the distinction can be argued at the level of character description: Charles Dickens's writing is predominantly metonymic (Micawber is represented by his cane in *David Copperfield* and Mrs Sparsit by her Roman nose in *Hard Times*), while Virginia Woolf's rendition of character is typically metaphoric (Clarissa Dalloway is repeatedly referred to as a bird but nothing she owns is ever solidly associated with her).

Lodge would be the first to urge limitations to, and reservations over, the theory, but, in general, the more literary styles, such as those of the modernists, tend towards dense, poetical imagery, the more they are likely to gravitate towards metaphor. Part of the emphasis on metaphor in modernism can be demonstrated from its use of symbols for allegorical or representational effect; a development from the *symbolistes* belief that the purpose of art is not to denote but to connote, to convey by symbols the transcendent reality behind appearances. In literature, symbolism had its origins in the work of Baudelaire and evolved partly against Zola's naturalism. While symbolism also flourished in drama and art, foremost among the *symbolistes* were the poets Rimbaud, Verlaine and Mallarmé, who, to varying degrees, abandoned the constraints of rhyme, form and metre in favour of a free verse which stressed rhythm and musicality in poems that frequently concentrated on death, the erotic and intense mystical and religious feelings.

Generally speaking, a symbol relies on the one hand on having a concrete, real signifier (for example the snow at the end of

Joyce's 'The Dead' in *Dubliners*) and also an elusive, suggestive, complex of signifieds. Symbolism often uses a method of uniting the internal and the external or projecting the internal onto the external, as in Conrad's *Heart of Darkness*, Kafka's 'Metamorphosis' or Lawrence's 'The Fox'. To take a longer example, in Woolf's *To the Lighthouse*, the beacon of light is an image of the characters' aspirations while its illumination of the dark connotes the individual's insight into experience and its circling movement mimics the turning of time. Additionally, to the characters, the lighthouse symbolises different things, and this changes over time.

One of the most symbolically rich texts of the 1920s is *A Passage to India*, E. M. Forster's last novel, published fifty years before his death though completed soon after the First World War and probably set before it, at the time of Forster's first visit to India in 1912–13. His most modernist novel, which incorporates both symbolism and realism (Lodge 1977: 97), *A Passage to India* is partly about what Forster and others have called the liberal dilemma: the opposition to political extremism and intolerance combined with a refusal to use force. It was generally agreed that the British Empire was split between paternalists, who thought that Britain had a moral and cultural supremacy over its colonies, and liberals such as Forster, who believed it right to spread values of understanding and education but disagreed with the Empire's military and commercial exploits. Throughout the novel, the constant emphasis on 'goodwill', 'friendship' and 'tolerance' is an assertion of Forster's liberal creed.

Two elements to the book can illustrate its modernist aspects: rhythm and symbolism. Forster and his critics have used the term 'rhythm' to denote the structural use in fiction of leitmotifs or 'repetition with variation', which depends upon reiterated words and phrases which accumulate resonances and meanings. 'Rhythm' then refers to the repeated use of expressions, incidents or characters to create a pulsating effect in the evolution of a text's themes. The technique is apparent in *A Passage to India* and, in particular, in the use made of the echo which haunts Adela and Mrs Moore after their visit to the Marabar Caves. All of the book is highly structured to create patterns, repetitions and rhythms. To begin with, it has a three-part structure: 'Mosque',

'Caves', 'Temple', three Indian spaces, representing Islam, Jainism (a fifth-century CE atheistic religion) and Hinduism. The book also follows a seasonal pattern in its three parts, from cold weather, to hot weather, to the rains.

The other key element to the book's construction is the central symbol of the caves, which has been interpreted in many ways. First, they appear a hollow, empty space to match Forster's perception of metaphysical emptiness in a Godless universe. Second, they arguably match Forster's view of India as a place of mystery and nullity. Third, the hollow caves can be read as a symbol of the main textual absence in the book, its missing centre: the enigma of what happened to Adela. A variation on this reading is offered by Brenda Silver, who describes the book's main technique as 'periphrasis', and the hollow caves in *A Passage to India* thus mimic the gap in the narrative that Forster leaves by never saying what actually happened at the Marabar. However, it is a periphrasis in another sense: the way in which the event, an alleged rape, is taken over by the Anglo-Indian community who 'protect' or conceal Adela and keep her in hiding, while generating views, theories and accusations themselves.

If we move to a wider consideration of the book, in one respect, the narrative concerns Adela's quest (hence her surname 'Quested') to discover 'the real India'. What she actually finds is the Marabar hills and an accompanying atmosphere of spiritual nullity, sexual fear and human inconsequence in the universe. There are arguments which say that India is reduced to the Marabar Caves in the novel. Everything we learn about the caves applies also to European views of the country: they are dark, empty, oppressive and mysterious. The common way of imagining India as a land occupied by monsoons, heat and dust rather than people is repeated in the fetishising of the caves in the novel. The caves are considered inexplicable and unknowable, remote and timeless, like India.

Forster said to his publisher in 1924 that he had been careful in *A Passage to India* 'not to allude to contemporary politics'. In 1960, he told his biographer that the book was not 'about the incompatibility of East and West [but] was really concerned with the difficulty of living in the universe'. In an essay, 'Three

Countries', Forster also said 'the book is not really about politics ... It's about the search of the human race for a more lasting home'. Overall, the novel suggests Forster's view that politics is opposed to, or at least always in tension with, friendship. Forster aims to make this a book about progressive, liberal-minded people, trying to be fair and amicable against a backdrop of politics and imperial administration: Fielding, we are told, 'was happiest in the give-and-take of private conversation. The world, he believed, is a globe of men who are trying to reach one another and can best do so by the help of goodwill plus culture and intelligence' (Forster 1983: 56). 'Goodwill' is one of the words most frequently mentioned in the novel, and personal factors are seen as ways of uniting people, while political factors are portrayed as sources of division. The easy familiarity of Fielding's first meeting with Aziz is contrasted with the formal and impersonal attempts at cross-cultural connection epitomised by the Collector's bridge party. The book's three-part structure even works on this level. At the end of 'Mosque', the first section, we are told: 'But they were friends, brothers. That part was settled, their compact had been subscribed by [Aziz showing Fielding his dead wife's] photograph, they trusted one another, affection had triumphed for once in a way' (Forster 1983: 113). At the end of the second section, 'Caves', Aziz and Fielding are separated, and Fielding returns to England. Then the last section, 'Temple', concludes with a pessimistic but ambivalent ending pointing up the difficulty of their mutually desired friendship.

In what the post-colonial critic Edward Said has called Orientalism, in his book of the same name, the 'Western benefits' of logic, efficiency and material well-being are accentuated by the positioning of India as illogical, inefficient and spiritual. Forster, for metaphysical reasons, repeatedly colludes with this representation of India in *A Passage to India*: 'they did *not* one thing which the non-Hindu would feel dramatically correct; this approaching triumph of India was a muddle (as we call it), a frustration of reason and form' (Forster 1983: 258). This sense of muddle and mystery is cultivated by Forster, and it becomes a feature of the narrative from 'what happened in the Marabar Caves' to whether the Nawab Bahadur's car accident is caused by an animal or a ghost and whether Adela sees a stick or a snake from the train. The book is riddled with inconclusive incidents, and Fielding's comment that 'A mystery is a muddle' (Forster 1983: 62) is used to reify even India's spiritualism into instances of simple human failure. Forster wrote about the incident at the caves:

> In the cave it is *either* a man, *or* the supernatural, *or* an illusion. If I say, it becomes whatever the answer a different book. And even if I know! My writing mind therefore is a bit of a blur here – i.e. I will it to remain a blur, and to be uncertain, as I am of many facts in daily life. This isn't a philosophy of aesthetics. *It's a particular trick I felt justified in trying because my theme was India.* It sprang straight from my subject matter. I wouldn't have attempted it in other countries, which though they contain mysteries or muddles, manage to draw rings round them.
>
> (E. M. Forster, quoted in Editor's Introduction to
> *A Passage to India*, 1983: 23)

Muddle extends over every part of the novel, from the chaos of 'mud' on the opening page to the final 'Temple' section, where the Hindu god and other offerings thrown into the river were 'emblems of passage; a passage not easy, not now, not here, not to be apprehended except when it is unattainable' (Forster 1983: 283). This mystery and misunderstanding spills over into the metaphysical realm in all aspects of the book. For example, the chief Indian exponent of muddle is Godbole, who is privileged with preternatural powers, with a 'telepathic appeal' that links him with Mrs. Moore. He typically says 'everything is anything and nothing something' (Forster 1983: 169).

In terms of modernism, such emphasis on muddle and obfuscation underlines the elements of doubt and uncertainty that pervade many early twentieth-century texts, in which scepticism over knowledge, God, identity, morality, civilisation and communication seem to undermine the imperial, masculine and Victorian certainties of the previous century. For Forster, *A Passage to India*, in many ways, represented all he had to say on the human predicament under modernity, and that is one reason why he never wrote another novel.

Like Forster's, W. B. Yeats's work is generally held to have heightened in formal sophistication during his career, but, in contrast to Forster, he continued publishing his best work up until his death, and it was between the wars that Yeats firmly established himself as one of the foremost modernists. His poetry here contains a fusing of form and content in clear rhythms and few adjectives, dense symbols and verse and rhyme patterns that match the thoughts they express. Yeats's symbolic system is described in *A Vision* (1925) and amounts to a theory of history influenced by the cyclical philosophy of Vico (1668–1744) and the Neoplatonism of Plotinus (205–69). Here, Yeats's central belief was that history can be interpreted as a series of expanding cones; each age, as it wears on, generates a centrifugal tendency which finally produces decadence or disintegration. And each cone is more precisely a double cone, since each age unwinds what its predecessor has wound, such that thesis and antithesis are in progress simultaneously. Yeats's term for this was a 'gyre', a spiralling movement (the image behind the title *The Winding Stair*) applicable to each individual's life as well as to history. For Yeats, history and life move through a 'millennium', 'the symbolic measure of a being that attains its flexible maturity and then sinks into rigid age'.

Yeats's symbolism can initially be thought of in terms of the work of the Swiss psychiatrist Carl Gustav Jung, who elaborated a theory of archetypal symbols which exist in the 'collective unconscious' and are common to all cultures, and Claude Lévi-Strauss, who claimed that an analysis of the structure of symbolism revealed universal principles of thought and reflected the human need to classify the world. Symbols not only act as signs which denote certain values and meanings, they also carry with them connotations of other meanings. In this way, all symbolism involves ambiguity and potential disagreement over meaning.

An extended discussion of one of Yeats's poems can illustrate his historical theories and his use of symbolism: 'Leda and the Swan' (1923) from *The Tower*. In Greek mythology, Leda was a queen of Sparta, the wife of Tyndarus. Zeus came to her in the form of a swan when she was bathing, and she gave birth to two eggs, from one of which came Clytemnestra, the wife and later murderer of Agamemnon, and from the other Helen of Troy, who married Agamemnon's brother Menelaus and whose abduction by Paris was the cause of the Trojan War. In the past, 'Leda and the Swan' has been seen as an admiration for and celebration of power and creative drive like Blake's 'Tiger Tiger', while more recently feminist critics have seen it instead as an objectionable 'celebration' of rape. In terms of Yeats's system of imagery, the city of Troy, or Ilium, is one of the most important elements. Troy was the city captured by the Greeks under Agamemnon after a ten-year siege as told by Homer in *The Iliad*. The city was considered imaginary until its existence was proved by excavations by Heinrich Schliemann at Hissarlik in Turkey, a few miles inland from the Aegean Sea. The excavation of Troy, from 1870 on, revealed ten periods of occupation and demonstrated to Yeats's generation a historical dimension to what had previously been thought of as myth. Troy, therefore, became to Yeats the primary symbol of a superior civilisation destroyed by the warring Greek princes under Agamemnon, who for Yeats destroyed a great empire and put in its place an 'intellectual anarchy'. Yeats considered Troy's fall to stand at a turning point in the gyres of history, a moment at which an annunciation had occurred. The occasion of this turning point is the conception of Helen of Troy, the product of a divine intervention in history, like Christ. In Book V of *A Vision*, called 'Dove or Swan', Yeats writes: 'I imagine the annunciation that founded Greece was made to Leda ... and that from one of her eggs came Love and from the other War'.

'Leda and the Swan', therefore, considers the pagan antecedents of Christianity, just as Yeats's later poem 'The Second Coming' (1919) envisions the eclipse of Christianity's 2,000-year reign and the arrival of a new phase of history with the 'rough beast' slouching toward its birth at Bethlehem. 'The Second Coming' is concerned with the foretelling of yet another historical cycle to follow those presaged by the two annunciations to Leda and to the Virgin Mary. These cycles, therefore, constitute a pattern to history. Each is a union of a god and a woman, and both produce momentous births, such as the latest human–divine birth about which Yeats conjectures in 'The Second Coming'. Leda's mating with Zeus gives rise to Homeric Greece, just as the Christian

Feast of the Annunciation on 25 March, exactly nine months before Christmas, celebrates the moment of the conception of Jesus, the start of Christianity. Both are the beginnings of one epoch and the end of another, caused by loss of control in a civilisation. The conception of Helen, announced in 'Leda and the Swan', marks the beginning of the Greek era and the demise of Troy; hence: 'A shudder in the loins engenders there / The broken wall, the burning roof and tower / And Agamemnon Dead'. Yeats originally meant the poem to be a comment on the French Revolution, but as he worked upon it, the political element faded away. He wrote:

> I thought nothing is now possible but some movement, or birth from above, preceded by some violent annunciation. My fancy began to play with Leda and the Swan for metaphor and I began this poem: but as I wrote, bird and lady took such possession of the scene that all politics went out of it.
>
> (Quoted in Johnsen 1991: 80)

For Yeats, Helen of Troy was also a personal symbol of his muse Maud Gonne, the revolutionary political activist he earlier compared to Helen in another poem, 'No Second Troy' (1908): 'Was there another Troy for her to burn?', alluding to the prophecy by Virgil (70–19 CE) in his fourth Eclogue that there will be another Troy – a premonition, according to some, of Christ's coming. The swans are archetypal symbols found throughout Yeats's work and allude to the Elizabethan poet Edmund Spenser, painting, Celtic myth and Lady Gregory's estate (see 'The Wild Swans at Coole' [1916]). The swan symbol builds in resonance over the course of his poetry, standing at different times for power, phallic strength and purity, and, thus, like Forster's rhythm, each mention of the swan adds to the intensity of the imagery while serving as shorthand for many complex ideas.

In 'Leda and the Swan', Yeats speculates repeatedly on the woman's position. He conjectures on whether Leda (and, by implication, Mary) by her impregnation became half or wholly divine. In the poem, 'shudder' describes the swan's ejaculation but also relates to Leda's fear. Both mother and child are 'mastered' by this power from the sky which is both above humanity (divine) and beneath it ('brute' animal). His will accomplished, Zeus is 'indifferent' to the woman and lets her 'drop', but not before, Yeats conjectures, Leda receives both knowledge, the annunciation and power, the divine ferocity which, through her child, the gods will come to impose upon men. Leda, thus, becomes the physical means by which terror enters history through a moment of violation. Agamemnon's death and the earlier deaths of all the heroes at Troy (such as Achilles, Hector and Paris) can therefore be seen as following from the brutality visited upon Leda.

In terms of analyses of modernism, such mythologising is frequently perceived as an attempt to escape from history, to avoid confronting the realities of modern life, from mass culture through to democracy, that writers steeped in classical education and 'high' culture found alienating and bewildering. For the modernists themselves, however, the point of using myth was to compensate for the dissatisfying fragmentation of the modern world: to create a controlling narrative that could be mapped onto and make sense of the rapid social changes of modernity.

In Jungian terms, myth, via the collective unconscious, performs the function of enabling humans to perceive basic truths. For example, in nearly all religions, there are myths of gods disguising themselves as animals, which is a way of coming to terms with the animal instincts in human nature, which the god represents in dream or myth. While Yeats's poetry is a complex expression of his theory of historical cycles initiated by the appearance or revelation of gods in the world, his concern is less with the supernatural than with insights into both reality and human affairs, an interest that links him with James Joyce, whose prose fiction begins from this very attempt by the artist, 'the priest of the imagination', to render in language the hidden significance of objects such that 'the quick intelligence may go beyond them to their meaning which is still unuttered' (Bolt 1981: 36). In this, both Yeats and Joyce aimed for a fusion of the material and the spiritual that was epitomised by the symbolist movement.

The manifestation of a divinity in the human world is called an epiphany. In his youth, Joyce wrote epiphanies, similar to prose poems, as an artistic exercise. He took the term from the

Bible, where it refers to a divine revelation, such as the manifestation of Christ to the Magi. For Joyce, however, an epiphany was the 'revelation of the whatness of the thing', the point at which 'the soul of the commonest object . . . seems to us radiant'. He felt there was an obligation on the artist to discover a spiritual truth 'in the vulgarity of speech or of gesture or in a memorable phase of the mind itself' (Joyce 1944: 188). This is the description Joyce gives in *Stephen Hero*, but cut from its reworked version as *A Portrait of the Artist as a Young Man*. However, each of the chapters of *A Portrait of the Artist as a Young Man*, which is in many ways a search for identity, ends with an epiphany, as Stephen sees in himself aspects of love, religion, art or understanding. Here, each epiphany is a synthesis of triumph which the next chapter destroys.

Epiphanies are a feature of Joyce's first book *Dubliners*, a sequence of stories that owes as much to naturalism as it does to modernism. The book's modernist characteristics are: uncertainty, particularly in the stories' endings, symbolism, linguistic intensity, an aesthetic rather than a moral focus, linguistic experimentation and a drive to throw off the old in favour of the new and an interest in the internal workings of the individual mind as much as a shared external reality. However, *Dubliners* only undoubtedly approaches a modernist form in 'The Dead', the final story, which was not a part of Joyce's original scheme for the book. Joyce's style in 'The Dead' has many influences and one worth mentioning again here is Walter Pater (1839–94). In this passage in the 'Conclusion' to *The Renaissance*, Pater dissolves the category of self under the name of reducing experience to purer subjectivity:

At first sight experience seems to bury us under a flood of external objects, pressing upon us with a sharp and importunate reality, calling us out of ourselves in a thousand forms of action. But when reflection begins to play upon those objects they are dissipated under its influence; the cohesive force seems suspended like some trick of magic; each object is loosed into a group of impressions – colour, odour, texture – in the mind of the observer. And if we continue to dwell in thought on this world, not of objects in the solidity with which language invests them, but of impressions, unstable, flickering, inconsistent, which burn and are extinguished with our consciousness of them, it contracts still further: the whole scope of observation is dwarfed into the narrow chamber of the individual mind. ... Every one of those impressions is the impression of the individual in his isolation, each mind keeping as a solitary prisoner its own dream of a world.

(Pater 1873: 182–3)

It is both the sentiment and style of a passage such as this that informs Joyce's presentation of Gabriel Conroy in 'The Dead'. In the final scene, Gabriel meditates on the living ghosts of Dublin (including himself) and looks forward, like Ibsen, to the time *When We Dead Awaken*. Gabriel's vision is both an epiphany and an enactment of Pater's description above and one which echoes Walter Pater's picture of experience which seems 'to bury us under a flood of objects' giving way to reflection and impressions:

A few light taps upon the pane made him turn to the window. It had begun to snow again. He watched sleepily the flakes, silver and dark, falling obliquely against the lamplight. The time had come for him to set out on his journey westward. Yes, the newspapers were right: snow was general all over Ireland. It was falling on every part of the dark central plain, on the treeless hills, falling softly upon the Bog of Allen and, farther westward, softly falling into the dark mutinous Shannon waves. It was falling, too, upon every part of the lonely churchyard on the hill where Michael Furey lay buried. It lay thickly drifted on the crooked crosses and headstones, on the spears of the little gate, on the barren thorns. His soul swooned slowly as he heard the snow falling faintly through the universe and faintly falling, like the descent of their last end, upon all the living and the dead.

(Joyce 1977)

The meaning of the symbol of the snow here is less important than the effects of language and imagery: repetition, alliteration, inversion, allusions to Celtic mythology and Christianity. The passage is a lyrical meditation on a 'journey westward': to the West of Ireland, to the Celtic lands, language and mythology, to

Gretta's home and to death, where the sun sets. The snow suggests a frozen people, a shroud over the land and the hibernation of winter before the regeneration of spring (compare with Eliot's 'forgetful snow' at the start of *The Waste Land*).

When Joyce repeats the style of such a lyrical passage in his next book, *A Portrait of the Artist as a Young Man*, as at the end of Chapter 4, it will be as a parody, both of Stephen's character and of his pretensions to be an artist. Joyce's use of language is remarkable because of its range: he can write moving poetical prose, as above, can pastiche myriad literary and popular styles, as in *Ulysses*, and can indulge himself in the most ludicrous puns and the most vulgar insults. Joyce's controversial use of language begins with the stories written for *Dubliners* (1914). The book was completed in its first form by 1905, but potential publishers were put off by possible libel suits and by the book's 'coarse' language. Joyce refused demands to change his text, and his stand is indicative of the importance of language to him at every level. For example, the first story of *Dubliners*, 'The Sisters', contains three key words for the entire collection: paralysis, gnomon and simony. To begin with, Joyce himself made his intention in writing *Dubliners* clear by telling various correspondents that his aim was to expose the numbing 'paralysis' which he felt was at the heart of Dublin, a city that had produced 'bat like souls' in its population: people who had had their individuality taken away from them, subsumed in a religion which removed responsibility from individuals. Second, a 'gnomon' is the central pillar of a sun dial and also a parallelogram with a section missing, which alerts the reader to the fact that the stories contain many important omissions, especially 'absent presences', such as Parnell in 'Ivy Day in the Committee Room' and Michael Furey in 'The Dead'. Lastly, the word 'simony' refers to the practice of selling religious relics and has come to represent a wider corruption within the church. Joyce hints at this in several ways, ranging from the sexual corruption of minors to the priests' unhealthy dominance of people's lives in Ireland. Consequently, in a world of stultification, absence and corruption, the positive forces of ambition, energy, determination and revolutionary zeal are all excised from *Dubliners*. Centuries of political domination by

England and the excessive power and status conferred on the clergy had resulted in a general paralysis of mind and free will, to be transcended only by death or emigration.

Recent discussions of Joyce's concern with language have frequently focused on colonial discourse, which several critics consider an important aspect to the modernist revolution in early twentieth-century Irish writers of a realist tradition associated with the rise of English colonialism. Towards the end of *A Portrait of the Artist as a Young Man*, Joyce has Stephen Dedalus try to compete with the British Empire on its own terms, using the words and phrases that constitute imperialist reality. Stephen realises, however, that everything he can say in the colonialists' language is always-already an 'English' expression. This is something acknowledged in a famous assertion of Stephen's frustration as he ponders his relationship with the Anglified Dean of Studies at university:

> The language in which we are speaking is his before it is mine. How different are the words *home*, *Christ*, *ale*, *master*, on his lips and on mine! I cannot speak or write these words without unrest of spirit. His language, so familiar and so foreign, will always be for me an acquired speech. I have not made or accepted its words. My voice holds them at bay. My soul frets in the shadow of his language.
>
> (Joyce 1960: 189)

*A Portrait of the Artist as a Young Man* ends with Stephen's decision to use the best weapons open to him: 'silence, exile, and cunning' (Joyce 1960: 247), implying that the only way he can come to terms with Catholicism, politics and colonialism in Ireland is to remove himself physically, linguistically and mentally from the arenas in which he has always been caught by pre-existing rules, beliefs and discourses. Stephen feels the need, in order to *be* himself, to 'fly the nets' of nationalism, religion and family, which are constraining and reductive of personal identity. The book moves through a series of searches for self – attempts to 'forge' an identity, yet it concludes in a dispersal as the diary entries end the book in fragments. It finishes with a Pater-like assertion of the individual as Stephen proclaims his self-origin and the creation of his own racial conscience. It also ends with a fractured ungrammatical language which mimics the language of the novel's beginning, when Stephen is a baby: it is one of Joyce's most remarkable feats to demonstrate Stephen's development through the growing sophistication of the narrator's language, so the fragmented conclusion suggests a new Stephen is about to be born. This intimation of rebirth is true in terms of the end of this novel, but it is also true in the sense that Stephen is reborn in Joyce's next book, *Ulysses*.

In both *Ulysses* and *A Portrait of the Artist as a Young Man*, the narrative frequently takes on the manner and often the language of the characters without actually using the first-person or transcribing their speech or thoughts. Only the final chapter is fully given over to the stream of consciousness of one character: Molly Bloom. A forty-page unpunctuated soliloquy reveals Molly, who has previously been an object more than a subject, to be anti-intellectual but to have a fecund mind, full of inner life.

The book's mythical method is both rich and complex. Harry Blamires's *The Bloomsday Book*, which recounts the story of *Ulysses* in more familiar realist prose, begins with this explanation:

> Joyce's symbolism cannot be explained mechanically in terms of one-for-one parallels, for his correspondences are neither exclusive nor continuously persistent. Nevertheless certain correspondences recur throughout *Ulysses*, establishing themselves firmly. Thus Leopold Bloom corresponds to Ulysses in the Homeric parallel, and Stephen Dedalus corresponds to Telemachus, Ulysses's son. At the beginning of Homer's *Odyssey* Telemachus finds himself virtually dispossessed by his mother's suitors in his own father's house, and he sets out in search of the lost Ulysses. In Joyce's first episode Stephen Dedalus feels that he is pushed out by his supposed friends from his temporary residence, and leaves it intending not to return.
>
> (Blamires 1966: 1)

From this opening, the novel pursues the central myth of Ulysses in such a way that its presence need not occur to the reader even though the simplest actions may have Homeric antecedents. For T. S. Eliot, whose use of mythology was just as great in *The Waste*

*Land*, the purpose of the symbolic level is less to supply meaning than structure:

> Joyce is pursuing a method which ... is simply a way of controlling, of ordering, of giving a shape and significance to the immense panorama of futility and anarchy which is contemporary history ... it is I sincerely believe a step towards making the world possible for art.
>
> ('Myth, Order and Ulysses' [1923])

However, the controlling imagery is not simply concerned with Homer and the level of events and actions. For example, in Chapter 1, Ireland appears to be symbolised in the decayed milkwoman and in old Mother Grogan in Buck Mulligan's story, while its subjugation is represented by the Englishman Haines's silver cigarette case with its central emerald and by the Martello Tower in which Stephen, Mulligan and Haines live. Thematic symbolism organises the chapters in terms of colour, food, science and art. In his first 1920 'summary-key skeleton-schema' for the novel, Joyce included a column listing the main symbols and leitmotifs of each chapter and in the second, a year later, he listed the correspondences between Homer's characters and his own. In the second scheme, he also refined his cardinal symbols to one per chapter: heir, horse, tide, nymph, Eucharist, caretaker, editor, constables, Stratford – London, citizens, barmaids, fenian, virgin, mothers, whore, sailors, comet, earth (see appendix to Ellmann 1972). Yet, in an important sense, all words were symbols for Joyce, who, more than any other writer, was attentive to the connotations of his language on many levels. As Sydney Bolt remarks, Joyce's use of the Eucharist symbol of recreation, of the word made flesh, 'is wrought upon the details of everyday life in *Ulysses*, to the extent that those details operate as symbols' (1981: 134).

Like its symbolism, the language of *Ulysses* is immensely varied, not least because it moves through a series of set pieces and parodies, with almost every chapter adopting a new style or number of styles. Each of these styles is appropriate to the chapter's subject: journalistic reporting and headlines in a newspaper office in 'Aeolus', romantic magazine fiction when dealing with sex and lust on Sandymount Strand in 'Nausicaa' and dramatic dialogue in the drunken brothel scene in 'Circe'. Some chapters use several styles for similar purposes: in 'Oxen of the Sun', the diverse nine styles represent stages in the evolution of the English language, creating a parallel with the nine months of development of a baby born in the hospital. In his schemes, Joyce included a list of 'technics', detailing the multiplicity of styles in the book, including monologue (male), catechism, dialectic, dialogue, prayer, soliloquy, oratory, narration, prose and monologue (female). These labels apply only to the construction of the chapters and give little indication of the differences between them, which multiply as the book develops, such that, while there is a straightforward methodology at work in the first half of the book, the later chapters follow a stylistic and linguistic trajectory far more than a narrative one, creating in 1922 an eccentric mosaic of techniques which no nineteenth-century realist writer would recognise as a novel.

Most importantly, *Ulysses* is a vastly detailed comic novel which acts as a compendium of modernist innovations, including stream of consciousness, representation of the flow of experience, images of the disintegrating self, a concern with the artist's aesthetic, a sense of history as tyranny, a fracturing of language, a delight in parody and pastiche, a reworking of myth and a celebration of urban experience. *Ulysses* is the book as world, but only inasmuch as the world is composed of correspondences, is itself a book of symbols. In *Finnegans Wake*, Joyce would attempt to (re)produce that world in a novel with a new language.

Joyce had two major Irish successors in Samuel Beckett and Flann O'Brien (1911–66), both of whom have been placed either side of, and even on, the modernist/postmodernist divide. In the Introduction, I discussed *Murphy*, the earliest and most clearly modernist of Beckett's novels, and I want to end by saying something about a book published the year after *Murphy*, in the same year as *Finnegans Wake*: O'Brien's *At Swim-Two-Birds* (1939). The book starts with an impoverished and drunken student narrator whose name the reader never learns. But this is only one level of the narrative and at the very beginning of the book while chewing a piece of bread he 'retires into the privacy of [his] own mind' (O'Brien 1972: 9), exactly like Murphy, and gives three examples of different openings for the novel he is going to write. Across these three levels, O'Brien launches one of the funniest and most sustained lambasts against the conventions of the realist novel, introducing the sensation novel, a morality tale, a cowboy Western, a heroic saga, mythology, a fairy tale and a parodic version of the narrative formulas associated with each. Above all, the book is an assault on the novel form itself and the distinction between levels of reality and fiction. As the narrator says: 'One beginning and one ending for a book was a thing I did not agree with' (O'Brien 1972: 9). The omniscient perspective of the realist text is broken up into fragments as narrative styles, from literary history and life, are juxtaposed with each other. The book takes to its limit modernism's attack on realist styles of narration and also pushes the novel's form towards a postmodernist idiom, with no attempt to represent rounded 'character', an intense self-reflexivity, little regard for the boundaries of time and space and a number of layers of narration which do not remain separate but bleed into each other. Published in the year the war began, *At Swim-Two-Birds* can serve as one marker of the end of the modernist revolution. After the war, new writers would not show fiction and 'human character', in Woolf's phrase, 'changed', but, rather, superseded. Through formal and linguistic experimentation modernists had overturned previous modes of representation, thereby laying the foundations for postmodernist writers to undermine the very categories of 'character', 'representation', 'reality' and even 'literature'.

# Glossary

**aestheticism**    A primarily nineteenth-century French artistic sensibility which espoused the idea of art for art's sake, claiming beauty had little to do with morality and was a higher pursuit for the artist. English aestheticists, such as Oscar Wilde, Arthur Symons and Charles Swinburne, claimed beauty as the only criterion for and gauge of art.

**art nouveau**    A pronouncedly asymmetrical and symbolical decorative style dominant in Europe at the end of the nineteenth and the start of the twentieth centuries.

**collective unconscious**    A term coined by Carl Gustav Jung to express his belief that there is a repository in all minds containing a pool of universal archetypes that express humanity's deep psychic nature.

**condensation/displacement**    As formulated by Sigmund Freud, mechanisms by which latent unconscious processes and symptoms are manifested to the conscious mind in dreams. In condensation, the content of one or more complex chains of association in the unconscious are reduced to a single idea in the dream. In displacement, a kind of mental censorship, the symptom is moved to another associated idea in order to alter its emphasis or intensity.

**dialectic**    Originally a method of argumentation in Greek philosophy, dialectic was used by the German philosopher G. W. F. Hegel to describe a process in which an idea or thesis when opposed by an antithesis, or counter-idea, leads to a new idea, or synthesis. In the phrase 'dialectical materialism', Karl Marx adapted Hegel's use of the term to describe a political struggle between two classes resulting in a new socio-economic order.

**discourse**    The idea of discourse in the sense used here is associated with the French theorist Michel Foucault and describes the power of institutionalised language in its naturalness, authority, professionalism, assertiveness and anti-theoretical directness. Discourses are established ways of thinking resulting from the power of institutionalised socio-historical forces which determine and delimit the meaning and worth of positions adopted in any given field or context, giving rise to shared assumptions within society. Thus power relations are always at work in 'legal discourse', 'discourses of patriarchy', 'post-colonial discourse' and so on. Over and above every opportunity for saying something, there stands a regularising collectivity that Foucault calls discourse. Discourses, which govern the production of culture, always give rise to counter-discourses.

**epistemology**  A term in philosophy for the theory, science or study of the method or basis of knowledge.

**free indirect discourse**  The representation of speech or thoughts without tags (such as 'he said' or 'she thought') or quotation marks.

**hegemony**  Most commonly used to describe the dominance of one country by another, it was taken up by the Italian Marxist Antonio Gramsci to describe the process by which non-repressive systems govern by consensus through the maintenance of shared assumptions, values and meanings that determine the way social reality is perceived within a particular culture.

**humanism**  Most often refers to an anthropocentric view which since the Renaissance has asserted the existence of a universal human nature, the right to freedom and self-determination. Secular humanism places 'man' instead of God at the centre of the conceptual universe, but post-war critics often argue that this universal 'man' masks the oppressive minority (in the numerical sense) interest of the white, middle-class, heterosexual European male.

**ideology**  Most commonly, ideology has referred in the past to individuals' consciously held socio-political beliefs or illusions about the world which underpin the way they live. Later Marxist critics consider ideology instead to encompass the imaginary relation that individuals believe they have to the world.

*langue/parole*  In his theory of how language functions, the influential Swiss linguist Ferdinand de Saussure distinguished between *langue*, the linguistic system, and *parole*, the individual linguistic utterance.

**Marxism**  A school of thought based on the writings of the German political philosopher Karl Marx. In Marx's view economic factors and the divisions between classes that they reinforce and reflect play a primary role in determining social institutions and activities.

**metonymy**  The substitution of a word referring to an attribute of a thing for the thing itself.

**mimesis**   A word used by Plato to describe the imitative representation of behaviour, reality, or human nature.

**mirror phase**   A term coined by the French psychoanalyst Jacques Lacan to describe the stage at which the child, between six and eighteen months, first (mis)recognises its (reflected) self and assumes a discrete image. That is to say, the child perceives and so apprehends a difference between its body and everything else.

**mythopoesis**   The creation of a mythic framework for literary works.

**naturalism**   A quasi-scientific mode of representation, developing from realism, that is detailed, detached and objective and stresses biological or social determinism. In literature it is most closely associated with a widespread movement of the late nineteenth century particularly associated with the French writers Émile Zola and the Goncourt brothers.

**New Woman**   A term used to describe women in the late nineteenth century who were in favour of emancipation and female independence.

**nihilism**   A term that denotes the refusal of established authorities and instituitions. In philosophy, an extreme form of scepticism that rejects all existing values and beliefs; more colloquially, a revolutionary doctrine of destruction for its own sake.

**polyphony**   Literally meaning many-voiced, in the works of the Russian theorist M. M. Bakhtin, polyphony refers to the presence within culture or a literary text of more than one language. More precisely, polyphony denotes the use of a number of speakers in dialogue, who are portrayed in the text as a plurality of consciousnesses with equal rights.

**poststructuralism**   After the French theorist Jacques Derrida's inauguration of deconstruction, from the late 1960s on poststructuralists, in such fields as psychoanalysis (Jacques Lacan and Julia Kristeva) and history (Michel Foucault and Hayden White), have decentred the bases of various traditional disciplines. Most importantly, under poststructuralism the individual is seen as without an 'essence', 'nature', or capacity for 'self-determination' and is, instead, perceived as being inserted in language and discourse. The individual, or rather the subject, is therefore not considered the centre of history and such categories as 'meaning' and 'experience' are also no longer authenticated by appeals to the individual consciousness. Such decentrings are often indebted to early writers, notably Nietzsche, Freud and Marx.

**signifier/signified**  For the Swiss linguist Ferdinand de Saussure, the signifier and signified are the two sides to the linguistic sign, which previously had been considered to be 'a word' and 'a thing'. The signifier refers to the sound image or written mark used to represent an abstract concept or idea, the signified. For Saussure the two were inseparable despite the relation between them being arbitrary.

**solipsism**  The philosophical theory that the self is the only thing that can be definitely known to exist.

**stream of consciousness**  The American philosopher William James in his *Principles of Psychology* (1890) made current the term 'stream of consciousness' to denote the flow and mixture in the mind of all past and present experience. In literature, it designates a technique that represents the movement of thoughts and impressions as they flow through the mind.

**structuralism**  A theoretical school heavily influenced by the linguistic study of Ferdinand de Saussure and based on the belief that all elements of culture can be understood in terms of and as parts of sign systems. For structuralists, anything that people do or use to convey information of any type is a sign. Influential European structuralists such as Roman Jakobson, Claude Lévi-Strauss and Roland Barthes attempted to develop a semiotics, or science of signs.

**symbolism**  Symbolism was a late nineteenth-century French style of poetry, indebted to Charles Baudelaire, realised by Stéphane Mallarmé and made widely known in Britain by Arthur Symons's book *The Symbolist Movement in Literature* (1899). Symbolists attempted to transcend materiality and to reach spiritual planes through the symbol, a concentrated moment or (sometimes mystical) vision in which the experience of life is expressed.

**teleology**  In philosophy, the study of design or purpose in nature, but, more generally, the belief that final causes exist and that there is an ultimate purpose to life.

**unreliable narrator**  A narrator who does not properly comprehend the world and whose judgements the reader mistrusts.

**verisimilitude**  The appearance or semblance of truth to nature or reality.

# Bibliography

Achebe, Chinua (1988) 'An Image of Africa: Racism in Conrad's Heart of Darkness', in *Hopes and Impediments: Selected Essays 1965–1987*, London: Heinemann.

Allen, Walter (1981) *The Short Story in English*, Oxford: Clarendon.

Armstrong, Tim (2005) *Modernism: A Cultural History*, Cambridge: Polity.

Arnold, Matthew (1857) 'On the Modern Element in Literature', in Vassiliki Kolocotroni, Jane Goldman and Olga Taxidou (eds) (1998) *Modernism: An Anthology of Sources and Documents*, Edinburgh: Edinburgh University, pp. 99–101.

Ayers, David (2004) *Modernism: A Short Introduction*, Oxford: Blackwell.

Baker, Houston A. (1987) *Modernism and the Harlem Renaissance*, Chicago, Ill.: Chicago University Press.

Barkan, Elazar and Bush, Ronald (eds) (1995) *Prehistories of the Future: The Primitivist Project and the Culture of Modernism*, Stanford, Calif.: Stanford University Press.

Barthes, Roland (1990) *S/Z*, trans. Richard Miller, Oxford: Blackwell. First published 1973.

Beckett, Samuel (1973) *Murphy*, London: Picador. First published 1938.

Bell, Michael (ed.) (1980) *The Context of English Literature 1900–1930*, London: Methuen.

Belsey, Catherine (1980) *Critical Practice*, London: Methuen.

Benjamin, Walter (1973) *Illuminations*, Glasgow: Fontana.

Berman, Marshall (1983) *All that is Solid Melts into Air: The Experience of Modernity*, London: Verso.

Bhabha, Homi K. (ed.) (1990) *Nation and Narration*, London: Routledge.

—— (1991) '"Race", Time and the Revision of Modernity', *Oxford Literary Review*, 13.

Blamires, Harry (1966) *The Bloomsday Book*, London: Methuen.

Bloch, Ernst, et al. (1977) *Aesthetics and Politics: Debates between Bloch, Lukacs, Brecht, Benjamin, Adorno*, London: Verso.

Boehmer, Elleke (2002) *Empire, the National, and the Postcolonial, 1890–1920: Resistance in Interaction*, Oxford: Oxford University Press.

Bolt, Sydney (1981) *A Preface to Joyce*, Essex: Longman.

Booth, Howard J. and Rigby, Nigel (eds) (2000) *Modernism and Empire*, Manchester: Manchester University Press.

Bradbury, Malcolm (1995) *Dangerous Pilgrimages: Trans-Atlantic Mythologies and the Novel*, London: Secker & Warburg.

Bradbury, Malcolm and McFarlane, James (eds) (1976) *Modernism: A Guide to European Literature 1890–1930*, Harmondsworth: Penguin.

Brecht, Bertolt (1975), 'The Popular and the Realistic', in David Craig (ed.) *Marxists on Literature*, Harmondsworth: Pelican, pp. 421–8.

Bristow, Joseph (1995) *Effeminate England: Homoerotic Writing after 1885*, Milton Keynes: Open University Press.

Brooker, Peter (ed.) (1992) *Modernism/Postmodernism*, London: Longman.

Brooker, Peter and Thacker, Andrew (2005) (eds) *Geographies of Modernism*, London: Routledge.

Brown, Dennis (1989) *The Modernist Self in Twentieth-Century English Literature*, London: Macmillan.

Brown, E. K. (1950) *Rhythm in the Novel*, Toronto: University of Toronto Press.

Butler, Christopher (1994) *Early Modernism: Literature, Music and Painting in Europe 1900–1916*, Oxford: Oxford University Press.

Butler, Lance St John (1990) *Victorian Doubt: Literary and Cultural Discourses*, Hemel Hempstead: Harvester.

Cahoone, Lawrence (ed.) (1996) *From Modernism to Postmodernism: An Anthology*, Oxford: Blackwell.

Cantor, Norman (1988) *Twentieth Century Culture, Modernism to Deconstruction*, London: Peter Lang.

Chabot, C. Barry (1997) *Writers for the Nation*, Tuscaloosa, Ala.: University of Alabama Press.

Childs, Peter (1999) *The Twentieth Century in Poetry*, London: Routledge.

Childs, Peter and Fowler, Roger (eds) (2005) *A Dictionary of Modern Critical Terms*, 2nd edn, London: Routledge.

Clark, Suzanne (1991) *Sentimental Modernism*, Indianapolis, Ind.: Indiana University Press.

Collins, Steven (1982) *Selfless Persons: Imagery and Thought in Theravāda Buddhism*, Cambridge: Cambridge University Press.

Collits, Terry (2005) *Postcolonial Conrad*, London: Routledge.

Comas, J. (1961) '"Scientific" Racism Again?', *Current Anthropology*, 2.

Connolly, Cyril (1979) *Enemies of Promise*, Harmondsworth, Penguin. First published 1938.

Conrad, Joseph (1973) *Heart of Darkness*, Harmondsworth: Penguin. First published 1902.

Darwin, Charles (1968) *The Origin of Species by Means of Natural Selection*, Harmondsworth: Penguin. First published 1859.

Dowling, David (1991) *Mrs Dalloway: Mapping Streams of Consciousness*, Boston, Mass.: Twayne.

Dowson, Jane (2002) *Women, Modernism and British Poetry, 1910–1939: Resisting Feminity*, Aldershot: Ashgate.

DuBois, W. E. B. (1994) *The Souls of Black Folk*, New York: Dover.

Dunbar, Pamela (1997) *Radical Mansfield: Double Discourse in Katherine Mansfield's Short Stories*, London: Macmillan.

DuPlessis, Rachel Blau (1985) *Writing Beyond the Ending: Narrative Strategies of Twentieth-Century Women Writers*, Bloomington, Ind.: Indiana University Press.

Eagleton, Terry (1970) *Exiles and Emigres*, London: Chatto & Windus.

—— (1983) *Literary Theory*, Oxford: Blackwell.

Easthope, Antony (1991) *Literary into Cultural Studies*, London: Routledge.

Eliot, T. S.(1922) *The Waste Land*, London: Faber.

—— (1932) *Selected Essays*, London: Faber.

—— (1988) *The Letters of T. S. Eliot, Volume I: 1898–1922*, New York, Harcourt Brace Jovanovich.

Ellmann, Richard (1972) *Ulysses on the Liffey*, London: Faber.

Ellmann, Richard and Feidelson, Charles (eds) (1965) *The Modern Tradition*, Oxford: Oxford University Press.

Faulkner, Peter (1977) *Modernism*, London: Methuen.

—— (ed.) (1986) *A Modernist Reader: Modernism in England 1910–1930*, London: Batsford.

Faulkner, William (1964) *The Sound and the Fury*, Harmondsworth: Penguin. First published 1929.

Felman, Shoshana (1982) 'Turning the Screw of Interpretation', in S. Felman (ed.), *Literature and Psychoanalysis: The Question of Reading: Otherwise*, Baltimore, Md.: Johns Hopkins University Press, pp. 94–207.

Fitzgerald, Penelope (1984) *Charlotte Mew and Her Friends*, London: Collins.

Fletcher, John (1964) *The Novels of Samuel Beckett*, London: Chatto & Windus.

Ford, Ford Madox (1972) *The Good Soldier: A Tale of Passion*, Harmondsworth: Penguin. First published 1915.

Forster, E. M. (1975) *Howards End*, Harmondsworth: Penguin. First published 1910.

—— (1983) *A Passage to India*, ed. Oliver Stallybrass, Harmondsworth: Penguin. First published 1924.

Foucault, Michel (1986) 'What is Enlightenment?', in Paul Rabinow (ed.) *The Foucault Reader*, Harmondsworth: Penguin.

Frank, Joseph (1963) 'Spatial Form in Modern Literature', in *The Widening Gyre: Crisis and Mastery in Modern Literature*, New Brunswick, N.J.: Prentice-Hall.

Friedman, Susan (1981) *Psyche Reborn*, Bloomington, Ind.: Indiana University Press.

Freud, Sigmund (1986) *The Essentials of Psychoanalysis*, Harmondsworth: Pelican.

—— (1991) *The Interpretation of Dreams*, Harmondsworth: Penguin. First published 1900.

Fullbrook, Kate (1986) *Katherine Mansfield*, Brighton: Harvester.

Furbank, P. N. and Kettle, Arnold (eds) (1973) *Modernism and Its Origins*, Milton Keynes: Open University Press.

Gikandi, Simon (1992). *Writing in Limbo: Modernism and Caribbean Literature*, Ithaca, N.Y.: Cornell University Press.

—— (1996) *Maps of Englishness: Writing Identity in the Culture of Colonialism*, New York: Columbia University Press.

—— (1997) 'Race and the Modernist Aesthetic', in Tim Youngs (ed.), *Writing and Race*, London: Longman, pp. 147–65.

Gilbert, Sandra M. (1989) 'Soldier's Heart: Literary Men, Literary Women, and the Great War', in Elaine Showalter (ed.), *Speaking of Gender*, London: Routledge.

Gillie, Christopher (1975) *Movements in English Literature 1900–1940*, Cambridge: Cambridge University Press.

Gilroy, Paul (1993) *The Black Atlantic: Modernity and Double Consciousness*, London: Verso.

Goldman, Jane (2004) *Modernism, 1910–1945: Image to Apocalypse*, Basingstoke: Palgrave Macmillan.

Habermas, Jürgen (1981) 'Modernity versus Postmodernity', *New German Critique*, 33: 3–14.

Harvey, David (1989) *The Condition of Postmodernity*, Oxford: Blackwell.

Hobsbawm, Eric (1987) *The Age of Empire, 1875–1914*, London: Weidenfeld & Nicholson.

Hughes, Langston (1958) 'Who's Passing for Who?', in *The Langston Hughes Reader*, New York: Braziller.

Hughes, Robert (1980) *The Shock of the New: Art and the Century of Change*, London: Thames & Hudson.

Hulme, T. E. (1924) 'Romanticism and Classicism', in David Lodge (ed.) *20th Century Literary Criticism*, London: Longman.

Huyssen, Andreas (1986) *After the Great Divide: Modernism, Mass Culture, Postmodernism*, Bloomington, Ind.: Indiana University Press.

Innes, Christopher (1999) 'Modernism in Drama', in Michael Levenson (ed.) *The Cambridge Companion to Modernism*, Cambridge: Cambridge University Press, pp. 130–56.

Innes, L. (2002) *A History of Black and Asian Writing in Britain, 1700–2000*, Cambridge: Cambridge University Press.

Isherwood, Christopher (1989) *Goodbye to Berlin*, London: Minerva. First published 1939.

James, C. L. R. (1980) *The Black Jacobins*, London: Allison & Busby.

James, Henry (1963) *Selected Literary Criticism*, ed. Morris Shapira, London: Heinemann.

—— (1969) 'The Turn of the Screw' (1898), in *The Turn of the Screw and Other Stories*, Harmondsworth: Penguin.

Jameson, Fredric (1984) 'Postmodernism, Or the Cultural Logic of Late Capitalism', *New Left Review*, 146: 53–93.

Jardine, Alice (1985) *Gynesis: Configurations of Woman and Modernity*, Ithaca, N.Y.: Cornell University Press.

Johnsen, William (1991) 'Textual/Sexual Politics in Yeats's "Leda and the Swan"', in Leonard Orr (ed.) *Yeats and Postmodernism*, Syracuse, N.Y.: Syracuse University Press.

Joyce, James (1944) *Stephen Hero*, London: Jonathan Cape.

—— (1960) *A Portrait of the Artist as a Young Man*, Harmondsworth: Penguin. First published 1916.

—— (1977) *Dubliners*, Hertfordshire: Panther. First published 1914.

—— (1969) *Ulysses*, Harmondsworth: Penguin. First published 1922.

Kaladjian, Walter (ed.) (2005) *The Cambridge Companion to American Modernism*, Cambridge: Cambridge University Press.

Kaplan, Sydney J. (1991) *Katherine Mansfield and the Origins of Modernist Ficton*, Ithaca, N.Y.: Cornell University Press.

Kenner, Hugh (1962) *Samuel Beckett: A Critical Study*, London: John Calder.

Kermode, F. (1966) *The Sense of an Ending*, Oxford: Oxford University Press.

Kiberd, Declan (1995) *Inventing Ireland*, London: Jonathan Cape.

Kiely, P. (1983) *Modernism Reconsidered*, Cambridge, Mass.: Harvard University Press.

226 BIBLIOGRAPHY

Kolocotroni, Vassiliki, Goldman, Jane and Taxidou, Olga (eds) (1998) *Modernism: An Anthology of Sources and Documents*, Edinburgh: Edinburgh University Press.

Larsen, Nella (1989) *Quicksand and Passing*, London: Serpent's Tail.

Lawrence, D. H. (1932) *Apocalypse*, London: Macmillan.

—— (1950) 'The Virgin and the Gipsy' (1930), in *St Mawr and The Virgin and the Gipsy*, Harmondsworth: Penguin.

—— (1971a) *A Selection from Phoenix*, Harmondsworth: Peregrine.

—— (1971b) *Fantasia of the Unconscious and Psychoanalysis and the Unconscious*, Harmondsworth: Penguin. First published 1923.

—— (1986) *Women in Love*, Harmondsworth: Penguin. First published 1920.

—— (1992) *Selected Poems*, ed. Mara Kalnins, London: Dent.

—— (1993) *The Rainbow*, London: Dent. First published 1915.

Ledger, Sally (1997) *The New Woman*, Manchester: Manchester University Press.

Lester, John A. (1968) *Journey through Despair*, Princeton, N.J.: Princeton University Press.

Levenson, Michael (1984) *A Genealogy of Modernism*, Cambridge: Cambridge University Press.

—— (1991) *Modernism and the Fate of Individuality*, Cambridge: Cambridge University Press.

—— (ed.) (1999) *The Cambridge Companion to Modernism*, Cambridge: Cambridge University Press.

Lloyd, David (1993) *Anomalous States: Irish Writing and the Post-Colonial Moment*, Dublin: Lilliput.

Locke, Alain (1968) *The New Negro*, New York: Arno Press.

Lodge, David (ed.) (1972) *20th Century Literary Criticism*, London: Longman.

—— (1977) *The Modes of Modern Writing: Metaphor, Metonymy, and the Typology of Modern Literature*, London: Arnold.

—— (1981) 'Modernism, Anti-Modernism, and Postmodernism', in *Working with Structuralism*, London: Routledge, pp. 1–16.

Logenbach, James (1988) *Stone Cottage: Pound, Yeats and Modernism*, Oxford: Oxford University Press.

London, Bette (1994) 'Of Mimicry and English Men: E. M. Forster and the Performance of Masculinity', in Tony Davies and Nigel Wood (eds) *A Passage to India*, Milton Keynes: Open University Press.

Lowry, Malcolm (1962) *Under the Volcano*, Harmondsworth: Penguin. First published 1947.

Lukács, Georg (1957) 'The Ideology of Modernism', in David Lodge (ed.) (1972) *20th Century Literary Criticism*, London: Longman, pp. 474–87.

McConnell, William S. (ed.) (2003) *Harlem Renaissance*, Farmington Hills, Mich.: Greenhaven.

McLeod, Hugh (1974) *Class and Religion in the Late Victorian City*, London: Croom Helm.

Mansfield, Katherine (1951) *The Garden Party and Other Stories*, Harmondsworth: Penguin. First published 1922.

—— (1962) *Bliss and Other Stories*, Harmondsworth: Penguin. First published 1920.

Marx, Karl, and Engels, Friedrich (1984) *Basic Writings on Politics and Philosophy*, Glasgow: Fontana.

Mahaffey, Vicki (2007) *Modernist Literature: Challenging Fiction*, Oxford: Blackwell.

Matthews, Steven (2004) *Modernism*, London: Hodder Arnold.

Mew, Charlotte (1997) *Collected Poems and Selected Prose*, ed. Val Warner. Manchester: Carcanet.

Moi, Toril (1985) *Sexual/Textual Politics: Feminist Literary Theory*, London: Methuen.

Moretti, Franco (1988) *Signs Taken for Wonders*, rev. edn, London: Verso.

Nebeker, Helen (1973) 'The Pear Tree: Sexual Implications in Katherine Mansfield's "Bliss"', *Modern Fiction Studies*, 18: 545–51.

Nicholls, Peter (1995) *Modernisms: A Literary Guide*, London: Macmillan.

Nietzsche, Friedrich (1961) *Thus Spoke Zarathustra: A Book for Everyone and No One*, trans. R. J Hollingdale, Harmondsworth: Penguin. First published 1883–92.

—— (1968) *Twilight of the Idols/The Anti-Christ*, trans. R. J. Hollingdale, Harmondsworth: Penguin. First published 1889 and 1895.

—— (1973) *Beyond Good and Evil: Prelude to a Philosophy of the Future*, trans. R. J. Hollingdale, Harmondsworth: Penguin. First published 1886.

—— (1979) *Ecce Homo: How One Becomes What One Is*, trans. R. J. Hollingdale, Harmondsworth: Penguin. First published 1908.

North, M. (1994) *The Dialect of Modernism*, Oxford: Oxford University Press.

—— (1999) *Reading 1922: A Return to the Scene of the Modern*, Oxford: Oxford University Press.

O'Brien, Flann (1972) *At Swim-Two-Birds*, Harmondsworth: Penguin. First published 1939.

Ouditt, Sharon (1994) *Fighting Forces, Writing Women: Identity and Ideology in the First World War*, London: Routledge.

Pater, Walter (1873) 'The Intensity of the Moment', in *Studies in the History of the Renaissance*, in R. Ellmann and C. Feidelson (eds) (1965) *The Modern Tradition*, Oxford: Oxford University Press, pp. 182–4.

Pollard, Charles W. (2004) *New World Modernisms: T. S. Eliot, Derek Walcott, and Kamau Brathwaite*, Charlottesville, Va.: University of Virginia Press.

Rainey, Lawrence (1998) *Institutions of Modernism: Literary Elites and Public Culture*, New Haven, Conn.: Yale University Press.

—— (ed.) (2005) *Modernism: An Anthology*, Oxford: Blackwell.

Reiss, Timothy (1982) *The Discourse of Modernism*, Ithaca, N.Y.: Cornell University Press.

Rich, Paul (1986) *Race and Empire in British Politics*, Cambridge: Cambridge University Press.

Ross, R. H. (1967) *The Georgian Revolt: Rise and Fall of a Poetic Ideal 1910–22*, London: Faber.

Rowell, Geoffrey (1974) *Hell and the Victorians*, Oxford: Clarendon.

Said, Edward (1978) *Orientalism*, Harmondsworth: Penguin.

—— (1990) 'Yeats and Decolonization', in Terry Eagleton, Fredric Jameson and Edward Said, *Nationalism, Colonialism, and Literature*, Minneapolis, Minn.: University of Minnesota Press.

—— (1991) 'Secular Criticism', in *The World, The Text, and The Critic*, London: Vintage. First published 1983.

—— (1993) *Culture and Imperialism*, London: Chatto & Windus.

Saussure, Ferdinand de (1974) *Course in General Linguistics*, trans. Wade Baskin, Glasgow: Fontana.

Scott, Bonnie Kime (ed.) (1990) *The Gender of Modernism*, Bloomington, Ind.: Indiana University Press.

—— (1995) *Refiguring Modernism*, 2 vols, Bloomington, Ind.: Indiana University Press.

Shaw, Valerie (1983) *The Short Story: A Critical Introduction*, London: Longman.

Showalter, Elaine (1985) *A Literature of their Own*, London: Virago. First published 1977.

—— (1986) *The Female Malady: Women, Madness, and English Culture (1830–1980)*, London: Pandora.

Silver, Brenda (1988) 'Periphrasis, Power and Rape in *A Passage to India*', *Novel*, 22 (fall): 86–105.

Smith Angela K. (ed.) (2000) *Women's Writing of the First World War: An Anthology*, Manchester: Manchester University Press.

Smith, Stan (1983) *20th Century Poetry*, London: Macmillan.

—— (1987) *The Origins of Modernism*, Hemel Hempstead: Harvester.

Stein, Gertrude (2006) *Three Lives and Q.E.D.*, ed. Marianne DeKoven, New York: Norton.

Stevenson, Randall (1992) *Modernist Fiction: An Introduction*, Hemel Hempstead: Harvester.

Sypher, Wylie (1960) *Rococo to Cubism in Art and Literature*, New York: Harper & Row.

Trodd, Anthea (1991) *An Introduction to Edwardian Literature*, Hemel Hempstead: Harvester.

Trotter, David (1993) *The English Novel in History 1895–1920*, London: Routledge.

Watts, Cedric (1982) *A Preface to Conrad*, London: Longman.

—— (1983) '"A Bloody Racist": About Achebe's View of Conrad', *Yearbook of English Studies*, 13: 196–209.

Waugh, Evelyn (1970) *Decline and Fall*, Harmondsworth: Penguin.

—— (1972) *Vile Bodies*, Harmondsworth: Penguin.

Waugh, Patricia (1992) *Practising Postmodernism/Reading Modernism*, London: Edward Arnold.

Wells, H. G. (1972a) *The Time Machine*, London: Dent. First published 1895.

—— (1972b) *Tono-Bungay*, London: Pan. First published 1909.

West, Rebecca (1982) *The Return of the Soldier*, Glasgow: Fontana. First published 1918.

Wheeler, Kathleen (1994) 'Dramatic Art in Katherine Mansfield's "Bliss"', in *'Modernist' Women Writers and Narrative Art*, London: Macmillan, pp. 121–40.

White, Allon (1981) *The Uses of Obscurity: the Fiction of Early Modernism*, London: Routledge.

Whitworth, Michael H. (ed.) (2007) *Modernism*, Oxford: Blackwell.

Wilde, Alan (1981) *Horizons of Assent: Modernism, Postmodernism and the Ironic Imagination*, Baltimore, Md.: Johns Hopkins University Press.

Williams, Raymond (1989) *The Politics of Modernism: Against the New Conformists*, London: Verso.

Wolff, Janet (1990) 'Feminism and Modernism', in *Feminine Sentences*, London: Polity.

Woolf, Virginia (1919) 'Modern Fiction', reprinted as 'The Novel of Consciousness' in Richard Ellmann and Charles Feidelson (eds) (1965) *The Modern Tradition*, Oxford: Oxford University Press.

—— (1924) 'Mr Bennett and Mrs Brown', reprinted in Peter Faulkner (ed.) (1986), *A Modernist Reader: Modernism in England 1910–1930*, London: Batsford.

—— (1973) *A Room Of One's Own*, London: Grafton. First published 1929.

—— (1976) *Mrs Dalloway*, London: Grafton. First published 1925.

—— (1978) *The Voyage Out*, London: Grafton.

—— (1988) 'Professions for Women', in *Women and Writing* (1931) London: Women's Press.

Wright, Anne (1984) *The Literature of Crisis, 1910–22*, London: Macmillan.

Yeats, W. B. (1980) *Collected Poems*, London: Macmillan.

Young, Allan (1981) *Dada and After: Extremist Modernism and English Literature*, Manchester: Manchester University Press.

Zavala, Iris (1992) *Colonialism and Culture: Hispanic Modernisms and the Social Imaginary*, Bloomington, Ind.: Indiana University Press.

# Index

'Farmer's Bride, The' (Mew) 137–38
Faulkner, William 185–86, 194–97
Feidelson, Charles 86
Felman, Shoshana 157
feminism 20, 135–36, 192
film 127–32
*Finnegans Wake* (Joyce) 66, 67, 68,
    199, 216
Fitzgerald, F. Scott 90
Flaubert, Gustave 15, 81, 82, 90, 119,
    149
Flint, F. S. 103, 107
Ford, Ford Madox 26, 58, 84, 103, 116,
    149, 150, 157–62
Forster, E.M. 34, 39, 41, 42, 67, 70, 74, 77,
    87, 132, 155, 197–98, 202–5, 206, 208
Foucault, Michel 17, 65
'Founding and Manifesto of Futurism,
    The' (Marinetti) 22
Fowler, Alastair 2
Fowler, Roger 2
Frank, Joseph 157
Frank, Waldo 90
Frazer, James 40, 66, 182
Freud, Sigmund 2, 21, 25, 37, 56–62,
    64, 66, 67, 72, 95, 113, 124, 126, 127,
    149, 150, 156, 165, 181, 200, 218, 221
Fry, Roger 87
Fuseli, Henri 126
Futurism 15, 22, 23, 27, 109, 121–23,
    125, 136

Galilei, Galileo 17
Galsworthy, John 83, 86, 87, 135
Galton, Francis 50
'Garden Party, The' (Mansfield) 15, 71,
    94, 98, 134, 139, 141, 143
Garnett, Edward 144
Gaskell, Elizabeth 81, 181
Genet, Jean 112
Gibson, Wilfred 100
Gide, André 2, 26
Gikandi, Simon 30, 32–33, 192–94
Gilbert, Sandra 176
Gilroy, Paul 18, 25, 34
Gissing, George 82, 101

Glaspell, Susan 114
Gobineau, Comte de 49
*Golden Bough, The* (Frazer) 40, 66, 182
Gonne, Maud 102, 198, 199, 208
*Good Soldier, The* (Ford) 58, 61, 77, 84,
    90, 116, 118, 149, 150, 157–62
*Goodbye to Berlin* (Isherwood) 124, 132
Gosse, Edmund 24
Goya, Francisco 126
Graves, Robert 15
Greene, Graham 6
Gregory, Lady 102, 198, 208
Gris, Juan 118

H. D. (Hilda Doolittle) 4, 5, 26, 27,
    103, 107, 108
Habermas, Jürgen 18
Haeckel, Ernst 56, 57, 62
Hall, Radclyffe 139
'Hamlet and his Problems' (Eliot) 105
Hardy, Thomas 14, 24, 66, 83, 100,
    134, 137, 181
Harris, Wilson 25, 31, 32
Harvey, David 19
Hawthorne, Nathaniel 91
*Heart of Darkness* (Conrad) 49, 70, 83,
    117, 148, 150–57, 161, 201, 202
Heidegger, Martin 68, 70, 72
Heisenberg, Werner 73
Hemingway, Ernest 6, 29, 90, 176, 185
Henley, W. E. 100
Hitler, Adolf 45
Hobbes, Thomas 17
Homer 199, 200, 207, 214, 215
Horkheimer, Max 16
*Howards End* (Forster) 39, 41, 77, 198,
Hughes, Langston 193
Hughes, Robert 76
Hulme, T. E. 17, 102, 103, 108
Hurston, Zora Neale 90
Huxley, Aldous 132
Huyssen, Andreas 24

Ibsen, Henrik 38, 110, 163, 211
'Ideology of Modernism, The' (Lukács)
    43